"A very useful addition to the nutrition literature . . . that can easily be understood without consulting other reference books or the complex scientific literature that is available. . . . It is a pleasure to find not merely cut-and-dried definitions presented but often a lively discussion with hard data, folklore, and anecdotal information. . . . It is my hope that the book will be widely referred to for popular reference information and that it will promote a more active interest and participation on the part of the reader-consumer. Good reading and good eating!"

—from the Introduction by Roy Brown, M.D., M.P.H.
Associate Professor of Community Medicine,
Mount Sinai School of Medicine

D1269968

Dictionary of Nutrition

*Richard Ashley
and Heidi Duggal*

Introduction by Roy Brown, M.D.

PUBLISHED BY POCKET BOOKS NEW YORK

POCKET BOOKS, a division of Simon & Schuster, Inc.
1230 Avenue of the Americas, New York, N.Y. 10020

Published by arrangement with St. Martin's Press
Library of Congress Catalog Card Number: 73-87397

ISBN: 0-671-49407-4

First Pocket Books printing February, 1976

15 14 13 12 11 10 9 8

POCKET and colophon are registered trademarks
of Simon & Schuster, Inc.

Printed in the U.S.A.

Contents

CONTENTS

CONTENTS

CONTENTS

CONTENTS

Authors' Introduction

The authors do not pretend to be "experts" in nutrition. We are simply persons who, attempting to eat in a healthy way, found how difficult it was to obtain objective information in an easily digestible form.

Anyone interested in the nutritional value of the foods he eats and in understanding the roles played by the various nutrients knows that there is no shortage of publications in these fields. If anything, there is an overabundance of them. But two major problems arise from this overabundance. First, there is the problem of conflicting information: for example, one book will cite the great value of vitamin E in relationship to sexual vigor, another will deny the claim. And, second, to acquire the most basic nutritional information necessitates the consulting of several volumes.

The *Dictionary of Nutrition* does not pretend to resolve the conflicting claims for various nutrients, but where such conflicts exist both sides of the question are given and the presence or absence of scientific data to support the claims is cited. Perhaps more importantly, the *Dictionary* is a one-volume source for all the nutritional information needed by the average person. Terms, both common and technical, are defined; the functions, sources, requirements, results of deficiencies, and the possible toxicity of the various vitamins, minerals, and other nutrients are given; the composition and nutrient values of some 400 foods are listed; and many factors which affect nutrition—food additives, pesticides, the nature of the soil, the Food and Drug Administration, and the like—are listed and discussed. It is a dictionary for laypeople by laypeople.

The information in the *Dictionary* comes from many

sources, ranging from the United States Department of Agriculture to Adelle Davis. We believe it to be a fair, objective compilation of the generally accepted data on nutrition.

Some tips on using the *Dictionary*:

Since this is a dictionary, it is arranged alphabetically. There are, however, some exceptions to strict alphabetical order. All vitamins are listed following VITAMINS, GENERAL. Thus one would not find biotin under B, but after VITAMINS, GENERAL. Similarly with the mineral iron, which is listed under MINERALS, GENERAL. Also, the bulk of the food entries follow general headings. For example chicken is not listed under C, but after the general heading POULTRY; beef after MEAT; carrots after VEGETABLES; and so on. When food items do not readily fall into categories, as in the cases of potato chips and ice cream, they are listed strictly alphabetically. References in the body of the text to other entries are indicated by an asterisk (*).

In the composition and nutrient value tables that accompany each food entry there are abbreviations which need explaining:

—means that though there is less than a trace amount of the nutrient present, there is reason to believe that *some* very small amount is present.

N.D. means simply that no data is available.

g stands for gram.

mg stands for milligram, 1/1,000 of a gram.

The composition and nutrient values in the food entries are taken chiefly from the U.S. Department of Agriculture, Home and Garden Bulletin No. 72, Revised January 1971. Those who compare the nutrient values listed in the *Dictionary* against some source they have previously used may find slight variations. This is because climate, soil, and several other factors affect nutrient values. As a result, the same quantities of a given food may have different nutrient values according to the time and place in which it was grown. The compilations of nutrient values take this into account, but slight variations occur, as they are bound to.

H.D.
R.A.

Calorie Chart

(g = gram and 28g = 1 ounce; cup = 8 oz.)

Calories

Alcohol:
   Gin, rum, vodka, whiskey, all have the
   same amount of calories but in each
   case calories increase as proof increases. Thus
   per 1/2 oz. of

80 proof	100
86 proof	105
90 proof	110
100 proof	125
Beer, 12 fl. oz.	150
Wine, table 3-1/2 fl. oz.	85
Wine, dessert 3-1/2 fl. oz	140
Bagel (one medium)	165
Baking powder biscuits (one 2″ dia.)	105
Bread:	
Cracked wheat (one slice)	65
Pumpernickel (one slice)	66
Rye (one slice)	60
White, enriched (one slice)	70
Whole wheat (one slice)	65
Breakfast cereals:	
Branflakes (cup)	105
Cornflakes (cup)	100
Granola (two oz.)	250
Oatmeal (two oz.)	130
Puffed Rice (cup)	60
Puffed Wheat (cup)	55
Shredded Wheat (biscuit)	90

Brewer's yeast (tablespoon)	25
Butter (2 pats, 14g)	100
Buttermilk (cup)	90
Cake or Pastry:	
Angelfood cake (slice, 53g)	135
Brownies (one, 20g)	85
Chocolate cake with icing (slice, 120g)	420
Danish (plain, small, 65g)	275
Devil's Food cake, chocolate icing (slice, 69g)	235
Doughnut, plain (one, 32g)	125
Fruitcake, dark (slice, 30g)	110
Gingerbread cake (slice, 63g)	175
Plain cake (slice, 86g)	315
Pound cake (slice, 30g)	140
Sponge cake (slice, 66g)	195
Cheese:	
Cheddar (1″ cube, 17g)	70
Cottage (cup, 245g)	260
Cream (ounce)	106
Processed (ounce)	105
Roquefort (ounce)	105
Swiss (ounce)	105
Chile:	
with beans (cup)	335
without beans (cup)	510
Chocolate:	
milk chocolate (ounce)	145
fudge (ounce)	115
Cocoa, (cup, made with milk)	245
Coffee (cup, black, no sugar)	3
Cookie (plain, hard, 25g)	82
Cream (tablespoon)	52
Dried Fruits:	
Apricots (cup)	390
Dates (cup)	490
Figs (8, 168g)	460
Prunes (8, 64g)	140
Raisins (cup)	480
Eggs:	
Raw, boiled, or poached (1)	80

Scrambled with milk and butter (1)   110
Farina (cup)   105
Fish:
  Flounder (3 oz., baked)   174
  Haddock (3 oz., breaded and fried)   140
  Halibut (3 oz., broiled)   156
  Salmon (3 oz., canned)   120
  Sardines (3 oz., canned)   175
  Shad (3 oz., baked)   170
  Swordfish (3 oz., broiled)   150
  Tuna (3 oz., canned)   170
Flour:
  All-purpose, enriched (cup, 115g)   420
  Cake or pastry, sifted (cup, 96g)   350
  Whole-wheat (cup, 120g)   400
French dressing (tablespoon, 16g)   65
Fruit:
  Apple (1)   70
  Apricot (3)   55
  Avocado (1/2)   185
  Banana (1)   100
  Blackberries (cup)   85
  Blueberries (cup)   85
  Cantaloupe (1/2)   60
  Cherries (cup)   65
  Grapefruit (1/2)   50
  Grapes (cup)   65
  Orange (1)   65
  Peach (1)   35
  Pear (1)   100
  Plum (1)   25
  Rhubarb (cup, cooked, sweetened)   385
  Strawberries (cup)   55
  Tangerine (1)   40
  Watermelon (4" $\times$ 8" wedge)   115
Fruit Juices:
  Apple (cup)   120
  Apricot (cup)   140
  Grape (cup)   165
  Grapefruit (cup, unsweetened)   100

Orange (cup)	110
Pineapple (cup)	135
Prune (cup)	200
Half and Half (cup)	325
Honey (tablespoon)	65
Ice Cream (cup)	255
Jam (tablespoon)	55
Jelly (tablespoon)	50
Malted Milk (2 cups, with ice cream)	690
Margarine (2 pats, 149g)	100
Maple Syrup (2 tablespoons)	100
Mayonnaise (tablespoon)	100
Meat:	
Bacon (2 slices, 15g)	90
Beef, Pot roast (3 oz., 85g)	245
Beef, Hamburger lean (3 oz)	185
Beef, Hamburger commercial (3 oz)	245
Beef, roast (3 oz)	375
Beef, sirloin steak, broiled (3 oz)	330
Beef, kidney, broiled (3 oz)	200
Beef, liver, fried (3 oz)	195
Bologna (2 slices, 26g)	80
Corned Beef (3 oz)	185
Frankfurter (1, 56g)	170
Ham (3 oz)	245
Lamb chop, broiled (3 oz)	300
Lamb, leg of, roasted (3 oz)	235
Pork chop (3-1/2 oz)	260
Pork roast (3 oz)	310
Veal cutlet, broiled (3 oz)	185
Milk:	
whole (cup)	160
skim (cup)	90
Mushrooms (cup, cooked or canned)	40
Nuts:	
Almonds (cup)	850
Cashews (cup)	785
Coconut (2" × 2" × 1/2" piece)	155
Peanuts (cup)	840

Pecans (cup)	740
Walnuts (cup)	790
Olives, green (10 large)	72
Olives, black (10 large)	105
Olive oil (tablespoon)	125
Pancakes (2)	120

Pasta:

Egg noodles (cup)	200
Macaroni (cup)	155
Macaroni and cheese (cup)	430
Spaghetti (cup)	155
Spaghetti with meatballs (cup)	330
Spaghetti, tomato sauce and cheese (cup)	260
Peanut butter (tablespoon)	95

Pie:

Apple (small slice)	350
Cherry (small slice)	350
Custard (small slice)	285
Lemon meringue (small slice)	305
Mince (small slice)	365
Pecan (small slice)	490
Pumpkin (small slice)	275
Pizza (1/8 of 14″ dia. pie)	185
Popcorn (cup)	40
Potato chips (10 med.)	115

Poultry:

Chicken breast (1/2 med. fried)	155
Chicken, broiled (3 oz)	115
Chicken, drumstick, fried (3 oz)	135
Chicken liver, fried (3-1/2 oz)	140
Turkey, roasted (3-1/2 oz)	265
Rice, brown (cup serving)	187
Rice, white (cup serving)	55
Rolls, hotdog or hamburger (1)	120
Saltines (4)	50

Shellfish:

Clams (3 oz)	45
Crabmeat (3 oz)	85
Lobster (3-1/2 oz)	92

Shrimp (3 oz)	100
Oysters (8-1/2 oz)	160

Soup:

Beef bouillon (cup)	30
Clam chowder, Manhattan (cup)	80
Clam chowder, New England (cup)	210
Cream of Chicken (cup)	180
Cream of Mushroom (cup)	215
Split pea, made with water (cup)	145
Split pea, made with milk (cup)	210
Tomato (cup)	90
Cream of Tomato (cup)	175
Vegetable (cup)	80
Sugar, brown (tablespoon)	50
Sugar, white (tablespoon)	48
Tea, no sugar (cup)	4
Thousand Island dressing (tablespoon)	80
Tomato catsup (tablespoon)	15

Vegetables:

Asparagus (4 spears)	10
Beans, green (cup)	30
Beans, lima (cup)	190
Beans, pea (cup)	225
Beans, red kidney (cup)	230
Bean sprouts (cup, uncooked)	17
Beets (cup)	55
Broccoli (cup)	40
Brussels sprouts (cup)	55
Cabbage (cup)	30
Carrots (1, raw)	30
Carrots (cup, cooked)	45
Cauliflower (cup)	25
Celery (1 stalk)	5
Collards (cup)	55
Corn (1 ear)	70
Endive (2 oz)	10
Eggplant (cup)	30
Onions (1 raw)	40
Onions, green (12 raw)	40
Peas (cup)	115

Potato, baked (1 med.)	90
Potato, french fried (20 pieces)	300
Soybeans (cup)	260
Spinach (cup)	40
Squash, summer (cup)	30
Squash, winter (cup)	130
Sweet potatoes, baked (1 med.)	155
Sweet potatoes, candied (1 med.)	295
Tomato (1)	40
Turnips (cup)	35
Vegetable Oils:	
Corn (tablespoon)	125
Cottonseed (tablespoon)	125
Peanut (tablespoon)	125
Safflower (tablespoon)	125
Soybean (tablespoon)	125
Yogurt, of partially skim milk (cup)	125

FOOD AND NUTRITION BOARD, NATIONAL ACADEMY OF SCIENCES—NATIONAL RESEARCH COUNCIL RECOMMENDED DAILY DIETARY ALLOWANCES,[a] Revised 1980

Designed for the maintenance of good nutrition of practically all healthy people in the U.S.A.

	Age (years)	Weight (kg)	Weight (lb)	Height (cm)	Height (in)	Protein (g)	Fat-Soluble Vitamins Vitamin A (µg RE)[b]	Vitamin D (µg)[c]	Vitamin E (mg α-TE)[d]
Infants	0.0–0.5	6	13	60	24	kg × 2.2	420	10	3
	0.5–1.0	9	20	71	28	kg × 2.0	400	10	4
Children	1–3	13	29	90	35	23	400	10	5
	4–6	20	44	112	44	30	500	10	6
	7–10	28	62	132	52	34	700	10	7
Males	11–14	45	99	157	62	45	1000	10	8
	15–18	66	145	176	69	56	1000	10	10
	19–22	70	154	177	70	56	1000	7.5	10

	(kg)	(lb)	(cm)	(in)				
23–50	70	154	178	70	56	1000	5	10
51+	70	154	178	70	56	1000	5	10
Females 11–14	46	101	157	62	46	800	10	8
15–18	55	120	163	64	46	800	10	8
19–22	55	120	163	64	44	800	7.5	8
23–50	55	120	163	64	44	800	5	8
51+	55	120	163	64	44	800	5	8
Pregnant					+30	+200	+5	+2
Lactating					+20	+400	+5	+3

[a] The allowances are intended to provide for individual variations among most normal persons as they live in the United States under usual environmental stresses. Diets should be based on a variety of common foods in order to provide other nutrients for which human requirements have been less well defined. See text for detailed discussion of allowances and of nutrients not tabulated. See Table 1 (p. 20) for weights and heights by individual year of age. See Table 3 (p. 23) for suggested average energy intakes.

[b] Retinol equivalents. 1 retinol equivalent = 1 μg retinol or 6 μg β carotene. See text for calculation of vitamin A activity of diets as retinol equivalents.

[c] As cholecalciferol. 10 μg cholecalciferol = 400 iu of vitamin D.

[d] α-tocopherol equivalents. 1 mg d-α tocopherol = 1 α-TE. See text for variation in allowances and calculation of vitamin E activity of the diet as α-tocopherol equivalents.

25

FOOD AND NUTRITION BOARD, NATIONAL ACADEMY OF SCIENCES—NATIONAL RESEARCH COUNCIL RECOMMENDED DAILY DIETARY ALLOWANCES,[a] Revised 1980

(CONTINUED)

Designed for the maintenance of good nutrition of practically all healthy people in the U.S.A.

| | Water-Soluble Vitamins | | | | | | | Minerals | | | | | |
	Vitamin C (mg)	Thiamin (mg)	Riboflavin (mg)	Niacin (mg NE)[e]	Vitamin B-6 (mg)	Folacin[f] (µg)	Vitamin B-12 (µg)	Calcium (mg)	Phosphorus (mg)	Magnesium (mg)	Iron (mg)	Zinc (mg)	Iodine (µg)
Infants	35	0.3	0.4	6	0.3	30	0.5[g]	360	240	50	10	3	40
	35	0.5	0.6	8	0.6	45	1.5	540	360	70	15	5	50
Children	45	0.7	0.8	9	0.9	100	2.0	800	800	150	15	10	70
	45	0.9	1.0	11	1.3	200	2.5	800	800	200	10	10	90
	45	1.2	1.4	16	1.6	300	3.0	800	800	250	10	10	120
Males	50	1.4	1.6	18	1.8	400	3.0	1200	1200	350	18	15	150
	60	1.4	1.7	18	2.0	400	3.0	1200	1200	400	18	15	150

60	1.5	1.7	19	2.2	400	3.0	800	800	350	10	15	150
60	1.4	1.6	18	2.2	400	3.0	800	800	350	10	15	150
60	1.2	1.4	16	2.2	400	3.0	800	800	350	10	15	150
Females												
50	1.1	1.3	15	1.8	400	3.0	1200	1200	300	18	15	150
60	1.1	1.3	14	2.0	400	3.0	1200	1200	300	18	15	150
60	1.1	1.3	14	2.0	400	3.0	800	800	300	18	15	150
60	1.0	1.2	13	2.0	400	3.0	800	800	300	18	15	150
60	1.0	1.2	13	2.0	400	3.0	800	800	300	10	15	150
Pregnant	+20	+0.4	+0.3	+2	+0.6	+400	+1.0	+400	+400	+150	h	+5	+25
Lactating	+40	+0.5	+0.5	+5	+0.5	+100	+1.0	+400	+400	+150	h	+10	+50

[d] 1 NE (niacin equivalent) is equal to 1 mg of niacin or 60 mg of dietary tryptophan.

[f] The folacin allowances refer to dietary sources as determined by Lactobacillus casei assay after treatment with enzymes (conjugases) to make polyglutamyl forms of the vitamin available to the test organism.

[g] The recommended dietary allowance for vitamin B-12 in infants is based on average concentration of the vitamin in human milk. The allowances after weaning are based on energy intake (as recommended by the American Academy of Pediatrics) and consideration of other factors, such as intestinal absorption; see text.

[h] The increased requirement during pregnancy cannot be met by the iron content of habitual American diets nor by the existing iron stores of many women; therefore the use of 30–60 mg of supplemental iron is recommended. Iron needs during lactation are not substantially different from those of nonpregnant women, but continued supplementation of the mother for 2–3 months after parturition is advisable in order to replenish stores depleted by pregnancy.

Reproduced from Recommended Dietary Allowances, National Academy Press, Washington, D.C., 1980.

Best† Nutritional Sources

Proteins
Egg yolk, milk, liver, kidney, lean red meats, seafood, cheese, brewer's yeast, wheat germ, soybeans.

Essentially Fatty Acids
Safflower oil, corn oil, soybean oil, peanut oil, cottonseed oil, wheat germ, nuts.

Vitamins
Vitamin A: liver, fish liver oil, butter, cheese, eggs, milk.
Vitamin B_1: brewer's or torula yeast, wheat germ, rice polish, whole-grain breads and cereals.
Vitamin B_2: liver, brewer's yeast, milk, whole-grain breads and cereals.
Vitamin B_6: brewer's yeast, wheat germ, wheat bran, liver, kidney, heart, blackstrap molasses.
Vitamin B_{12}: liver, kidney, milk, eggs, cheese, and most meats.
Biotin: brewer's yeast, egg yolk, milk, liver.
Choline: brains, liver, kidney, wheat germ, brewer's yeast, egg yolk.
Folic acid: liver, kidney, green vegetables, nuts.
Inositol: liver, brewer's yeast, wheat germ, whole-grain breads and cereals, oatmeal, corn.
Niacin: brewer's yeast, liver, kidney, wheat germ.
Para-aminobenzoic acid: liver, kidney, whole-grain breads and cereals, brewer's yeast.
Pantothenic acid: liver, kidney, whole-grain breads and cereals, brewer's yeast, green vegetables.
Bioflavonoids: the pulp (especially the white of the rind)

† For other sources, consult individual entries in body of text.

of citrus fruits, black and red currants, rose hips, asparagus, apricots.

Vitamin C: citrus fruits, guavas, ripe bell peppers, rose hips.

Vitamin D: fish-liver oils, milk fortified with vitamin D.

Vitamin E: unrefined vegetable oils (e.g., corn, soy, cottonseed), wheat germ, whole-grain breads and cereals, nuts.

Vitamin K: green vegetables.

Minerals

Bromide: green leafy vegetables, whole grain breads and cereals, seafood, liver, kidney.

Calcium: milk, yogurt, cheese, cultured buttermilk.

Chlorine: table salt, green leafy vegetables.

Chromium: same as Bromide.

Cobalt: same as Bromide.

Copper: green leafy vegetables, seafood, liver, whole-grain breads and cereals, kidney, dried fruits, egg yolk.

Fluoride: drinking water tested with fluoride.

Iodine: iodized salt, seafood.

Iron: pork and beef liver, egg yolk, wheat germ, brewer's yeast, apricots, beans, peas.

Magnesium: whole-grain breads and cereals, nuts, soybeans.

Manganese: green leafy vegetables, wheat germ, whole-grain breads and cereals, nuts, beans, liver.

Molybdenum: same as Bromide.

Phosphorus: same as Calcium.

Potassium: vegetables, fruits, whole-grain breads and cereals, meat, nuts.

Sodium: table salt.

Sulphur: protein-rich foods, brussels sprouts, lentils, onions.

Zinc: shellfish, liver, kidney, and green leafy vegetables and nuts if grown in soil with adequate zinc deposits.

Introduction

I have no doubt that the *Dictionary of Nutrition* will be a very useful addition to the nutrition literature, serving as a practical guide to the "No-man's Land" of nutrition. It is an unpretentious guide to sorting out and organizing the nutritional information with which the public is currently being bombarded. The subjects have been researched carefully, and the authors have produced a distillate that can easily be understood without consulting other reference books or the complex scientific literature that is available. The terms that are defined come from both technical and commonplace parlance. One would certainly not expect this modest book to resolve all the nutritional controversies, but the authors have no hesitation in presenting the reader with evidence from both sides of a given question.

The system of organization in the *Dictionary of Nutrition* makes it easy to use as a handy reference guidebook. The reader can consult the major category of foodstuff or the category of micro-nutrient such as vitamins or minerals and find convenient sub-groupings and cross-indexing.

It is a pleasure to find not merely cut-and-dried definitions presented but often a lively discussion with hard data, folklore, and anecdotal information presented in the form of an essay that blends together the various points of view. The authors do not pull their punches; they freely criticize where justified the food industry, the government agencies, and the scientific nutrition community as well as the ignorant consumer. There is a smattering of medical information presented throughout the text, all of which will be easily comprehensible to the lay reader. Important information is given about the possible dangers and the nutritional losses that occur in association with certain additives, processing techniques and cooking.

It is a positive experience to have a useful reference book that is written with a concern for being comprehensive, while at the same time keeping a keen sense of humor. Frozen foods are described as "an American way of life." And when one looks up "gin," the definition is "an alcoholic beverage . . . popular with those who 'drink' their lunch." It is also to the credit of the authors that a full caloric chart is given with references for everyday foods, including all sorts of alcoholic beverages and various types of meat, fish, vegetables, fruit, and even bagels. In fact, food composition and nutrient values are presented for nearly four hundred different foods.

It is my hope that the book will be widely referred to for popular reference information and that it will promote a more active interest and participation on the part of the reader-consumer. Good reading and good eating!

Roy Brown, M.D., M.P.H.
Associate Professor
          of Community Medicine
Mount Sinai School of Medicine

Dictionary
of Nutrition

Ac'cent
International Mineral & Chemical Corp.'s trade name for monosodium glutamate.*

acetic acid
A simple organic acid, of which vinegar is a dilute solution.

achlorhydria
Hydrochloric acid deficiency in the secretion of gastric juices.

acid foods and alkaline foods
The minerals phosphorus, sulphur, and chlorine are acid-forming, while potassium, sodium, calcium and magnesium are base-forming. Whether a given food leaves an acid or alkaline residue is determined by which of these predominate in the food. Milk, vegetables, and some fruits leave an alkaline residue. Meat, fish, eggs, cheese, and cereals leave an acid residue. Sugars and fats have no minerals and thus are neutral.

acidophilus milk
Unfermented milk containing a high concentration of viable *Lactobacillus acidophilus*, a bacteria which when present in the intestine is thought to increase its efficiency.

acids and alkalis
Chemicals used to control the degree of acidity or alkalinity in processed foods. For example, most of the "fruit"-type soft drinks have their flavors modified by citric, malic, or tartaric acid, while the "zesty tang" of the

cola drinks is imparted by phosphoric acid. Cookies, candies, and soda crackers are made more alkaline by the addition of ammonium carbonate which is used as a leavening agent. By law, all additives must be listed on the product's label or package.

See Additives

additives

All those materials, natural and synthetic, which aid in the storage, manufacture, and preservation of food. It is estimated that some ten thousand chemicals are used for these purposes in America. Not all of them are harmless, and many which may be harmless individually may not be so in combination with others. Then, too, what may be harmless to one individual is not necessarily harmless to another. To date, very little hard data are available on the overall effect on the nation's health of the additives present in our food.

According to the Food Protection committee of the National Academy of Sciences, which rules on the safety of food additives, every chemical added to our foods must serve one or more of the following purposes:

—improve its keeping qualities
—improve its availability
—facilitate its preparation
—enhance its quality or consumer acceptability
—improve its nutritional value

To improve the keeping qualities of food products—that is, to prevent spoilage and deterioration—is certainly a necessary and worthwhile objective. The problems inherent in shipping and storing large quantities of perishable foods are such that an urban, technological society could not survive in the absence of sophisticated methods of preserving its foodstuffs. We pay a price, however, the precise amount of which has not been calculated. We do not know the long-term effects of the dozens of preservatives we ingest daily. Many of them in constant use are being reexamined for their possibly deleterious effect on humans, and some banned in other countries for this very reason are still in use here. For example, sodium diacetate, a mold-inhibitor used in bread, is banned in Great Britain, but allowed and used here.

Again, the making of foods more readily available to the consumer is a praiseworthy objective. But in reality the true objective here is often the convenience of the distributor rather than that of the consumer. It doesn't matter to the New York consumers whether they get their iceberg lettuce from Long Island or California, but since the New York distributors apparently find it more convenient to process refrigerator boxcars than fresh produce from truck, the New York consumer eats California produce when Long Island produce is available.

Perhaps equally unnecessary but an objective which cannot be blamed on the food processors—who are catering to the demands of the public for "convenience" foods —is facilitating the preparation of food. In this category fall all those instant foods: mashed, diced, and sliced foods, cake mixes and the like which greatly reduce the time required to prepare a meal. The vast majority of them are heavily dosed with chemicals.

In the same vein, the majority of chemicals added to foods to "enhance its quality or consumer acceptability" seem completely unnecessary. Coloring agents used to make meat "red," and butter "yellow," and oranges "orange," serve no useful purpose other than to make these products look like our ideal image of them—an image that owes more to advertising than to nature.

The improvement of the nutritional value of foods is of course a most worthwhile objective. Unfortunately, only a handful of the thousands of additives in use have anything to do with nutritional values. And with certain exceptions —e.g., adding vitamin D to milk, wheat germ to whole wheat bread—the chief purpose of adding nutrients is to replace those removed or destroyed by the processing methods, a purpose only partially served insofar as the replacement rarely equals that which was removed or destroyed.

The central question about food additives is their safety over a long period of time. Not only have a goodly percentage of additives *not* been subjected to long-term testing, but the long-term testing now in effect makes it unlikely that the question can be correctly answered. For example, additives that show no cancerous effects on laboratory animals tested over a two-year period may well have such an effect on humans eating them over a twenty-year period. Then, too, some individuals are more susceptible to cancer than others, and this differentiation cannot be properly evaluated in small populations of laboratory test animals.

Nor is very much known about the possible synergistic effects of the heady mixture of additives we eat: additives not individually harmful may in combination be very harmful. By law, all additives used in or applied to foods and drinks must be listed on the label or package of the product. The law does not require, however, that a warning similar to that on cigarette packages be printed next to those additives being currently tested as suspect.

As of 1958, the Additive Foods Amendment required that no additive could be used in foods or drinks until the manufacturer had proved to the Food and Drug Administration (FDA) that it was safe for human consumption. But exempt from this premarketing testing were those more than six hundred additives (both natural and synthetic) on the Generally Recognized as Safe* (GRAS) list. These were additives which had been added to foods for a long time and which qualified scientists had recognized as safe for human consumption when used as intended. Awareness of the inadequacy of the testing of additives in general and the complete lack of testing of the GRAS list in particular, has led to a program of testing items on the GRAS list. But due to limitations of funds and manpower, only one hundred of those most suspect are on the initial test list. And just how soon we will benefit from this testing is open to question. For example, FDA scientists warned about the cancer-causing possibilities of the cyclamate sweeteners in 1958, but cyclamates were not banned from use until 1969.

See the following for a description of the main categories of additives:

Acids and alkalis
Bleaching and maturing agents
Buffers and neutralizers
Coloring agents
Emulsifiers
Flavoring agents
Leavening agents
Moisture-control agents
Nutrition supplements
Preservatives
Stabilizers and thickeners

aging
(1) A term applied to the treatment of flour with oxidizing agents, an aging process that improves its baking qualities.
(2) The hanging of meat to soften the muscles which have been hardened by rigor mortis.
(3) The slow oxidation and formation of esters in wine which reduces its initial harshness and develops its bouquet and mellowness.

albumin(s)
The word "albumins" is often used as a synonym for the simple proteins which are soluble in water and coagulate under heat.
See Lactalbumin

albumin index
The ratio of the height of the egg white (albumin) to its width when laid on a flat surface. Used to measure the quality of eggs. As an egg deteriorates, the egg white gets thinner, i.e., the albumin index decreases. In practical terms, the faster an egg spreads in a pan, the older it is.

alcohol
A name usually referring to ethyl alcohol (C_2H_5OH), produced by the yeast fermentation of carbohydrates, and which is the intoxicating agent (through the depression of the central nervous system) in fermented and distilled bev-

erages. Alcohol has been used as an intoxicant for at least five thousand years and very few societies in the world do without it. Even those societies whose chief religion forbids its use seem to have it available in ample quantities.

Beer made by fermenting cereals, and wine, made by fermenting the juice of grapes, or other fruits, were the most popularly used intoxicants up until the 18th century. The distilling process which produced hard liquors was invented in the 9th century but hard liquors were not widely used until the 18th century when gin and whisky as we know them were invented. Alcohol destroys many essential nutrients (and especially the B vitamins), and usually causes a loss of appetite. Alcoholics, therefore, almost always suffer from very serious nutritional deficiencies. In addition, the regular intake of large amounts of alcohol has a cumulative and adverse effect on the tissues and vital organs of the body. Moderate consumption by normal persons eating a balanced diet does not appear to have any obvious adverse effects, but as with all aspects of nutrition, the response to alcohol is individual and for some persons even small quantities of it are detrimental.

See Beer; Gin; Rum; Whisky; Wine; and Vodka for composition and nutrient values.

alginates
Salts of alginic acid found in many seaweeds. Ammonium alginate and salts of iron and magnesium are used as thickeners, stabilizers, binding and emulsifying agents in food processing, especially in the manufacture of ice cream and artificial whipped cream.

alkaloids
Organic compounds containing nitrogen and found in plants. A great many drugs and poisons are essentially alkaloids. Some examples: codeine, morphine, nicotine, quinine, and strychnine.

amino acids
All proteins are composed of combinations of 22 amino acids.

Eight of these—the essential amino acids—must be provided if adequate nutrition is to be maintained. These are: lysine, methionine, leucine, threonine, valine, tryptophane, isoleucine, and phenylalanine.

Twelve—the nonessential amino acids—are synthesized in the body if an adequate source of nitrogen is present in the diet. These are: glycine, alanine, proline, serine, cystine, tyrosine, hydroxyproline, aspartic acid, glutamic acid, hydroxyglutamic acid, norlevelne, and di-iodo-tyrosine.

Two more—arginine* and histidine*—are generally considered to be essential for children to support growth, nonessential for adults.

See Protein

amphetamines

In a nutritional context, used to control weight by reducing the desire for food. Almost all "diet pills" are amphetamine-based. They do, in fact, inhibit the appetite, but their drawback is that they are habit-forming and long-term use has many unpleasant side-effects including, of course, dependence on the drug.

anemia

Generally used to refer to a condition resulting from the body's not producing enough red blood cells and/or hemoglobin and which is frequently caused by a deficiency of either protein,* iodine,* iron,* vitamin C,* vitamin B_{12},* or folic acid.*

The commonest form of anemia is iron-deficiency anemia, a condition thought to afflict more than 25 percent of the population. In iron-deficiency anemia the number of red blood cells usually remains normal but the hemoglobin, the iron-containing protein component of the red blood cells, lacks color due to its deficiency in iron. Symptoms include lack of energy, muscular weakness, shortness of breath when exercising, and excessive feelings of fatigue.

Pernicious anemia, so named because it was once invariably fatal, is the result of deficiencies of both vitamin B_{12} and folic acid.

animal starch
    See Glycogen

antibodies
Any of various proteins in the blood, produced by the
liver, in reaction to various bacteria, bacterial toxins, and
possibly viruses. They combine with and render these in-
truders harmless. In short, they are one of the body's
mechanisms for fighting infection. Their production is dependent on an adequate intake of protein.
    See Phagocytes, Protein

anti-caking agents
Chemical compounds (such as calcium phosphate, magnesium silicate, sodium silico aluminate) which are mixed
into salt, sugar, powdered food products, instant whips
and the like to prevent the formation of lumps caused by
the absorption of moisture.
    Anticaking agents must, by law, be listed on the prod-
uct's label or package.
    See Additives

aphrodisiacs
Concoctions of various and sundry kinds which allegedly
have a stimulating or intensifying effect on the consumer's
sexual drive and desires. Since this has been a subject of
more than average interest, not to say apprehension among
the world's male population, it is not surprising that
aphrodisiac properties have been attributed to a staggering
variety of foods and drinks. There is no reliable evidence,
however, indicating that they have the sought-after effect,
except indirectly in those cases where certain drugs are
added to foods or drinks. For example, hashish into cookies, marijuana into brownies, LSD-25 or Spanish fly into
drinks. And even in these cases, the effects are not always
what is expected or desired.
    In the absence of organic malfunctions or serious psy-
chological disturbances, the most likely cause of a marked

decrease in sexual vigor is the serious lack of one or more of the essential nutrients, or of sleep.

arachidonic acid
See Essential Fatty Acids

arginine
An amino acid considered nonessential for adults, but since children cannot make enough arginine to support adequate growth rates, it is an essential amino acid for them.

ariboflavinosis
Name given to set of symptoms caused by vitamin B_2 deficiency. It is characterized by cracking at the corners of the mouth, and swollen, cracked, bright red lips among others.

ascorbic acid
Vitamin C*

aspartic acid
A nonessential amino acid.*

atherosclerosis
A form of arteriosclerosis caused by excessive deposits of cholesterol in the walls of the arteries. At least three of the B vitamins—inositol, choline, and B_6—help maintain normal blood cholesterol, which becomes excessive when any of these vitamins are undersupplied. Blood cholesterol has been shown to drop when patients are treated with the B vitamins.

avidin
A substance in raw egg white. When combined with biotin it makes biotin unavailable to the body. Consequently anyone whose diet includes a large amount of raw eggs may be in danger of inducing biotin deficiency. How large an amount is not known. Volunteers on adequate diets who were fed one-half cup of powdered raw egg whites per

day developed symptoms of biotin deficiency. On the other hand, volunteers who were fed 36 raw eggs per day in a later study developed no deficiency symptoms.

See Biotin; Egg white injury

bagel
A doughnut-shaped roll made by immersing plain yeast dough in boiling water and then baking.

COMPOSITION AND NUTRIENT VALUE PER bagel (55 g)

Protein	6 g	Phosphorous	N.D. mg
Carbohydrate	30 g	Potassium	N.D. mg
Fat	2 g	Sodium	N.D. mg
Saturated Fatty Acids	— g	Vitamin A	I.U.
Oleic Acid	— g	Vitamin B_1	0.15 mg
Linoleic Acid	— g	Vitamin B_2	0.11 mg
Iron	1.2 mg	Niacin	1.40 mg
Calcium	8 mg	Vitamin C	0 mg
		Calories	165

baking powder
Any powder used as a substitute for yeast in baking. It is usually a mixture of sodium bicarbonate, starch, and tartaric acid, and is not toxic.

basal metabolic rate
The rate at which energy is used to maintain body temperature, heart beat, respiration, the tension of the muscles, and the like—measured when the body is at complete rest in moderate temperature and some twelve to fourteen hours after a meal. The BMR is controlled by the thyroid gland and increased if the thyroid gland is hyperactive and decreased when underactive. Deficiencies in vitamin E or iodine adversely affect the function of the thyroid gland and hence the BMR.

beer (light or dark)
An alcoholic beverage brewed from malt and flavored

with hops. Relatively high in calories, and often consumed in quantity—hence the term "beer belly."

COMPOSITION AND NUTRIENT VALUE PER 12 fluid ounces (360 g)

Protein	1 g	Phosphorous	N.D. mg
Carbohydrate	14 g	Potassium	N.D. mg
Fat	0 g	Sodium	N.D. mg
Saturated Fatty Acids	0 g	Vitamin A	— I.U.
Oleic Acid	0 g	Vitamin B_1	0.01 mg
Linoleic Acid	0 g	Vitamin B_2	0.11 mg
Iron	Trace mg	Niacin	2.20 mg
Calcium	18 mg	Vitamin C	— mg
		Calories	150

beet sugar
Sucrose extracted from the sugar beet.
   See Sugar

beriberi
A disease which results from a severe vitamin B_1 deficiency, occurring chiefly in areas where white (polished) rice is the mainstay of the diet and where other sources of B_1 are not well supplied. There are two forms: wet beriberi, where edema is the obvious feature, and dry beriberi where emaciation is the obvious feature. In both forms there is a degeneration of the nerves, stomach disorders, personality changes, mental depression and an enlarged heart with an increased heart beat. Death frequently results from cardiac failure.
   See Vitamin B_1

bioflavonoids
   See Vitamins

biotin
   See Vitamin B complex

biscuits (Baking powder, with "enriched flour")

COMPOSITION AND NUTRIENT VALUE PER 2 inches in diameter biscuit (28 g)

Protein	2 g	Phosphorous	N.D. mg
Carbohydrate	13 g	Potassium	N.D. mg
Fat	5 g	Sodium	N.D. mg
Saturated Fatty Acids	1 g	Vitamin A	Trace I.U.
Oleic Acid	2 g	Vitamin B_1	0.06 mg
Linoleic Acid	1 g	Vitamin B_2	0.06 mg
Iron	0.4 mg	Niacin	0.10 mg
Calcium	34 mg	Vitamin C	Trace mg
		Calories	105

blanching
A process of partial precooking performed on fruits and vegetables prior to canning, freezing, or dehydrating. It can result in losses of from 10 percent to 20 percent of protein, sugars and salts and as much as 33-1/3 percent of the vitamin C. Vitamins B_1, B_2, and niacin are also adversely affected.

bleaching
   See Flour, Refining and Bleaching

bleaching and maturing agents
When freshly ground flour is stored it undergoes a maturing process which results in a stronger and more resilient dough and slowly bleaches the original pale yellow to white. Since storage is expensive both in terms of space and spoilage, flour processors employ chemicals to hasten the bleaching and maturing process. Some of these, e.g., benzoyl peroxide, bleach the flour without improving the baking qualities. Others, such as chlorine dioxide, have both a bleaching and improving (maturing) effect.

Bleaching does seem to destroy what few nutrients are left in flour after the refining process, but so little *is* left that bleaching is not in itself a significant factor in the loss of nutritive values in our daily diet. Bread from refined but unbleached flour, however, does taste better.

See Additives; Flour, Refining and Bleaching; Bread

blood sugar
Also called glucose and dextrose. The production of energy is directly related to the amount of sugar available to the cells of the body. Analysis of the blood of normal persons who have not eaten for twelve hours shows an average of 90-95 milligrams of sugar in 100 cc of blood. At this level energy is adequately produced, but as the blood sugar is used and the blood sugar level falls to approximately 70 milligrams, hunger and fatigue are felt. If the blood sugar is not renewed from dietary sources at this point, fatigue becomes exhaustion and, frequently, attendant headache, muscular weakness, and sometimes even nausea and vomiting occur. If the blood sugar level drops dangerously low, blackouts and fainting may result.

See Protein—Functions and Properties for a particularly relevant discussion of the importance of adequate protein for breakfast in relation to the blood sugar level.

bone meal
The bones of cattle ground into powder. It is rich in calcium, phosphorous, and trace elements, and is used as a food supplement.

botulin
Any of several nerve toxins found in improperly canned or improperly smoked foods.

See Botulism

botulism
A frequently fatal food poisoning caused by botulin. Symptoms include vomiting, abdominal cramps, muscular weakness, and visual disturbances.

bran flakes
A breakfast cereal made from bran, the outer coat covering

the germ of cereal grains which is separated from the grain during the milling process.

COMPOSITION AND NUTRIENT VALUE PER Cup (35 g) (40% bran, thiamin and iron added)

Protein	4 g	Phosphorous	N.D. mg
Carbohydrate	28 g	Potassium	N.D. mg
Fat	1 g	Sodium	N.D. mg
Saturated Fatty Acids	— g	Vitamin A	0 I.U.
Oleic Acid	— g	Vitamin B_1	0.14 mg
Linoleic Acid	— g	Vitamin B_2	0.06 mg
Iron	12.3 mg	Niacin	2.2 mg
Calcium	25 mg	Vitamin C	0 mg
		Calories	105

bread

A basic food usually made from flour or meal—in America usually wheat or rye—which is mixed with a liquid and a leavening agent and baked into loaves or rolls.

Most breads available today are "enriched" breads—that is, approximately one-third of the iron, vitamin B_1, and niacin removed in the refining process of flour is replaced. Unfortunately most of the other nutrients are not replaced, and commercial breads are not comparable in nutrient value to breads made from stone-ground whole-wheat flours. The modern methods of flour refining especially destroy what was once the most readily available source of the B-vitamin complex. Before these methods were employed, it seems unlikely that many people suffered from B-vitamin deficiencies since the breads, cereals, and foods prepared from grains and flours processed by the older methods retained the B vitamins.

According to the Department of Agriculture, white bread as compared to whole wheat bread has lost the following percentage of nutrients: vitamin B_1, 90 percent; B_2, 61 percent; niacin, 80 percent; calcium, 60 percent; potassium, 74 percent; iron, 76 percent; magnesium, 78 percent; linoleic acid, 50 percent. In addition, the protein of the wheat germ which is rich in the essential amino acids is discarded in the making of white bread.

bread, cracked-wheat

COMPOSITION AND NUTRIENT VALUE PER slice (25 g)

Protein	2 g	Phosphorous	25 mg
Carbohydrate	13 g	Potassium	50 mg
Fat	1 g	Sodium	125 mg
Saturated Fatty Acids	— g	Vitamin A	Trace I.U.
Oleic Acid	— g	Vitamin B$_1$	0.03 mg
Linoleic Acid	— g	Vitamin B$_2$	0.02 mg
Iron	0.3 mg	Niacin	0.30 mg
Calcium	22 mg	Vitamin C	Trace mg
		Calories	65

bread, pumpernickel

COMPOSITION AND NUTRIENT VALUE PER slice (25 g)

Protein	2 g	Phosphorous	N.D. mg
Carbohydrate	13 g	Potassium	N.D. mg
Fat	Trace g	Sodium	N.D. mg
Saturated Fatty Acids	— g	Vitamin A	Trace I.U.
Oleic Acid	— g	Vitamin B$_1$	0.06 mg
Linoleic Acid	— g	Vitamin B$_2$	0.03 mg
Iron	0.6 mg	Niacin	0.30 mg
Calcium	21 mg	Vitamin C	0 mg
		Calories	66

bread, rye

COMPOSITION AND NUTRIENT VALUE PER slice (25 g)

Protein	2 g	Phosphorous	29 mg
Carbohydrate	13 g	Potassium	52 mg
Fat	Trace g	Sodium	120 mg
Saturated Fatty Acids	— g	Vitamin A	0 I.U.
Oleic Acid	— g	Vitamin B$_1$	0.05 mg

Linoleic Acid	— g	Vitamin B_2	0.02 mg
Iron	0.4 mg	Niacin	0.40 mg
Calcium	19 mg	Vitamin C	0 mg
		Calories	60

bread, white (enriched)

COMPOSITION AND NUTRIENT VALUE PER slice (25 g)

Protein	2 g	Phosphorous	33 mg
Carbohydrate	13 g	Potassium	36 mg
Fat	1 g	Sodium	132 mg
Saturated Fatty Acids	— g	Vitamin A	Trace I.U.
Oleic Acid	— g	Vitamin B_1	0.06 mg
Linoleic Acid	— g	Vitamin B_2	0.05 mg
Iron	0.6 mg	Niacin	0.60 mg
Calcium	21 mg	Vitamin C	Trace mg
		Calories	70

bread, whole wheat

COMPOSITION AND NUTRIENT VALUE PER slice (28 g)

Protein	3 g	Phosphorous	54 mg
Carbohydrate	14 g	Potassium	40 mg
Fat	1 g	Sodium	144 mg
Saturated Fatty Acids	— g	Vitamin A	Trace I.U.
Oleic Acid	— g	Vitamin B_1	0.09 mg
Linoleic Acid	— g	Vitamin B_2	0.03 mg
Iron	0.8 mg	Niacin	0.80 mg
Calcium	24 mg	Vitamin C	Trace mg
		Calories	65

See Flour, Refining and Bleaching; Refined Foods

breakfast cereals
Despite manufacturers' claims to the contrary, the com-

mercial breakfast cereals marketed in this country are not very nutritious, as the following sampling illustrates. One exception, Granola, is listed. There are others, but we did not have the information needed for composition and nutrient values.

Corn Flakes (plain, "enriched")

COMPOSITION AND NUTRIENT VALUE PER Cup (25 g)

Protein	2 g	Phosphorous	15 mg
Carbohydrate	21 g	Potassium	40 mg
Fat	Trace g	Sodium	165 mg
Saturated Fatty Acids	— g	Vitamin A	0 I.U.
Oleic Acid	— g	Vitamin B$_1$	0.11 mg
Linoleic Acid	— g	Vitamin B$_2$	0.02 mg
Iron	0.4 mg	Niacin	0.50 mg
Calcium	4 mg	Vitamin C	0 mg
		Calories	100

Granola

COMPOSITION AND NUTRIENT VALUE (extrapolated from package contents listing) PER two ounces (56 g)

Protein	9 g	Phosphorous	160 mg
Carbohydrate	38 g	Potassium	N.D. mg
Fat	9 g	Sodium	N.D. mg
Saturated Fatty Acids	N.D. g	Vitamin A	0 I.U.
Oleic Acid	N.D. g	Vitamin B$_1$	0.42 mg
Linoleic Acid	N.D. g	Vitamin B$_2$	0.17 mg
Iron	1 mg	Niacin	1.8 mg
Calcium	N.D. mg	Vitamin C	0 mg
		Calories	250

Oats, rolled (Oatmeal)
A breakfast cereal.

COMPOSITION AND NUTRIENT VALUE PER Cup (240 g), cooked

Protein	5 g	Phosphorous	140 mg
Carbohydrate	23 g	Potassium	142 mg
Fat	2 g	Sodium	508 mg
Saturated Fatty Acids	— g	Vitamin A	0 I.U.
Oleic Acid	— g	Vitamin B$_1$	0.19 mg
Linoleic Acid	1 g	Vitamin B$_2$	0.05 mg
Iron	1.4 mg	Niacin	0.20 mg
Calcium	22 mg	Vitamin C	0 mg
		Calories	130

Puffed Rice ("enriched")

A breakfast cereal.

COMPOSITION AND NUTRIENT VALUE PER Cup (15 g)

Protein	1 g	Phosphorous	82 mg
Carbohydrate	13 g	Potassium	57 mg
Fat	Trace g	Sodium	Trace mg
Saturated Fatty Acids	— g	Vitamin A	0 I.U
Oleic Acid	— g	Vitamin B$_1$	0.07 mg
Linoleic Acid	— g	Vitamin B$_2$	0.01 mg
Iron	0.3 mg	Niacin	0.70 mg
Calcium	3 mg	Vitamin C	0 mg
		Calories	60

Puffed Wheat ("enriched")

A breakfast cereal.

COMPOSITION AND NUTRIENT VALUE PER Cup (15 g)

Protein	2 g	Phosphorous	N.D. mg
Carbohydrate	12 g	Potassium	N.D. mg
Fat	Trace g	Sodium	N.D. mg
Saturated Fatty Acids	— g	Vitamin A	0 I.U.
Oleic Acid	— g	Vitamin B$_1$	0.08 mg
Linoleic Acid	— g	Vitamin B$_2$	0.03 mg
Iron	0.6 mg	Niacin	1.2 mg
Calcium	4 mg	Vitamin C	0 mg
		Calories	55

Shredded Wheat

A breakfast cereal.

COMPOSITION AND NUTRIENT VALUE PER Biscuit (25 g)

Protein	2 g	Phosphorous	122 mg
Carbohydrate	20 g	Potassium	116 mg
Fat	1 g	Sodium	1 mg
Saturated Fatty Acids	— g	Vitamin A	0 I.U.
Oleic Acid	— g	Vitamin B_1	0.06 mg
Linoleic Acid	— g	Vitamin B_2	0.03 mg
Iron	0.9 mg	Niacin	1.10 mg
Calcium	11 mg	Vitamin C	0 mg
		Calories	90

brewer's yeast

A preparation containing yeast cells and inert material, used as a leavening agent and a dietary supplement. Brewer's yeast is a by-product of the beer-making process, but there are other yeast products such as torula,* which are grown in laboratories and contain essentially the same nutrients. Brewer's yeast is a particularly concentrated source of the B-vitamin complex, and is, in addition, a good source of complete protein.*

COMPOSITION AND NUTRIENT VALUE PER Tablespoon (8 g)

Protein	3 g	Phosphorous	148 mg
Carbohydrate	3 g	Potassium	158 mg
Fat	Trace g	Sodium	10 mg
Saturated Fatty Acids	— g	Vitamin A	Trace I.U.
Oleic Acid	— g	Vitamin B_1	1.25 mg
Linoleic Acid	— g	Vitamin B_2	0.34 mg
Iron	1.4 mg	Niacin	3 mg
Calcium	17 mg	Vitamin C	Trace mg
		Calories	25

buffers and neutralizers

Chemicals such as ammonium bicarbonate, tartaric acid, and sodium aluminum phosphate (to name a few) which are added to foods and drinks to control acidity or alkalinity. By law, all such additives must be listed on the product's label or package.

See Acids and Alkalis; Additives

butter

A dairy product made by churning the cream separated from milk until it becomes solid. The finished butter, which must contain more than 80 percent fat and not more than 15 percent water, is usually whitish or pale yellow. The deep yellow of the butter one buys comes from artificial coloring agents. Salt is usually added to enhance the butter's keeping qualities. Butter to which salt has not been added is called sweet butter. Butter is a rich source of vitamin A and a relatively poor source of vitamin D, both of which are present in significantly higher amounts in butter made in the summer than that made in winter.

COMPOSITION AND NUTRIENT VALUE PER 1/4 pound (113 g)

Protein	1 g	Phosphorous	0 mg
Carbohydrate	1 g	Potassium	28 mg
Fat	92 g	Sodium	990 mg
Saturated Fatty Acids	51 g	Vitamin A	3750 I.U.
Oleic Acid	30 g	Vitamin B_1	0 mg
Linoleic Acid	3 g	Vitamin B_2	Trace mg
Iron	0 mg	Niacin	Trace mg
Calcium	23 mg	Vitamin C	0 mg
		Calories	810

buttermilk

The residue left after churning butter. It has a slightly sour taste but it is almost fat-free and thus very low in calories. With the exception of its relatively low vitamin A content, it is the nutritional equivalent of whole milk.

COMPOSITION AND NUTRIENT VALUE PER Cup (245 g)

Protein	9 g	Phosphorous	270 mg
Carbohydrate	12 g	Potassium	52 mg
Fat	Trace g	Sodium	19 mg
Saturated Fatty Acids	— g	Vitamin A	10 I.U.
Oleic Acid	— g	Vitamin B_1	0.10 mg
Linoleic Acid	— g	Vitamin B_2	0.44 mg
Iron	0.1 mg	Niacin	0.2 mg
Calcium	296 mg	Vitamin C	2 mg
		Calories	90

caffeine

An alkaloid found in coffee and tea and much abused in this country. An average-sized cup of coffee contains 100 milligrams of caffeine, tea a little less. In small doses caffeine is beneficial as a stimulant and is said to alleviate migraine headaches. In large doses—and some people consume the equivalent of 100 to 200 cups of coffee in caffeine tablets per day—it frequently results in symptoms severe enough to be classed as psychotic.

See Coffee for the effects of caffeine on vitamin B

cake

A baked mixture of flour, liquids and other ingredients, sometimes with eggs and almost invariably with a considerable amount of sugar.

angel food cake

COMPOSITION AND NUTRIENT VALUE PER Piece, 1/12 of 10-inch diam. cake (53 g)

Protein	3 g	Phosphorous	N.D. mg
Carbohydrate	32 g	Potassium	N.D. mg
Fat	Trace g	Sodium	N.D. mg
Saturated Fatty Acids	— g	Vitamin A	0 I.U.

Oleic Acid	— g	Vitamin B$_1$	Trace mg
Linoleic Acid	— g	Vitamin B$_2$	0.06 mg
Iron	0.2 mg	Niacin	0.10 mg
Calcium	50 mg	Vitamin C	0 mg
		Calories	135

brownies

COMPOSITION AND NUTRIENT VALUE PER brownie (20 g) made from packaged mix.

Protein	1 g	Phosphorous	N.D. mg
Carbohydrate	13 g	Potassium	N.D. mg
Fat	4 g	Sodium	N.D. mg
Saturated Fatty Acids	1 g	Vitamin A	20 I.U.
Oleic Acid	2 g	Vitamin B$_1$	0.03 mg
Linoleic Acid	1 g	Vitamin B$_2$	0.02 mg
Iron	0.4 mg	Niacin	0.10 mg
Calcium	9 mg	Vitamin C	Trace mg
		Calories	85

chocolate cake, with fudge icing

COMPOSITION AND NUTRIENT VALUE PER slice (120 g)

Protein	5 g	Phosphorous	38 mg
Carbohydrate	70 g	Potassium	165 mg
Fat	14 g	Sodium	52 mg
Saturated Fatty Acids	4 g	Vitamin A	50 I.U.
Oleic Acid	8 g	Vitamin B$_1$	Trace mg
Linoleic Acid	1 g	Vitamin B$_2$	Trace mg
Iron	0.8 mg	Niacin	0.30 mg
Calcium	29 mg	Vitamin C	Trace mg
		Calories	420

danish pastry, plain

COMPOSITION AND NUTRIENT VALUE PER piece, 4 1/2″ × 1″ (65 g)

Protein	5 g	Phosphorous	N.D. mg
Carbohydrate	30 g	Potassium	N.D. mg
Fat	15 g	Sodium	N.D. mg
Saturated Fatty Acids	5 g	Vitamin A	200 I.U.
Oleic Acid	7 g	Vitamin B_1	0.05 mg
Linoleic Acid	3 g	Vitamin B_2	0.10 mg
Iron	0.6 mg	Niacin	0.5 mg
Calcium	33 mg	Vitamin C	Trace mg
		Calories	275

devil's food cake (2-layer, with chocolate icing)

COMPOSITION AND NUTRIENT VALUE PER slice, 1/16 of 9-inch diam. cake (69 g)

Protein	3 g	Phosphorous	N.D. mg
Carbohydrate	40 g	Potassium	N.D. mg
Fat	9 g	Sodium	N.D. mg
Saturated Fatty Acids	3 g	Vitamin A	100 I.U.
Oleic Acid	4 g	Vitamin B_1	0.02 mg
Linoleic Acid	1 g	Vitamin B_2	0.06 mg
Iron	0.6 mg	Niacin	0.20 mg
Calcium	41 mg	Vitamin C	Trace mg
		Calories	235

doughnut, plain (from "enriched" flour)

COMPOSITION AND NUTRIENT VALUE PER one (32 g)

Protein	1 g	Phosphorous	63 mg
Carbohydrate	16 g	Potassium	26 mg
Fat	6 g	Sodium	80 mg
Saturated Fatty Acids	1 g	Vitamin A	30 I.U.
Oleic Acid	4 g	Vitamin B_1	0.05 mg
Linoleic Acid	Trace g	Vitamin B_2	0.05 mg
Iron	0.4 mg	Niacin	0.40 mg
Calcium	13 mg	Vitamin C	Trace mg
		Calories	125

fruitcake (dark, made with "enriched" flour)

COMPOSITION AND NUTRIENT VALUE PER slice (30 g)

Protein	2 g	Phosphorous	38 mg
Carbohydrate	18 g	Potassium	165 mg
Fat	4 g	Sodium	52 mg
Saturated Fatty Acids	1 g	Vitamin A	40 I.U.
Oleic Acid	2 g	Vitamin B_1	0.04 mg
Linoleic Acid	Trace g	Vitamin B_2	0.04 mg
Iron	0.8 mg	Niacin	0.20 mg
Calcium	22 mg	Vitamin C	Trace mg
		Calories	110

gingerbread

COMPOSITION AND NUTRIENT VALUE PER piece, 1/9 of 8-inch square cake (63 g)

Protein	2 g	Phosphorous	33 mg
Carbohydrate	32 g	Potassium	222 mg
Fat	4 g	Sodium	119 mg
Saturated Fatty Acids	1 g	Vitamin A	Trace I.U.
Oleic Acid	2 g	Vitamin B_1	0.02 mg
Linoleic Acid	1 g	Vitamin B_2	0.06 mg
Iron	1 mg	Niacin	0.50 mg
Calcium	57 mg	Vitamin C	Trace mg
		Calories	175

plain cake

COMPOSITION AND NUTRIENT VALUE PER piece, 1/9 of 9-inch square cake without icing (86 g)

Protein	4 g	Phosphorous	N.D. mg
Carbohydrate	48 g	Potassium	N.D. mg
Fat	12 g	Sodium	N.D. mg
Saturated Fatty Acids	3 g	Vitamin A	150 I.U.

Oleic Acid	6 g	Vitamin B_1	0.02 mg
Linoleic Acid	2 g	Vitamin B_2	0.08 mg
Iron	0.3 mg	Niacin	0.20 mg
Calcium	55 mg	Vitamin C	Trace mg
		Calories	315

pound cake

COMPOSITION AND NUTRIENT VALUE PER slice (30 g)

Protein	2 g	Phosphorous	N.D. mg
Carbohydrate	14 g	Potassium	N.D. mg
Fat	9 g	Sodium	N.D. mg
Saturated Fatty Acids	2 g	Vitamin A	80 I.U.
Oleic Acid	4 g	Vitamin B_1	0.01 mg
Linoleic Acid	1 g	Vitamin B_2	0.03 mg
Iron	0.2 mg	Niacin	0.10 mg
Calcium	6 mg	Vitamin C	0 mg
		Calories	140

sponge cake

COMPOSITION AND NUTRIENT VALUE PER slice, 1/12 of 10-inch cake (66 g)

Protein	5 g	Phosphorous	N.D. mg
Carbohydrate	36 g	Potassium	N.D. mg
Fat	4 g	Sodium	N.D. mg
Saturated Fatty Acids	1 g	Vitamin A	300 I.U.
Oleic Acid	2 g	Vitamin B_1	0.03 mg
Linoleic Acid	Trace g	Vitamin B_2	0.09 mg
Iron	0.8 mg	Niacin	0.10 mg
Calcium	20 mg	Vitamin C	Trace mg
		Calories	195

calorie
Also called the kilocalorie or large calorie, it is defined as the unit of heat equal to the amount of heat required to

raise the temperature of one kilogram of water by 1° Centigrade at one atmosphere of pressure.

Intake of food is measured in calories because the number of calories ingested is directly related to the energy available to the body. If the energy expended is less than that available, the usual result is weight gain.

See Energy

cane sugar
Sucrose extracted from sugar cane.
See Sugar

carbohydrates
Various organic compounds consisting only of carbon, hydrogen and oxygen—such as sugars, starches, and cellulose (plant starch). The sugars and starches break down in the digestive process into simple sugars such as glucose, fructose and galactose. Cellulose and certain other carbohydrates are not broken down in the digestive process and do not serve as a dietary source of energy (e.g., pectins, agar-agar). These are termed the "unavailable" carbohydrates.

Carbohydrates form the chief part of the diet in most parts of the world and hence are the major source of energy for most of the world's population. They contribute about 45 percent of the daily calorie intake in highly developed countries and upwards of 90 percent of the daily calorie intake in the developing countries. Superfluous carbohydrate contributes to the buildup of fat in the body.

SOURCES
With the exception of meats, fats, salad oils, and a few other nutrients, almost everything we ingest contains carbohydrates.

REQUIREMENTS
There are no specific requirements established for carbohydrates. If anything, Americans eat far too many carbohydrates.

DEFICIENCIES
No known deficiencies except in cases of starvation.

EXCESS
Leads to gains in weight, usually unwanted.

carotene
A yellow pigment occurring in plants from which animals and humans form Vitamin A. The yellow color is hidden in many plants by the green color of chlorophyll.
See Vitamin A

casein
The chief protein of milk. Lactalbumin and lactoglobulin are the others. Since casein is precipitated under acid conditions and lactalbumin and lactoglobulin are not, cheese contains casein but not the other two proteins.
See Cheese; Milk

cellulose
The main constituent of all plant tissues and fibers. It cannot be digested by man, but it is useful insofar as it provides the bulk necessary for intestinal functioning.
See Roughage

cereal
(1) Any edible grain or grass that may be used as food (e.g., wheat, corn, rice, barley).
(2) The dried preparations manufactured from grains or seeds that are consumed in large quantities at breakfast.

The vast majority of this latter group are made from refined grains by a process requiring great heat. Consequently, most of the nutrients are either destroyed or discarded. The manufacturers attempt to rectify this by adding vitamins, minerals, and protein to their product. The resulting cereal, however, is rarely of much nutritional value—a fact revealed by repeated investigations.

certified raw milk
Certified raw milk is milk produced by disease-free cows,

which are milked by sterilized machines in hygienic surroundings. The cows receive regular veterinary inspection, and their milk is regularly tested for the presence of microorganisms. It is not pasteurized. (Pasteurization,* while it inactivates most of the disease-causing microorganisms often present in whole milk, also reduces its nutritional value and destroys the phosphatase enzymes necessary for the absorption of calcium and phosphorus.) *Certified* means that the milk was produced in compliance with the strict laws governing every phase of the production. It is more nutritious than its pasteurized counterpart.

See Milk

cheese

A solid food made from the curd precipitated from milk by the action of lactic acid or the enzyme rennin or both. Cheeses are classed as either hard (cheddar, swiss), semihard (Roquefort, Gorgonzola), or soft (Brie, cottage).

All the natural cheeses are very good sources of complete protein, as well as minerals and vitamin A if the cheese is made from whole milk.

cheese, cheddar

COMPOSITION AND NUTRIENT VALUE PER One-inch cube (17 g)

Protein	4 g	Phosphorous	128 mg
Carbohydrate	Trace g	Potassium	30 mg
Fat	6 g	Sodium	180 mg
Saturated Fatty Acids	3 g	Vitamin A	230 I.U.
Oleic Acid	2 g	Vitamin B_1	0.01 mg
Linoleic Acid	Trace g	Vitamin B_2	0.08 mg
Iron	0.2 mg	Niacin	Trace mg
Calcium	129 mg	Vitamin C	0 mg
		Calories	70

cheese, cottage (creamed)

COMPOSITION AND NUTRIENT VALUE PER Cup (245 g)

Protein	33 g	Phosphorous	360 mg
Carbohydrate	7 g	Potassium	170 mg
Fat	10 g	Sodium	625 mg
Saturated Fatty Acids	6 g	Vitamin A	420 I.U.
Oleic Acid	3 g	Vitamin B_1	0.07 mg
Linoleic Acid	Trace g	Vitamin B_2	0.61 mg
Iron	0.7 mg	Niacin	0.2 mg
Calcium	230 mg	Vitamin C	0 mg
		Calories	260

cheese, cottage (uncreamed)

COMPOSITION AND NUTRIENT VALUE PER Cup (200 g)

Protein	34 g	Phosphorous	380 mg
Carbohydrate	5 g	Potassium	180 mg
Fat	1 g	Sodium	620 mg
Saturated Fatty Acids	Trace g	Vitamin A	20 I.U.
Oleic Acid	Trace g	Vitamin B_1	0.06 mg
Linoleic Acid	Trace g	Vitamin B_2	0.56 mg
Iron	0.8 mg	Niacin	0.2 mg
Calcium	180 mg	Vitamin C	0 mg
		Calories	170

cheese, cream

COMPOSITION AND NUTRIENT VALUE PER Ounce (28 g)

Protein	2 g	Phosphorous	170 mg
Carbohydrate	1 g	Potassium	25 mg
Fat	11 g	Sodium	180 mg
Saturated Fatty Acids	6 g	Vitamin A	440 I.U.
Oleic Acid	4 g	Vitamin B_1	Trace mg
Linoleic Acid	Trace g	Vitamin B_2	0.07 mg
Iron	0.07 mg	Niacin	Trace mg
Calcium	18.0 mg	Vitamin C	0 mg
		Calories	106

cheese, processed

Cheese is processed to temporarily arrest the deterioration in flavor that occurs in natural cheeses after a short period of time.

COMPOSITION AND NUTRIENT VALUE PER Ounce (28 g)

Protein	7 g	Phosphorous	190 mg
Carbohydrate	1 g	Potassium	22 mg
Fat	9 g	Sodium	370 mg
Saturated Fatty Acids	5 g	Vitamin A	350 I.U.
Oleic Acid	3 g	Vitamin B_1	0.01 mg
Linoleic Acid	Trace g	Vitamin B_2	0.12 mg
Iron	0.3 mg	Niacin	Trace mg
Calcium	198 mg	Vitamin C	0 mg
		Calories	105

cheese, Roquefort (or Bleu)

COMPOSITION AND NUTRIENT VALUE PER Ounce (28 g)

Protein	6 g	Phosphorous	100 mg
Carbohydrate	1 g	Potassium	22 mg
Fat	9 g	Sodium	284 mg
Saturated Fatty Acids	5 g	Vitamin A	350 I.U.
Oleic Acid	3 g	Vitamin B_1	0.01 mg
Linoleic Acid	Trace g	Vitamin B_2	0.17 mg
Iron	0.1 mg	Niacin	0.3 mg
Calcium	89 mg	Vitamin C	0 mg
		Calories	105

cheese, Swiss

COMPOSITION AND NUTRIENT VALUE PER Ounce (28 g)

Protein	8 g	Phosphorous	140 mg
Carbohydrate	1 g	Potassium	25 mg
Fat	8 g	Sodium	225 mg

Saturated Fatty Acids	4 g	Vitamin A	320 I.U.
Oleic Acid	3 g	Vitamin B$_1$	Trace mg
Linoleic Acid	Trace g	Vitamin B$_2$	0.11 mg
Iron	0.3 mg	Niacin	Trace mg
Calcium	262 mg	Vitamin C	0 mg
		Calories	105

chili con carne

(Or "Chili with meat." A spicy dish made of ground chili peppers, meat, various seasonings, and sometimes beans.)

COMPOSITION AND NUTRIENT VALUE PER Cup, with beans (250 g)

Protein	19 g	Phosphorous	350 mg
Carbohydrate	30 g	Potassium	500 mg
Fat	15 g	Sodium	1060 mg
Saturated Fatty Acids	7 g	Vitamin A	150 I.U.
Oleic Acid	7 g	Vitamin B$_1$	0.08 mg
Linoleic Acid	Trace g	Vitamin B$_2$	0.18 mg
Iron	4.2 mg	Niacin	3.20 mg
Calcium	80 mg	Vitamin C	0 mg
		Calories	335

Chinese restaurant syndrome

Name given to a set of symptoms which include headache, chest pain, and numbness reported by the sufferer after dining on Chinese food. It is thought that monosodium glutamate (MSG)*—a food additive in high favor in most such restaurants—is the responsible agent.

chlorophyll

The green coloring matter of plants, which enables the process of photosynthesis* to proceed, and through which plants are able to manufacture their own complex foods. Animals, on the other hand, must be supplied with ready-made complex foods.

chocolate

A preparation made from the cured and roasted seeds of

the cocoa bean, called "cocoa" or "chocolate nib," refined and mixed with sugar, cocoa butter, lecithin, and, in the case of milk chocolate, milk solids.

chocolate, milk

COMPOSITION AND NUTRIENT VALUE PER Ounce (28 g) of milk chocolate

Protein	2 g	Phosphorous	N.D. mg
Carbohydrate	16 g	Potassium	N.D. mg
Fat	9 g	Sodium	N.D. mg
Saturated Fatty Acids	5 g	Vitamin A	80 I.U.
Oleic Acid	3 g	Vitamin B_1	0.02 mg
Linoleic Acid	Trace g	Vitamin B_2	0.10 mg
Iron	0.3 mg	Niacin	0.10 mg
Calcium	65 mg	Vitamin C	Trace mg
		Calories	145

fudge, plain

COMPOSITION AND NUTRIENT VALUE PER Ounce (28 g)

Protein	1 g	Phosphorous	N.D. mg
Carbohydrate	21 g	Potassium	N.D. mg
Fat	4 g	Sodium	N.D. mg
Saturated Fatty Acids	2 g	Vitamin A	Trace I.U.
Oleic Acid	1 g	Vitamin B_1	0.01 mg
Linoleic Acid	Trace g	Vitamin B_2	0.03 mg
Iron	0.3 mg	Niacin	0.10 mg
Calcium	22 mg	Vitamin C	Trace mg
		Calories	115

cholesterol

The most common animal sterol and a universal tissue constituent occurring especially in the brain, bile, blood cells, plasma, liver and kidney of humans and animals, and in milk, egg yolk, and animal fats and oils.

Many researchers believe cholesterol to be an important

factor in causing various cardiovascular diseases. A diet rich in the saturated fatty acids (found chiefly in meats and dairy products) causes a rise in the blood cholesterol. Conversely, if the diet contains mostly unsaturated fatty acids (from vegetables and fish) the blood cholesterol will usually be lowered.

Since cholesterol is essential to the body processes it cannot be entirely eliminated. It forms the raw material from which vitamin D, bile salts, and the sex and adrenal hormones are made. And cholesterol is manufactured from starch and sugar by the liver whether or not cholesterol has been excluded from the diet.

See Fats; Lecithin; Sterols

choline
See under Vitamin B complex

citrus fruit
A genus which includes lemons, limes, grapefruit, oranges, and tangerines. They are our most dependable source of vitamin C and their pulp, especially the white of the rind, is particularly rich in bioflavonoids.*

See individual citrus fruits under FRUITS for composition and nutrient values.

cocoa bean
The bean is left to ferment and then is roasted. After roasting, it is cracked, the shell removed, and the remainder (called the nib) is used as the basic material for a number of products.

Chocolate is made from cocoa nibs from which the rich fat content (54 percent) has not been removed. The beverage cocoa is made from nibs from which the fat has been extracted, as is the cocoa used as a flavoring.

cocoa
A beverage made from the ground nibs of the cocoa bean (after roasting) and warm milk. It contains sizeable amounts of caffeine, a fact not generally known by the parents giving it to children.

COMPOSITION AND NUTRIENT VALUE PER Cup (250 g) made with milk

Protein	10 g	Phosphorous	212 mg
Carbohydrate	27 g	Potassium	50 mg
Fat	12 g	Sodium	19 mg
Saturated Fatty Acids	7 g	Vitamin A	400 I.U.
Oleic Acid	4 g	Vitamin B$_1$	0.10 mg
Linoleic Acid	Trace g	Vitamin B$_2$	0.45 mg
Iron	1 mg	Niacin	0.5 mg
Calcium	295 mg	Vitamin C	3 mg
		Calories	245

cod-liver oil
A rich source of vitamin A and D. The average sample of cod-liver oil contains from 400-4,000 I.U. of vitamin A and from 40-400 I.U. of vitamin D.

coenzymes
Substances needed by certain enzymes to assist in their functions. Most coenzymes are members of the vitamin B complex. For example, coenzyme A contains pantothenic acid, and coenzyme I contains niacin.

coffee
A beverage, made from ground coffee beans and water, consumed in great quantities in this country. Some researchers have produced data indicating that animals fed coffee develop vitamin B deficiencies, a result both of the caffeine and water content of the coffee. The caffeine stimulates the heartbeat which in turn increases the flow of blood plasma through the kidneys, which together with the liquid content of the coffee causes a loss of B vitamin through excretion of a greater volume of urine.
    See Caffeine

COMPOSITION AND NUTRIENT VALUE PER Cup (230 g) black, unsweetened

Protein	Trace g	Phosphorous	9 mg
Carbohydrate	1 g	Potassium	40 mg
Fat	0 g	Sodium	2 mg
Saturated Fatty Acids	0 g	Vitamin A	0 I.U.
Oleic Acid	0 g	Vitamin B_1	0 mg
Linoleic Acid	0 g	Vitamin B_2	Trace mg
Iron	0.2 mg	Niacin	0.6 mg
Calcium	9 mg	Vitamin C	0 mg
		Calories	3

coloring agents

Various materials, some natural but most synthetic, applied or mixed into foods to enhance, retain, or recreate the natural color of the food. For example, dyes are used to make butter yellow and meat red. The coloring agents have neither preservative nor nutritive value but add unneeded chemicals to the body in the cause of esthetics.

By law, the coloring agents used must be stated on the product's label.

See Additives

complete proteins

Those proteins which supply adequate amounts of the essential amino acids.

See Essential Amino Acids; subheading *Sources* under Protein

cookies

Essentially the same ingredients as cake* but dried to low moisture content.

cookie, hard

COMPOSITION AND NUTRIENT VALUE PER cookie (25 g)

Protein	1 g	Phosphorous	N.D. mg
Carbohydrate	12 g	Potassium	N.D. mg
Fat	3 g	Sodium	N.D. mg
Saturated Fatty Acids	— g	Vitamin A	14 I.U.

Oleic Acid	— g	Vitamin B_1	0.1 mg
Linoleic Acid	— g	Vitamin B_2	0.1 mg
Iron	0.1 mg	Niacin	0.10 mg
Calcium	6 mg	Vitamin C	Trace mg
		Calories	82

fig bars

COMPOSITION AND NUTRIENT VALUE PER bar (14 g)

Protein	1 g	Phosphorous	N.D. mg
Carbohydrate	11 g	Potassium	N.D. mg
Fat	1 g	Sodium	N.D. mg
Saturated Fatty Acids	— g	Vitamin A	20 I.U.
Oleic Acid	— g	Vitamin B_1	Trace mg
Linoleic Acid	— g	Vitamin B_2	0.01 mg
Iron	0.2 mg	Niacin	0.10 mg
Calcium	11 mg	Vitamin C	Trace mg
		Calories	50

cooking, effect on nutritional values

Vegetables lose most of their vitamin C when boiled in water. Steaming or cooking in very little water minimizes the loss. In general, the water-soluble vitamins and minerals are leached into the water. It is advisable, therefore, to use no more water than is necessary for the cooking operation and to not discard it. The proteins are not affected, nor are the fat-soluble vitamins except at frying temperatures. For example, frying destroys 10 percent of B_1, 10 percent of B_2, and 15 percent of niacin, and the longer the food is subjected to high temperatures the greater the loss. Stewing destroys 75 percent of B_1, 30 percent of B_2, and 50 percent of niacin.

See Fat-soluble vitamins; Water-soluble vitamins.

cream

The fatty part of unhomogenized milk that accumulates at the surface. (Heavy or whipping.)

See also Half and half

COMPOSITION AND NUTRIENT VALUE PER Cup (238 g)

Protein	5 g	Phosphorous	70 mg
Carbohydrate	7 g	Potassium	65 mg
Fat	90 g	Sodium	50 mg
Saturated Fatty Acids	50 g	Vitamin A	3670 I.U.
Oleic Acid	30 g	Vitamin B_1	0.05 mg
Linoleic Acid	3 g	Vitamin B_2	0.26 mg
Iron	0.1 mg	Niacin	0.1 mg
Calcium	179 mg	Vitamin C	2 mg
		Calories	840

cretinism
A condition resulting from the underactivity of the thyroid gland and characterized by arrested growth and mental retardation. It can be caused by a dietary deficiency of iodine.
   See Iodine; Thyroid Gland

cyanocobalamin
Vitamin B_{12}
   See Vitamins

dairy products
Those foods such as butter and cheese which are made from milk, and of course milk itself. Dairy products are good sources of complete protein* and many minerals and vitamins.
   See individual dairy product entries for nutritive values

dark adaptation
The change that takes place in the retina to assist vision in dim light. A pigment, visual purple which is necessary for seeing in dim light, is formed from vitamin A, aldehyde, and a protein. When there is a vitamin A deficiency, the result is poor dark adaptation.
   See Visual Purple; Vitamin A

dehydration
The process by which the water content of various foods is removed through evaporation. The heat applied in the process destroys some of the nutrients and the air oxidizes others.

dental caries
Tooth decay—and the most widespread disease in America. Surveys comparing Americans and other nationalities with respect to the number of teeth decayed or missing, strongly suggest that the most important factor in our lead in this area is our high intake of sticky carbohydrate foods with heavy concentrations of refined sugar (coffee cakes, candy bars, and the like). But there are many other factors that affect the health of the teeth. Adequate amounts of protein, calcium, phosphorus, vitamin A, vitamin C, and vitamin D are all necessary for the healthy development of the teeth and their supporting structures, and calcium and vitamin D are essential to the prevention of tooth decay. In addition, though many people have healthy teeth without the aid of fluorides, it has been demonstrated that those who drink water containing 1 to 2 ppm of fluoride have considerably less tooth decay than those who drink water with much lower amounts of fluoride.
See Fluoride

desiccated liver
A rich and concentrated source of iron, complete protein, and the B complex of vitamins sold in tablets, capsules, and powder. It is made by drying liver (after the lining, connective tissues, and external fat are removed) at low temperature in a vacuum chamber, a process which preserves the nutrients.

dextrose
A synonym for glucose.*

dietary supplements
See Food supplements

diets

Prescribed courses—including the amount and preparation of selected foods and food supplements*—for the purpose of (1) preventing nutritional deficiencies; (2) correcting nutritional deficiencies; (3) attaining in specific illnesses a therapeutically correct balance of nutrients (e.g. a diet excluding as much sugar as possible in diabetes, and salt-free diet* in certain heart diseases); (4) losing weight; and (5) gaining weight.

With the exception of (1), the eating of a balanced diet to prevent nutritional deficiencies—an activity for which all persons should acquire the necessary information—no one should undertake a special diet unless it is carried out under the supervision of a competent physician.

See Reducing

digestibility

The proportion of a given food absorbed from the digestive tract into the bloodstream, measured as the difference between intake and fecal output with allowance for the portion of feces not derived from undigested food. Normal digestibility for most foods is 90-95 percent.

digestion

The breaking down of foods into simpler constituents by the digestive enzymes—proteins to amino acids, fats to glycerol and fatty acids, starch to glucose—which are then absorbed into the bloodstream.

See Intestinal Juice

disaccharide

Any of a class of carbohydrates, including lactose and sucrose, yielding two monosaccharides on hydrolysis.

dizziness

One of the symptoms manifested through a variety of nutritional deficiencies. These include deficiencies in choline, folic acid, pantothenic acid, niacin, and vitamin B_6.

DNA
Desoxyribonucleic acid.
See Nucleic Acids

dried fruits
Fruits such as grapes (raisins), plums (prunes), apricots, peaches and figs which are dehydrated in the sun or by the application of chemicals. Most commercially produced dried fruits are dehydrated by chemicals, the application of sulphur dioxide gas being one of the more common methods.

The vitamin and mineral content of the fruits is decreased and the sugar content increased during the drying process. The commercial sulphuring procedure does, however, prevent the loss of vitamin C.

apricots, dried

COMPOSITION AND NUTRIENT VALUE PER Cup (150 g)

Protein	8 g	Phosphorous	150 mg
Carbohydrate	100 g	Potassium	1560 mg
Fat	1 g	Sodium	38 mg
Saturated Fatty Acids	— g	Vitamin A	16,350 I.U.
Oleic Acid	— g	Vitamin B_1	0.02 mg
Linoleic Acid	— g	Vitamin B_2	0.23 mg
Iron	8.2 mg	Niacin	4.90 mg
Calcium	100 mg	Vitamin C	19 mg
		Calories	390

dates, dried

COMPOSITION AND NUTRIENT VALUE PER Cup (178 g)

Protein	4 g	Phosphorous	110 mg
Carbohydrate	130 g	Potassium	1300 mg
Fat	1 g	Sodium	1 mg
Saturated Fatty Acids	— g	Vitamin A	90 I.U.
Oleic Acid	— g	Vitamin B_1	0.16 mg

Linoleic Acid	— g	Vitamin B$_2$	0.17 mg
Iron	5.3 mg	Niacin	3.90 mg
Calcium	105 mg	Vitamin C	0 mg
		Calories	490

figs, dried

COMPOSITION AND NUTRIENT VALUE PER 2 figs (42 g)

Protein	2 g	Phosphorous	55 mg
Carbohydrate	30 g	Potassium	390 mg
Fat	Trace g	Sodium	15 mg
Saturated Fatty Acids	— g	Vitamin A	40 I.U.
Oleic Acid	— g	Vitamin B$_1$	0.04 mg
Linoleic Acid	— g	Vitamin B$_2$	0.04 mg
Iron	1.2 mg	Niacin	0.20 mg
Calcium	52 mg	Vitamin C	0 mg
		Calories	120

prune
A partially dried plum.

COMPOSITION AND NUTRIENT VALUE PER 4 (32 g), raw

Protein	1 g	Phosphorous	N.D. mg
Carbohydrate	18 g	Potassium	N.D. mg
Fat	Trace g	Sodium	N.D. mg
Saturated Fatty Acids	— g	Vitamin A	440 I.U.
Oleic Acid	— g	Vitamin B$_1$	0.02 mg
Linoleic Acid	— g	Vitamin B$_2$	0.04 mg
Iron	1.1 mg	Niacin	0.40 mg
Calcium	14 mg	Vitamin C	1 mg
		Calories	70

prunes (cooked, unsweetened)

COMPOSITION AND NUTRIENT VALUE PER Cup (270 g)

| Protein | 2 g | Phosphorous | 100 mg |
| Carbohydrate | 78 g | Potassium | 810 mg |

Fat	1 g	Sodium	10 mg
Saturated Fatty Acids	— g	Vitamin A	1860 I.U.
Oleic Acid	— g	Vitamin B$_1$	0.08 mg
Linoleic Acid	— g	Vitamin B$_2$	0.18 mg
Iron	4.5 mg	Niacin	1.70 mg
Calcium	78 mg	Vitamin C	2 mg
		Calories	295

raisins (seedless)
Partially dried grapes.

COMPOSITION AND NUTRIENT VALUE PER Cup (165 g)

Protein	4 g	Phosphorous	224 mg
Carbohydrate	128 g	Potassium	1050 mg
Fat	Trace g	Sodium	38 mg
Saturated Fatty Acids	— g	Vitamin A	30 I.U.
Oleic Acid	— g	Vitamin B$_1$	0.18 mg
Linoleic Acid	— g	Vitamin B$_2$	0.13 mg
Iron	5.8 mg	Niacin	0.80 mg
Calcium	102 mg	Vitamin C	2 mg
		Calories	480

edema
An excess accumulation of fluid in the body tissues.
There are many causes, some of which are dietary, such
as deficiencies in the essential fatty acids, potassium, and
certain amino acids.
See Potassium; Sodium-Potassium Balance

eggs
The oval, thin-shelled ova of domestic fowl, especially
chickens, used as food. Eggs are a valuable source of complete protein, iron, and much of the ·B complex of vitamins. They are rich in cholesterol, but they contain
lecithin, choline, and inositol—a combination which prevents cholesterol from being deposited in the blood vessels
and liver.
See Egg white injury

eggs (raw, boiled or poached)

COMPOSITION AND NUTRIENT VALUE PER Egg (50 g)

Protein	6 g	Phosphorous	205 mg
Carbohydrate	Trace g	Potassium	129 mg
Fat	6 g	Sodium	122 mg
Saturated Fatty Acids	2 g	Vitamin A	590 I.U.
Oleic Acid	3 g	Vitamin B_1	0.05 mg
Linoleic Acid	Trace g	Vitamin B_2	0.15 mg
Iron	1.1 mg	Niacin	0 mg
Calcium	27 mg	Vitamin C	Trace mg
		Calories	80

eggs (scrambled with milk and fat)

COMPOSITION AND NUTRIENT VALUE PER egg (64 g)

Protein	7 g	Phosphorous	222 mg
Carbohydrate	1 g	Potassium	140 mg
Fat	8 g	Sodium	338 mg
Saturated Fatty Acids	3 g	Vitamin A	690 I.U.
Oleic Acid	3 g	Vitamin B_1	0.05 mg
Linoleic Acid	Trace g	Vitamin B_2	0.18 mg
Iron	1.1 mg	Niacin	Trace mg
Calcium	51 mg	Vitamin C	0 mg
		Calories	110

egg yolk

COMPOSITION AND NUTRIENT VALUE PER yolk (17 g), raw, boiled or poached

Protein	3 g	Phosphorous	175 mg
Carbohydrate	Trace g	Potassium	33 mg
Fat	5 g	Sodium	9 mg
Saturated Fatty Acids	2 g	Vitamin A	580 I.U.
Oleic Acid	2 g	Vitamin B_1	0.04 mg

Linoleic Acid	Trace g	Vitamin B$_2$	0.07 mg
Iron	0.9 mg	Niacin	Trace mg
Calcium	24 mg	Vitamin C	0 mg
		Calories	60

egg white injury
A term describing biotin deficiency induced by a diet excessively high in raw eggs.
  See Avidin; Biotin

emulsifiers
(Also called "surface-active agents"). Substances such as lecithin, propylene glycol alginate, the diglycerides, and the monoglycerides which aid the uniform dispersion of oil in water—and, consequently, form such emulsions as margarine, mayonnaise, salad dressing, ice cream, and the like. Stabilizers* keep these emulsions in stable form.
  Emulsifiers are also used in baked products to aid the incorporation of fat into the dough and to keep the crumb soft.
  Lecithin, a natural compound, was formerly the chief emulsifier used in processed foods, but today almost all emulsifiers are synthetic chemical compounds. By law, all such additives must be listed on the product's label or package.
  See Additives; Stabilizers and Thickeners

emulsifying salts
Sodium citrate, sodium tartrate, and sodium phosphate, used in the manufacture of dairy products.

energy
The ability to do work. The energy the body requires for its metabolic processes, the maintenance of body temperature, and muscular activity, comes from the oxidation of foods, specifically, carbohydrates, fats, and whatever proteins are available after tissue-building needs are met. The energy expended by the body is measured in the number of calories used. Energy is stored in the body as fat.

enriched or fortified foods
Usually processed foods to which synthetic nutrients are added in order to replace those either entirely or partially destroyed by pasteurizing, precooking, milling, refining, bleaching, and the like.

Unfortunately, the "enriched" foods are rarely the nutritive equivalent of these same foods before processing. The exception is when additional nutrients are added to a food even though its nutrients have not been destroyed or removed, as when wheat germ is added to whole grain breads.

See Additives; Bread; Flour, Refining and Bleaching

enzymes
Any of the many proteins or conjugated protein produced by and functioning as biochemical catalysts in living organisms such as plants, animals and humans. Some enzymes need the help of coenzymes,* the majority of which are members of the vitamin B complex.*

ergosterol
A sterol isolated from yeast which when treated with ultraviolet rays is converted to vitamin D_2. This is the way in which synthetic vitamin D is made.

See Synthetic Vitamins; Vitamin D

essential fatty acids
The name given to three unsaturated fatty acids—linoleic, arachidonic, and linolenic. Arachidonic is found in animal tissues and linoleic and linolenic in vegetable oils, especially safflower, sunflower, and corn oils. (Some texts do not include linolenic among the essential fatty acids because though it can substitute for linoleic with respect to supporting growth, it cannot do so with respect to supporting health.)

The need for the essential fatty acids in human diets has not been established, but the evidence gathered from laboratory animals suggests that it is very important. A deficiency of fatty acids in these animals causes, among other things, restriction in growth, damage to vital organs, (including the reproductive system), and abnormalities of the skin and hair.

See Fats

estrogens

Female sex hormones. The synthetic female sex hormones stilbestrol and hexoestrol, are used to increase the growth rate of cattle, a practice beneficial to cattlemen but of very doubtful benefit to the consumer.

farina ("enriched")

A flourlike substance made from durum wheat after the germ and bran have been removed. It is almost pure starch, consequently most farina products are "enriched."

COMPOSITION AND NUTRIENT VALUE PER Cup (245 g), cooked

Protein	3 g	Phosphorous	N.D. mg
Carbohydrate	22 g	Potassium	N.D. mg
Fat	Trace g	Sodium	N.D. mg
Saturated Fatty Acids	— g	Vitamin A	0 I.U.
Oleic Acid	— g	Vitamin B_1	0.12 mg
Linoleic Acid	— g	Vitamin B_2	0.07 mg
Iron	0.7 mg	Niacin	1.0 mg
Calcium	147 mg	Vitamin C	0 mg
		Calories	105

fats

Organic substances which are compounds of carbon, hydrogen, and oxygen, similar to carbohydrates but containing less oxygen. They are derived from plants and animals and usually occur in combination with proteins and carbohydrates.

Fats are broken down in the digestive process to glycerine and fatty acids. The latter are of two types, saturated and unsaturated (either monounsaturated or polyunsaturated). The unsaturated fatty acids are three in number: linoleic, arachidonic, and linolenic. Collectively they are known as the essential fatty acids* (though some texts do not include linolenic among the essential fatty acids).

Fats oxidize quickly when exposed to air and become rancid, a process which destroys Vitamin E and makes the assimilation of other fat-soluble vitamins (A, D, and K) difficult. Similarly, the most common manufacturing methods used to extract vegetable oils (an important source of the essential fatty acids) involve a heating process which seriously depletes or destroys the nutrients. The overheating of fats and oils during cooking also seriously reduces their nutritive values, as does the hydrogenation of refining of vegetable oils.

FUNCTION OR PROPERTIES

All of the body cells utilize essential fatty acids to aid in repairing and replacing themselves and for immediate energy. Fat supports the internal organs, especially the kidneys. It also forms a protective sheath around the nerves and likewise protects the muscles. In addition it helps maintain body temperature. A reserve of fat can also be an important source of energy when food intake is insufficient. Fat is also necessary for the absorption and protection of the fat-soluble vitamins, A, D, E, and K. The adrenal cortex and sex gland hormones are made of specific fats.

SOURCES

Fats are either saturated or unsaturated. Natural vegetable oils are rich sources of unsaturated fats and are preferred to the saturated animal fats to reduce cholesterol levels.

Sources for unsaturated fats are the natural vegetable oils such as safflower, corn, soybean, peanut, cottonseed; wheat germ and nuts, mayonnaise, and salad dressings. Safflower oil contains the highest amount of the essential fatty acids and the greatest amount of linoleic acid, the most important of them. Fatty meats, butter, cream, egg yolk, and lard are sources of saturated fats.

REQUIREMENTS

Though essential to growth and health, no requirements have been set for fats. An excessive intake of fats, whether saturated or unsaturated, results in fatty deposits in the body which in turn can lead to heart ailments and other diseases.

DEFICIENCIES

Laboratory animals deprived of the essential fatty acids suffer restriction in growth, damage to vital organs (including the reproductive organs) and abnormalities of the skin and hair. Very little work has been done on humans in this respect, although there is evidence that eczema often results from low-fat diets and has been alleviated by the addition of vegetable oils to the diet, and that the abnormalities produced in laboratory animals lacking linoleic acid also show up in humans lacking it.

Some nutritionists, including Adelle Davis, feel that eating too little fat is possibly a major factor in overweight, for three reasons: (1) many apparently overweight persons are in fact only waterlogged—they suffer an edema which the addition of salad oils to their diet eliminates; (2) when essential fatty acids are deficient in the diet, the body changes sugar to fat far more rapidly than is normal. As a consequence, the blood sugar level drops precipitously and a great hunger is felt, causing one to overeat; and (3) fats are more satisfying than other foods in the sense of giving one a feeling of being "full." Thus forgoing eating fat at a meal may leave you feeling so hungry after that you eat many more times the calories than would have been provided by the fats.

Insufficient fat in the diet, particularly the unsaturated fats, results in the inability to properly absorb and protect the fat-soluble vitamins.

fat-soluble vitamins

Vitamins A, D, E, and K. They occur in food in solution with fats and are stored in the body to a greater degree than the water-soluble vitamins.

See Fats; Hydrogenation; Water-Soluble Vitamins

fermented milk
A semiliquid product made by the fermentation of milk with any of several lactic-acid-producing bacteria. A wide variety of such products are made in various countries, some of them alcoholic. The best known, however, is probably yogurt.*

fiber
In a nutritional context, a term referring to the indigestible parts of food.

firming agents
Pectin in fresh fruits and vegetables keeps the cells together. The heating required for canned fruits and vegetables breaks down the pectin and they become soft and break up. Canners therefore add firming agents (such as calcium lactate and calcium chloride) which together with the pectin form a gel which protects the canned fruits and vegetables from softening.
   See Additives

fish
Any of a great variety of cold-blooded aquatic vertebrates having fins, gills, and a streamlined body, and eaten as food. They are a fine source of complete protein.

   fish sticks
A fish fillet—frequently haddock or cod—which has been breaded and cut into an oblong shape.

COMPOSITION AND NUTRIENT VALUE PER 10 sticks (227 g), breaded

Protein	38 g	Phosphorous	360 mg
Carbohydrate	15 g	Potassium	280 mg
Fat	20 g	Sodium	— mg
Saturated Fatty Acids	5 g	Vitamin A	— I.U.
Oleic Acid	4 g	Vitamin B$_1$	0.9 mg

Linoleic Acid	10 g	Vitamin B_2	0.16 mg
Iron	0.9 mg	Niacin	3.6 mg
Calcium	25 mg	Vitamin C	0 mg
		Calories	400

flounder

COMPOSITION AND NUTRIENT VALUE PER 3.5 ounces (100 g), baked

Protein	30 g	Phosphorous	344 mg
Carbohydrate	0 g	Potassium	585 mg
Fat	8 g	Sodium	235 mg
Saturated Fatty Acids	— g	Vitamin A	0 I.U.
Oleic Acid	— g	Vitamin B_1	Trace mg
Linoleic Acid	— g	Vitamin B_2	Trace mg
Iron	1.4 mg	Niacin	1.6 mg
Calcium	22 mg	Vitamin C	0 mg
		Calories	200

haddock

COMPOSITION AND NUTRIENT VALUE PER 3 ounces (85 g), breaded and fried

Protein	17 g	Phosphorous	200 mg
Carbohydrate	5 g	Potassium	510 mg
Fat	5 g	Sodium	56 mg
Saturated Fatty Acids	1 g	Vitamin A	— I.U.
Oleic Acid	3 g	Vitamin B_1	0.03 mg
Linoleic Acid	Trace g	Vitamin B_2	0.06 mg
Iron	1 mg	Niacin	2.7 mg
Calcium	34 mg	Vitamin C	2 mg
		Calories	140

halibut

COMPOSITION AND NUTRIENT VALUE PER 3.5 ounces (100 g), broiled

Protein	26 g	Phosphorous	267 mg
Carbohydrate	0 g	Potassium	540 mg
Fat	8 g	Sodium	56 mg
Saturated Fatty Acids	— g	Vitamin A	440 I.U.
Oleic Acid	— g	Vitamin B$_1$	Trace mg
Linoleic Acid	— g	Vitamin B$_2$	Trace mg
Iron	0.8 mg	Niacin	9.2 mg
Calcium	14 mg	Vitamin C	0 mg
		Calories	182

salmon

COMPOSITION AND NUTRIENT VALUE PER 3 ounces (85 g), canned

Protein	17 g	Phosphorous	280 mg
Carbohydrate	0 g	Potassium	340 mg
Fat	5 g	Sodium	45 mg
Saturated Fatty Acids	1 g	Vitamin A	60 I.U.
Oleic Acid	1 g	Vitamin B$_1$	0.03 mg
Linoleic Acid	Trace g	Vitamin B$_2$	0.16 mg
Iron	0.7 mg	Niacin	6.8 mg
Calcium	167 mg	Vitamin C	0 mg
		Calories	120

sardines

Any of a variety of small edible herrings or related fishes of the family Clupeidae.

COMPOSITION AND NUTRIENT VALUE PER 3 oz. (85 g) canned in oil, drained

Protein	20 g	Phosphorous	490 mg
Carbohydrate	0 g	Potassium	540 mg
Fat	9 g	Sodium	480 mg
Saturated Fatty Acids	— g	Vitamin A	190 I.U.
Oleic Acid	— g	Vitamin B$_1$	0.02 mg

Linoleic Acid	— g	Vitamin B$_2$	0.17 mg
Iron	2.5 mg	Niacin	4.6 mg
Calcium	372 mg	Vitamin C	0 mg
		Calories	175

shad

COMPOSITION AND NUTRIENT VALUE PER 3 ounces (85 g), Baked

Protein	20 g	Phosphorous	300 mg
Carbohydrate	0 g	Potassium	350 mg
Fat	10 g	Sodium	75 mg
Saturated Fatty Acids	— g	Vitamin A	20 I.U.
Oleic Acid	— g	Vitamin B$_1$	0.11 mg
Linoleic Acid	— g	Vitamin B$_2$	0.22 mg
Iron	0.5 mg	Niacin	7.3 mg
Calcium	20 mg	Vitamin C	0 mg
		Calories	170

swordfish

COMPOSITION AND NUTRIENT VALUE PER 3 ounces (85 g), broiled

Protein	24 g	Phosphorous	225 mg
Carbohydrate	0 g	Potassium	700 mg
Fat	5 g	Sodium	45 mg
Saturated Fatty Acids	— g	Vitamin A	1750 I.U.
Oleic Acid	— g	Vitamin B$_1$	0.03 mg
Linoleic Acid	— g	Vitamin B$_2$	0.04 mg
Iron	1.1 mg	Niacin	9.3 mg
Calcium	23 mg	Vitamin C	0 mg
		Calories	150

tuna

COMPOSITION AND NUTRIENT VALUE PER 3 ounces (85 g), canned, drained

Protein	24 g	Phosphorous	300 mg
Carbohydrate	0 g	Potassium	240 mg
Fat	7 g	Sodium	700 mg
Saturated Fatty Acids	2 g	Vitamin A	70 I.U.
Oleic Acid	1 g	Vitamin B_1	0.04 mg
Linoleic Acid	1 g	Vitamin B_2	0.10 mg
Iron	1.6 mg	Niacin	10.1 mg
Calcium	7 mg	Vitamin C	0 mg
		Calories	170

flavoring agents

A wide variety of natural and synthetic substances which are added to various processed foods in order to create, modify, mask or enhance their taste or odor. There are some two thousand in use, of which five hundred are natural and the rest synthetic. Both kinds are widely used in soft drinks, ice cream, baked goods and candy among other things.

Natural and artificial sweeteners are also classed as flavoring agents inasmuch as they contribute the basic taste to many foods and drinks. Sugar and honey are natural sweeteners; saccharin (500 times sweeter than sugar), and the cyclamate compounds (30 to 50 times sweeter and now banned from use), are synthetic sweeteners.

In addition certain "fruit acids" are widely used in products containing fruit. Of these citric acids is the most commonly used.

The flavor "enhancers" intensify the natural taste of a food, though they have no inherent flavor of their own. Of these monosodium glutamate (MSG) is the most widely used.

See Additives; GRAS; Monosodium Glutamate

flour, refining and bleaching

A process which destroys most of the nutrients available in the grains prior to refining. (Before flour was refined and bleached, bread was made from flour ground from whole grains which contained all the nutrients available in the grains.)

In the modern refining process, the bran and germ of

the grains—the constituents which contain most of the nutrients—are separated from the endosperm (consisting mostly of starch) and discarded. The starchy endosperm is then ground into flour. The flour is bleached (usually with chlorine dioxide) to make it whiter than white and to increase its keeping qualities. (In a complex, technological society, the ability to store flour for long periods of time is important. It must be shipped long distances to urban centers and warehoused till made into food products.) Unfortunately, the flour which emerges from these processes is almost totally devoid of nutrients, and bread and other products made from it are purely starch foods. Most commercial bakers thoughtfully "enrich" their products by adding vitamins, minerals, and occasionally protein along with the host of chemical additives designed to keep the product soft and "fresh." Since they rarely replace more than one-third of the nutrients lost in the refining process, their products are not the nutritional equivalent of similar ones made from unrefined and unbleached flour.

See Bread; Refined Foods

flour (all-purpose, "enriched")

COMPOSITION AND NUTRIENT VALUE PER Cup (115g)

Protein	12 g	Phosphorous	87 mg
Carbohydrate	88 g	Potassium	86 mg
Fat	1 g	Sodium	1 mg
Saturated Fatty Acids	— g	Vitamin A	0 I.U.
Oleic Acid	— g	Vitamin B_1	0.51 mg
Linoleic Acid	— g	Vitamin B_2	0.30 mg
Iron	3.3 mg	Niacin	4 mg
Calcium	18 mg	Vitamin C	0 mg
		Calories	420

flour, cake or pastry (sifted)

COMPOSITION AND NUTRIENT VALUE PER Cup (96 g)

Protein	7 g	Phosphorous	N.D. mg
Carbohydrate	76 g	Potassium	N.D. mg
Fat	1 g	Sodium	N.D. mg
Saturated Fatty Acids	— g	Vitamin A	0 I.U.
Oleic Acid	— g	Vitamin B_1	0.03 mg
Linoleic Acid	— g	Vitamin B_2	0.03 mg
Iron	0.5 mg	Niacin	0.70 mg
Calcium	16 mg	Vitamin C	0 mg
		Calories	350

flour, whole-wheat

COMPOSITION AND NUTRIENT VALUE PER Cup (120 g)

Protein	16 g	Phosphorous	464 mg
Carbohydrate	85 g	Potassium	445 mg
Fat	2 g	Sodium	3 mg
Saturated Fatty Acids	Trace g	Vitamin A	0 I.U.
Oleic Acid	1 g	Vitamin B_1	0.66 mg
Linoleic Acid	1 g	Vitamin B_2	0.14 mg
Iron	4 mg	Niacin	5.20 mg
Calcium	49 mg	Vitamin C	0 mg
		Calories	400

fluorine
See Minerals

folacin
Former name for folic acid.*

folic acid
See under Vitamin B Complex

food
That which we eat in order to maintain life and growth and which for some individuals provides their most intense pleasure.

food and drug administration (FDA)

A federal agency charged with the administration of the Food, Drug and Cosmetic Act of 1938 (since amended many times) which superseded the Pure Food and Drug Act of 1906. Included in the act and its amendments are criteria for the purity and nutritional value of foods, regulations pertaining to manufacturing and processing foods, to the use of additives, to packaging, labeling, and almost every aspect of the food industry. Thus to administer the law, the FDA must test foods and chemicals, formulate standards for labeling and packaging, inspect facilities and methods, and the like.

The FDA has wide powers to seize and confiscate contaminated foods, to stop the production of products, and to even close down manufacturing and processing facilities which do not conform to the law. Critics of the FDA contend that it is too understaffed to do its work properly and, moreover, that its enforcement policies are in themselves insufficiently strict.

food and nutrition board

Short for Food and Nutrition Board, National Academy of Sciences—National Research Council of the United States. A very official-sounding organization which is, in fact, a private organization funded by industry. Since 1940 it has, in its own words, "developed formulations of daily nutrient intakes which were judged to be adequate for the maintenance of good nutrition in the population of the United States."

See Recommended Dietary Allowances

food faddists

Sometimes they are zealots following the unjustified claims of those exploiting them for commercial gain; at other times simple crackpots who mistake their visions for truth. More frequently, a term applied by food-industry spokesmen to anyone who disputes the claims made for the nutritional sufficiency of their products.

food poisoning
Poisoning caused by eating foods contaminated by bacteria, toxic food additives, and toxic pesticides. The commonest bacterial poisoning is caused by *Staphylococcus* and *Salmonellae*. The former causes symptoms of abdominal cramp, nausea, vomiting, and diarrhea within two to four hours. After twelve to twenty-four hours, the latter causes similar symptoms (of greater intensity) which may persist for weeks. It is not often fatal.
  See Botulin; Botulism

food supplements
All those products—such as vitamins, minerals, protein powders—designed to provide nutrients in a concentrated, packaged form, as distinguished from nutrients occurring in their natural sources.

Though most nutritionists feel it is preferable to use natural sources whenever possible, there seem to be two good reasons for using food supplements: (1) to prevent or serve as insurance against inadequacies in the diet, and (2) to treat diseases which may have a nutritional basis.

It should be noted that people often make the error of taking a single nutrient to alleviate a particular problem, without a proper awareness that good health is built on a sufficiency of *all* essential nutrients and in particular not being aware that large doses of one nutrient can be counter-productive. For example, the B-vitamin complex is interdependent insofar as a proper balance among them being necessary for each to work efficiently in the body. Taking large amounts of B_1 while maintaining an ordinary and normally sufficient intake of the other B vitamins results in a B-vitamin-complex deficiency.

For new FDA regulations concerning the labeling, promotion, and sale of vitamins and minerals *see* Vitamins.

french dressing
A seasoned salad dressing of oil and vinegar.

COMPOSITION AND NUTRIENT VALUE PER Tablespoon (16 g)

Protein	Trace g	Phosphorous	0 mg
Carbohydrate	3 g	Potassium	0 mg
Fat	6 g	Sodium	— mg
Saturated Fatty Acids	1 g	Vitamin A	— I.U.
Oleic Acid	1 g	Vitamin B$_1$	— mg
Linoleic Acid	3 g	Vitamin B$_2$	— mg
Iron	0.1 mg	Niacin	— mg
Calcium	2 mg	Vitamin C	0 mg
		Calories	65

frozen foods

An American way of life. Freezing inhibits the action of the microorganisms that spoil foods and thus allows prolonged storage. The process does not result in significant losses in nutritive values and if kept at the proper temperature (0° Farenheit or below), frozen foods can be stored for long periods of time and retain their nutritive values. At 10° or above, however, the vitamin loss is considerable. Deterioration is rapid after thawing, and defrosted foods should not be refrozen.

The freezing of food does affect its taste, texture, and appearance, but not enough to discourage most Americans from buying them.

fructose

A six-carbon sugar found as the free sugar in honey and in some fruits. Along with glucose it is the fastest form of energy, passing directly into the bloodstream unchanged.

fruit

The fleshy, seed-bearing part of plants, notwithstanding that some, such as the tomato, are generally called vegetables. They contain very little protein and fat, and from 3 to 25 percent carbohydrate (which occurs as glucose, sucrose, fructose, starch, pectin, and cellulose). During the ripening process, the starch changes to sugars. Fruits are a good source of vitamin C and potassium and some serve as sources of carotene and iron. Canning destroys about 50 percent of the vitamin content.

apple

COMPOSITION AND NUTRIENT VALUE PER one (150 g), raw

Protein	Trace g	Phosphorous	13 mg
Carbohydrate	18 g	Potassium	130 mg
Fat	Trace g	Sodium	1 mg
Saturated Fatty Acids	— g	Vitamin A	50 I.U.
Oleic Acid	— g	Vitamin B_1	0.04 mg
Linoleic Acid	— g	Vitamin B_2	0.02 mg
Iron	0.4 mg	Niacin	0.10 mg
Calcium	8 mg	Vitamin C	3 mg
		Calories	70

applesauce

COMPOSITION AND NUTRIENT VALUE PER Cup (244 g), canned, unsweetened

Protein	1 g	Phosphorous	N.D. mg
Carbohydrate	26 g	Potassium	N.D. mg
Fat	Trace g	Sodium	N.D. mg
Saturated Fatty Acids	— g	Vitamin A	100 I.U.
Oleic Acid	— g	Vitamin B_1	0.05 mg
Linoleic Acid	— g	Vitamin B_2	0.02 mg
Iron	1.2 mg	Niacin	0.10 mg
Calcium	10 mg	Vitamin C	2 mg
		Calories	100

apricot

COMPOSITION AND NUTRIENT VALUE PER 3 (114 g), raw

Protein	1 g	Phosphorous	30 mg
Carbohydrate	14 g	Potassium	280 mg
Fat	Trace g	Sodium	1 mg

Saturated Fatty Acids	— g	Vitamin A	2890 I.U.
Oleic Acid	— g	Vitamin B$_1$	0.03 mg
Linoleic Acid	— g	Vitamin B$_2$	0.04 mg
Iron	0.5 mg	Niacin	0.70 mg
Calcium	18 mg	Vitamin C	10 mg
		Calories	55

apricots, canned in heavy syrup

COMPOSITION AND NUTRIENT VALUE PER Cup (259 g)

Protein	1 g	Phosphorous	37 mg
Carbohydrate	57 g	Potassium	600 mg
Fat	Trace g	Sodium	2 mg
Saturated Fatty Acids	— g	Vitamin A	4510 I.U.
Oleic Acid	— g	Vitamin B$_1$	0.05 mg
Linoleic Acid	— g	Vitamin B$_2$	0.06 mg
Iron	0.8 mg	Niacin	0.90 mg
Calcium	28 mg	Vitamin C	10 mg
		Calories	220

avocado
A fruit, eaten as a vegetable

COMPOSITION AND NUTRIENT VALUE PER 1/2 large (108 g)

Protein	2 g	Phosphorous	42 mg
Carbohydrate	6 g	Potassium	600 mg
Fat	18 g	Sodium	4 mg
Saturated Fatty Acids	4 g	Vitamin A	310 I.U.
Oleic Acid	8 g	Vitamin B$_1$	0.1 mg
Linoleic Acid	2 g	Vitamin B$_2$	0.2 mg
Iron	0.6 mg	Niacin	1.7 mg
Calcium	11 mg	Vitamin C	15 mg
		Calories	185

banana

COMPOSITION AND NUTRIENT VALUE PER 1 medium (175 g)

Protein	1 g	Phosphorous	52 mg
Carbohydrate	26 g	Potassium	468 mg
Fat	Trace g	Sodium	2 mg
Saturated Fatty Acids	— g	Vitamin A	230 I.U.
Oleic Acid	— g	Vitamin B$_1$	0.06 mg
Linoleic Acid	— g	Vitamin B$_2$	0.07 mg
Iron	0.8 mg	Niacin	0.80 mg
Calcium	10 mg	Vitamin C	12 mg
		Calories	100

blackberries

COMPOSITION AND NUTRIENT VALUE PER Cup (144 g), fresh

Protein	2 g	Phosphorous	46 mg
Carbohydrate	19 g	Potassium	220 mg
Fat	1 g	Sodium	Trace mg
Saturated Fatty Acids	— g	Vitamin A	290 I.U.
Oleic Acid	— g	Vitamin B$_1$	0.05 mg
Linoleic Acid	— g	Vitamin B$_2$	0.06 mg
Iron	1.3 mg	Niacin	0.50 mg
Calcium	46 mg	Vitamin C	30 mg
		Calories	85

blueberries

COMPOSITION AND NUTRIENT VALUE PER Cup (140 g), fresh

Protein	1 g	Phosphorous	N.D. mg
Carbohydrate	21 g	Potassium	N.D. mg
Fat	1 g	Sodium	N.D. mg
Saturated Fatty Acids	— g	Vitamin A	140 I.U.
Oleic Acid	— g	Vitamin B$_1$	0.04 mg
Linoleic Acid	— g	Vitamin B$_2$	0.08 mg
Iron	1.4 mg	Niacin	0.60 mg
Calcium	21 mg	Vitamin C	20 mg
		Calories	85

cantaloupe

COMPOSITION AND NUTRIENT VALUE PER 1/2 medium (385 g)

Protein	1 g	Phosphorous	64 mg
Carbohydrate	14 g	Potassium	910 mg
Fat	Trace g	Sodium	40 mg
Saturated Fatty Acids	— g	Vitamin A	6540 I.U.
Oleic Acid	— g	Vitamin B$_1$	0.08 mg
Linoleic Acid	— g	Vitamin B$_2$	0.06 mg
Iron	0.8 mg	Niacin	1.20 mg
Calcium	27 mg	Vitamin C	63 mg
		Calories	60

cherries (fresh)

COMPOSITION AND NUTRIENT VALUE PER Cup (114 g), raw

Protein	1 g	Phosphorous	20 mg
Carbohydrate	15 g	Potassium	270 mg
Fat	Trace g	Sodium	1 mg
Saturated Fatty Acids	— g	Vitamin A	620 I.U.
Oleic Acid	— g	Vitamin B$_1$	Trace mg
Linoleic Acid	— g	Vitamin B$_2$	Trace mg
Iron	0.4 mg	Niacin	0.50 mg
Calcium	18 mg	Vitamin C	10 mg
		Calories	65

cherries (canned)

COMPOSITION AND NUTRIENT VALUE PER Cup (244 g), canned, pitted, unsweetened

Protein	2 g	Phosphorous	30 mg
Carbohydrate	26 g	Potassium	135 mg
Fat	Trace g	Sodium	8 mg
Saturated Fatty Acids	— g	Vitamin A	1660 I.U.

Oleic Acid	— g	Vitamin B$_1$	Trace mg
Linoleic Acid	— g	Vitamin B$_2$	Trace mg
Iron	0.7 mg	Niacin	0.50 mg
Calcium	37 mg	Vitamin C	12 mg
		Calories	105

cranberry sauce

COMPOSITION AND NUTRIENT VALUE PER Cup (277 g),
canned, sweetened

Protein	Trace g	Phosphorous	27 mg
Carbohydrate	104 g	Potassium	150 mg
Fat	1 g	Sodium	3 mg
Saturated Fatty Acids	— g	Vitamin A	60 I.U.
Oleic Acid	— g	Vitamin B$_1$	0.03 mg
Linoleic Acid	— g	Vitamin B$_2$	0.03 mg
Iron	0.6 mg	Niacin	0.10 mg
Calcium	17 mg	Vitamin C	6 mg
		Calories	405

fruit cocktail

COMPOSITION AND NUTRIENT VALUE PER Cup (256 g),
canned, in heavy syrup

Protein	1 g	Phosphorous	30 mg
Carbohydrate	50 g	Potassium	350 mg
Fat	Trace g	Sodium	12 mg
Saturated Fatty Acids	— g	Vitamin A	360 I.U.
Oleic Acid	— g	Vitamin B$_1$	0.05 mg
Linoleic Acid	— g	Vitamin B$_2$	0.03 mg
Iron	1 mg	Niacin	1.30 mg
Calcium	23 mg	Vitamin C	5 mg
		Calories	195

grapefruit (pink or red)

COMPOSITION AND NUTRIENT VALUE PER 1/2 (241 g)

Protein	1 g	Phosphorous	54 mg
Carbohydrate	13 g	Potassium	290 mg
Fat	Trace g	Sodium	4 mg
Saturated Fatty Acids	— g	Vitamin A	540 I.U.
Oleic Acid	— g	Vitamin B_1	0.05 mg
Linoleic Acid	— g	Vitamin B_2	0.02 mg
Iron	0.5 mg	Niacin	0.20 mg
Calcium	20 mg	Vitamin C	44 mg
		Calories	50

grapefruit (white)

COMPOSITION AND NUTRIENT VALUE PER 1/2 (241 g)

Protein	1 g	Phosphorous	54 mg
Carbohydrate	12 g	Potassium	290 mg
Fat	Trace g	Sodium	4 mg
Saturated Fatty Acids	— g	Vitamin A	10 I.U.
Oleic Acid	— g	Vitamin B_1	0.05 mg
Linoleic Acid	— g	Vitamin B_2	0.02 mg
Iron	0.5 mg	Niacin	0.20 mg
Calcium	19 mg	Vitamin C	44 mg
		Calories	45

grapes (American type, e.g., Concord)

COMPOSITION AND NUTRIENT VALUE PER Cup (153 g)

Protein	1 g	Phosphorous	30 mg
Carbohydrate	15 g	Potassium	120 mg
Fat	1 g	Sodium	5 mg
Saturated Fatty Acids	— g	Vitamin A	100 I.U.
Oleic Acid	— g	Vitamin B_1	0.05 mg
Linoleic Acid	— g	Vitamin B_2	0.03 mg
Iron	0.4 mg	Niacin	0.20 mg
Calcium	15 mg	Vitamin C	3 mg
		Calories	65

grapes (European type, e.g., Muscat, Tokay)

COMPOSITION AND NUTRIENT VALUE PER Cup (160 g)

Protein	1 g	Phosphorous	30 mg
Carbohydrate	25 g	Potassium	240 mg
Fat	Trace g	Sodium	6 mg
Saturated Fatty Acids	— g	Vitamin A	140 I.U.
Oleic Acid	— g	Vitamin B_1	0.07 mg
Linoleic Acid	— g	Vitamin B_2	0.04 mg
Iron	0.6 mg	Niacin	0.40 mg
Calcium	17 mg	Vitamin C	6 mg
		Calories	95

oranges

COMPOSITION AND NUTRIENT VALUE PER 1 medium (180 g)

Protein	1 g	Phosphorous	40 mg
Carbohydrate	16 g	Potassium	300 mg
Fat	Trace g	Sodium	Trace mg
Saturated Fatty Acids	— g	Vitamin A	260 I.U.
Oleic Acid	— g	Vitamin B_1	0.13 mg
Linoleic Acid	— g	Vitamin B_2	0.05 mg
Iron	0.05 mg	Niacin	0.50 mg
Calcium	54 mg	Vitamin C	66 mg
		Calories	65

papaya

COMPOSITION AND NUTRIENT VALUE PER Cup (182 g)

Protein	1 g	Phosphorous	32 mg
Carbohydrate	18 g	Potassium	470 mg
Fat	Trace g	Sodium	6 mg
Saturated Fatty Acids	— g	Vitamin A	3190 I.U.

Oleic Acid	— g	Vitamin B_1	0.07 mg
Linoleic Acid	— g	Vitamin B_2	0.08 mg
Iron	0.5 mg	Niacin	0.50 mg
Calcium	36 mg	Vitamin C	102 mg
		Calories	70

peach

COMPOSITION AND NUTRIENT VALUE PER 1 medium, yellow (114 g)

Protein	1 g	Phosphorous	22 mg
Carbohydrate	10 g	Potassium	31 mg
Fat	Trace g	Sodium	5 mg
Saturated Fatty Acids	— g	Vitamin A	1320 I.U.
Oleic Acid	— g	Vitamin B_1	0.02 mg
Linoleic Acid	— g	Vitamin B_2	0.05 mg
Iron	0.5 mg	Niacin	1 mg
Calcium	9 mg	Vitamin C	7 mg
		Calories	35

peach (canned in heavy syrup)

COMPOSITION AND NUTRIENT VALUE PER Cup (257 g)

Protein	1 g	Phosphorous	35 mg
Carbohydrate	52 g	Potassium	310 mg
Fat	Trace g	Sodium	6 mg
Saturated Fatty Acids	— g	Vitamin A	1100 I.U.
Oleic Acid	— g	Vitamin B_1	0.02 mg
Linoleic Acid	— g	Vitamin B_2	0.06 mg
Iron	0.8 mg	Niacin	1.4 mg
Calcium	10 mg	Vitamin C	7 mg
		Calories	200

peach (frozen)

COMPOSITION AND NUTRIENT VALUE PER 12 ounces (340 g)

Protein	1 g	Phosphorous	N.D. mg
Carbohydrate	77 g	Potassium	N.D. mg
Fat	Trace g	Sodium	N.D. mg
Saturated Fatty Acids	— g	Vitamin A	2210 I.U.
Oleic Acid	— g	Vitamin B_1	0.03 mg
Linoleic Acid	— g	Vitamin B_2	0.14 mg
Iron	1.7 mg	Niacin	2.4 mg
Calcium	77 mg	Vitamin C	135 mg
		(most added by mfg)	
		Calories	300

pear

COMPOSITION AND NUTRIENT VALUE PER 1 Medium (182 g), fresh

Protein	1 g	Phosphorous	29 mg
Carbohydrate	25 g	Potassium	182 mg
Fat	1 g	Sodium	3 mg
Saturated Fatty Acids	— g	Vitamin A	30 I.U.
Oleic Acid	— g	Vitamin B_1	0.04 mg
Linoleic Acid	— g	Vitamin B_2	0.07 mg
Iron	0.5 mg	Niacin	0.20 mg
Calcium	13 mg	Vitamin C	7 mg
		Calories	100

pear (canned in heavy syrup)

COMPOSITION AND NUTRIENT VALUE PER Cup (255 g)

Protein	1 g	Phosphorous	30 mg
Carbohydrate	50 g	Potassium	75 mg
Fat	1 g	Sodium	12 mg
Saturated Fatty Acids	— g	Vitamin A	Trace I.U.
Oleic Acid	— g	Vitamin B_1	0.03 mg
Linoleic Acid	— g	Vitamin B_2	0.05 mg
Iron	0.5 mg	Niacin	0.30 mg
Calcium	13 mg	Vitamin C	4 mg
		Calories	195

pineapple (fresh, diced)

COMPOSITION AND NUTRIENT VALUE PER Cup (140 g)

Protein	1 g	Phosphorous	12 mg
Carbohydrate	19 g	Potassium	210 mg
Fat	Trace g	Sodium	1 mg
Saturated Fatty Acids	— g	Vitamin A	100 I.U.
Oleic Acid	— g	Vitamin B_1	0.12 mg
Linoleic Acid	— g	Vitamin B_2	0.04 mg
Iron	0.7 mg	Niacin	0.30 mg
Calcium	24 mg	Vitamin C	24 mg
		Calories	75

pineapple (canned in heavy syrup, sliced)

COMPOSITION AND NUTRIENT VALUE PER Large slice (122 g)

Protein	Trace g	Phosphorous	90 mg
Carbohydrate	24 g	Potassium	150 mg
Fat	Trace g	Sodium	1 mg
Saturated Fatty Acids	— g	Vitamin A	50 I.U.
Oleic Acid	— g	Vitamin B_1	0.09 mg
Linoleic Acid	— g	Vitamin B_2	0.03 mg
Iron	0.4 mg	Niacin	0.20 mg
Calcium	13 mg	Vitamin C	8 mg
		Calories	90

plum (fresh)

COMPOSITION AND NUTRIENT VALUE PER 1 large (160 g)

Protein	Trace g	Phosphorous	10 mg
Carbohydrate	7 g	Potassium	100 mg
Fat	Trace g	Sodium	Trace mg
Saturated Fatty Acids	— g	Vitamin A	140 I.U.

Oleic Acid	— g	Vitamin B$_1$	0.02 mg
Linoleic Acid	— g	Vitamin B$_2$	0.02 mg
Iron	0.3 mg	Niacin	0.30 mg
Calcium	7 mg	Vitamin C	3 mg
		Calories	25

plum (canned in syrup)

COMPOSITION AND NUTRIENT VALUE PER Cup (256 g)

Protein	1 g	Phosphorous	25 mg
Carbohydrate	53 g	Potassium	213 mg
Fat	Trace g	Sodium	2 mg
Saturated Fatty Acids	— g	Vitamin A	2970 I.U.
Oleic Acid	— g	Vitamin B$_1$	0.05 mg
Linoleic Acid	— g	Vitamin B$_2$	0.05 mg
Iron	2.2 mg	Niacin	0.90 mg
Calcium	22 mg	Vitamin C	4 mg
		Calories	205

rasperries (red, raw)

COMPOSITION AND NUTRIENT VALUE PER Cup (123 g)

Protein	1 g	Phosphorous	N.D. mg
Carbohydrate	17 g	Potassium	N.D. mg
Fat	1 g	Sodium	N.D. mg
Saturated Fatty Acids	— g	Vitamin A	160 I.U.
Oleic Acid	— g	Vitamin B$_1$	0.04 mg
Linoleic Acid	— g	Vitamin B$_2$	0.11 mg
Iron	1.1 mg	Niacin	1.10 mg
Calcium	27 mg	Vitamin C	31 mg
		Calories	70

raspberries (red, frozen)

COMPOSITION AND NUTRIENT VALUE PER 10 oz. carton (284 g)

Protein	2 g	Phosphorous	N.D. mg
Carbohydrate	70 g	Potassium	N.D. mg
Fat	1 g	Sodium	N.D. mg
Saturated Fatty Acids	— g	Vitamin A	200 I.U.
Oleic Acid	— g	Vitamin B_1	0.06 mg
Linoleic Acid	— g	Vitamin B_2	0.17 mg
Iron	1.7 mg	Niacin	1.70 mg
Calcium	37 mg	Vitamin C	59 mg
		Calories	275

rhubarb (cooked, sweetened)

COMPOSITION AND NUTRIENT VALUE PER Cup (272 g)

Protein	1 g	Phosphorous	N.D. mg
Carbohydrate	98 g	Potassium	N.D. mg
Fat	Trace g	Sodium	N.D. mg
Saturated Fatty Acids	— g	Vitamin A	220 I.U.
Oleic Acid	— g	Vitamin B_1	0.06 mg
Linoleic Acid	— g	Vitamin B_2	0.15 mg
Iron	1.6 mg	Niacin	0.70 mg
Calcium	212 mg	Vitamin C	17 mg
		Calories	385

strawberries (raw)

COMPOSITION AND NUTRIENT VALUE PER Cup (149 g)

Protein	1 g	Phosphorous	34 mg
Carbohydrate	13 g	Potassium	220 mg
Fat	1 g	Sodium	3 mg
Saturated Fatty Acids	— g	Vitamin A	90 I.U.
Oleic Acid	— g	Vitamin B_1	0.04 mg
Linoleic Acid	— g	Vitamin B_2	0.10 mg
Iron	1.5 mg	Niacin	1 mg
Calcium	31 mg	Vitamin C	88 mg
		Calories	55

tangerine

COMPOSITION AND NUTRIENT VALUE PER 1 medium
(116 g)

Protein	1 g	Phosphorous	23 mg
Carbohydrate	10 g	Potassium	110 mg
Fat	Trace g	Sodium	2 mg
Saturated Fatty Acids	— g	Vitamin A	360 I.U.
Oleic Acid	— g	Vitamin B_1	0.05 mg
Linoleic Acid	— g	Vitamin B_2	0.02 mg
Iron	0.3 mg	Niacin	0.10 mg
Calcium	34 mg	Vitamin C	27 mg
		Calories	40

watermelon

COMPOSITION AND NUTRIENT VALUE PER 4″ x 8″ wedge
(925 g)

Protein	2 g	Phosphorous	96 mg
Carbohydrate	27 g	Potassium	600 mg
Fat	1 g	Sodium	2 mg
Saturated Fatty Acids	— g	Vitamin A	2510 I.U.
Oleic Acid	— g	Vitamin B_1	0.13 mg
Linoleic Acid	— g	Vitamin B_2	0.13 mg
Iron	2.1 mg	Niacin	0.70 mg
Calcium	30 mg	Vitamin C	30 mg
		Calories	115

fruit juices

All fruit juices contain various vitamins, minerals, simple
sugars, and acids in varying amounts. They are especially rich in vitamins A and C, and potassium. For all practical purposes, the best juice source of vitamin C comes
from the citrus fruits (oranges, grapefruit, lemon). The
unstrained juice of raw fruits containing the fibers is to be
preferred to the strained inasmuch as the cellulose of

these fibers helps in the absorption of the nutrients and provides roughage as well. Canned fruit juices have much of their nutritive value destroyed by the high temperatures used in canning. The canners then "enrich" their product by adding vitamins and minerals. And a large number of fruit "drinks"—"orange" drinks, "grape" drinks, "orange-ades" and etc.—are marketed which contain very little of the juices mentioned in the name of the product. It is wise, therefore, to check the listed contents before buying.

apple juice

COMPOSITION AND NUTRIENT VALUE PER Cup (248 g)

Protein	Trace g	Phosphorous	12 mg
Carbohydrate	30 g	Potassium	200 mg
Fat	Trace g	Sodium	5 mg
Saturated Fatty Acids	— g	Vitamin A	— I.U.
Oleic Acid	— g	Vitamin B_1	0.02 mg
Linoleic Acid	— g	Vitamin B_2	0.05 mg
Iron	1.5 mg	Niacin	0.20 mg
Calcium	15 mg	Vitamin C	2 mg
		Calories	120

apricot nectar
The juice of the apricot.

COMPOSITION AND NUTRIENT VALUE PER Cup (251 g), canned

Protein	1 g	Phosphorous	30 mg
Carbohydrate	37 g	Potassium	440 mg
Fat	Trace g	Sodium	Trace mg
Saturated Fatty Acids	— g	Vitamin A	2380 I.U.
Oleic Acid	— g	Vitamin B_1	0.03 mg
Linoleic Acid	— g	Vitamin B_2	0.03 mg
Iron	0.5 mg	Niacin	0.50 mg
Calcium	23 mg	Vitamin C	8 mg
		Calories	140

grape juice (canned or bottled)

COMPOSITION AND NUTRIENT VALUE PER Cup (253 g)

Protein	1 g	Phosphorous	33 mg
Carbohydrate	42 g	Potassium	450 mg
Fat	Trace g	Sodium	1 mg
Saturated Fatty Acids	— g	Vitamin A	— I.U.
Oleic Acid	— g	Vitamin B$_1$	0.10 mg
Linoleic Acid	— g	Vitamin B$_2$	0.05 mg
Iron	0.8 mg	Niacin	0.50 mg
Calcium	28 mg	Vitamin C	Trace mg
		Calories	165

grape juice (frozen, diluted)

COMPOSITION AND NUTRIENT VALUE PER Cup (250 g)

Protein	1 g	Phosphorous	N.D. mg
Carbohydrate	33 g	Potassium	N.D. mg
Fat	Trace g	Sodium	N.D. mg
Saturated Fatty Acids	— g	Vitamin A	10 I.U.
Oleic Acid	— g	Vitamin B$_1$	0.05 mg
Linoleic Acid	— g	Vitamin B$_2$	0.08 mg
Iron	0.3 mg	Niacin	0.50 mg
Calcium	8 mg	Vitamin C	0 mg
		(unless fortified)	
		Calories	135

grapefruit juice (unsweetened, canned, white)

COMPOSITION AND NUTRIENT VALUE PER Cup (247 g)

Protein	1 g	Phosphorous	40 mg
Carbohydrate	24 g	Potassium	280 mg
Fat	Trace g	Sodium	2 mg
Saturated Fatty Acids	— g	Vitamin A	20 I.U.
Oleic Acid	— g	Vitamin B$_1$	0.07 mg
Linoleic Acid	— g	Vitamin B$_2$	0.04 mg

Iron	1 mg	Niacin	0.40 mg
Calcium	20 mg	Vitamin C	84 mg
		Calories	100

grapefruit juice (unsweetened, frozen, white)

COMPOSITION AND NUTRIENT VALUE PER Cup (247 g)

Protein	1 g	Phosphorous	40 mg
Carbohydrate	24 g	Potassium	280 mg
Fat	Trace g	Sodium	2 mg
Saturated Fatty Acids	— g	Vitamin A	20 I.U.
Oleic Acid	— g	Vitamin B_1	0.10 mg
Linoleic Acid	— g	Vitamin B_2	0.04 mg
Iron	0.2 mg	Niacin	0.50 mg
Calcium	25 mg	Vitamin C	96 mg
		Calories	100

lemon juice

COMPOSITION AND NUTRIENT VALUE PER Cup (244 g)

Protein	1 g	Phosphorous	26 mg
Carbohydrate	20 g	Potassium	160 mg
Fat	Trace g	Sodium	8 mg
Saturated Fatty Acids	— g	Vitamin A	50 I.U.
Oleic Acid	— g	Vitamin B_1	0.07 mg
Linoleic Acid	— g	Vitamin B_2	0.02 mg
Iron	0.5 mg	Niacin	0.20 mg
Calcium	17 mg	Vitamin C	112 mg
		Calories	60

lemon juice (frozen, diluted)

COMPOSITION AND NUTRIENT VALUE PER Cup (248 g)

Protein	Trace g	Phosphorous	N.D. mg
Carbohydrate	28 g	Potassium	N.D. mg
Fat	Trace g	Sodium	N.D. mg

Saturated Fatty Acids	— g	Vitamin A	Trace I.U.
Oleic Acid	— g	Vitamin B_1	Trace mg
Linoleic Acid	— g	Vitamin B_2	0.02 mg
Iron	Trace mg	Niacin	0.20 mg
Calcium	2 mg	Vitamin C	17 mg
		Calories	110

lime juice

COMPOSITION AND NUTRIENT VALUE PER Cup (246 g)

Protein	1 g	Phosphorous	N.D. mg
Carbohydrate	22 g	Potassium	N.D. mg
Fat	Trace g	Sodium	N.D. mg
Saturated Fatty Acids	— g	Vitamin A	20 I.U.
Oleic Acid	— g	Vitamin B_1	0.05 mg
Linoleic Acid	— g	Vitamin B_2	0.02 mg
Iron	0.5 mg	Niacin	0.20 mg
Calcium	22 mg	Vitamin C	79 mg
		Calories	65

orange juice (fresh)

COMPOSITION AND NUTRIENT VALUE PER Cup (248 g)

Protein	2 g	Phosphorous	42 mg
Carbohydrate	26 g	Potassium	500 mg
Fat	1 g	Sodium	2 mg
Saturated Fatty Acids	— g	Vitamin A	500 I.U.
Oleic Acid	— g	Vitamin B_1	0.22 mg
Linoleic Acid	— g	Vitamin B_2	0.07 mg
Iron	0.5 mg	Niacin	1 mg
Calcium	27 mg	Vitamin C	124 mg
		Calories	110

orange juice (frozen, diluted)

COMPOSITION AND NUTRIENT VALUE PER Cup (249 g)

Protein	2 g	Phosphorous	N.D. mg
Carbohydrate	29 g	Potassium	N.D. mg
Fat	Trace g	Sodium	N.D. mg
Saturated Fatty Acids	— g	Vitamin A	550 I.U.
Oleic Acid	— g	Vitamin B$_1$	0.22 mg
Linoleic Acid	— g	Vitamin B$_2$	0.02 mg
Iron	0.2 mg	Niacin	1 mg
Calcium	25 mg	Vitamin C	120 mg
		Calories	110

pineapple juice (canned)

COMPOSITION AND NUTRIENT VALUE PER Cup (249 g)

Protein	1 g	Phosphorous	22 mg
Carbohydrate	34 g	Potassium	370 mg
Fat	Trace g	Sodium	2 mg
Saturated Fatty Acids	— g	Vitamin A	120 I.U.
Oleic Acid	— g	Vitamin B$_1$	0.12 mg
Linoleic Acid	— g	Vitamin B$_2$	0.04 mg
Iron	0.7 mg	Niacin	0.50 mg
Calcium	37 mg	Vitamin C	22 mg
		Calories	135

prune juice (canned or bottled)

COMPOSITION AND NUTRIENT VALUE PER Cup (256 g)

Protein	1 g	Phosphorous	100 mg
Carbohydrate	49 g	Potassium	625 mg
Fat	Trace g	Sodium	5 mg
Saturated Fatty Acids	— g	Vitamin A	— I.U.
Oleic Acid	— g	Vitamin B$_1$	0.03 mg
Linoleic Acid	— g	Vitamin B$_2$	0.03 mg
Iron	10.5 mg	Niacin	1 mg
Calcium	36 mg	Vitamin C	5 mg
		Calories	200

g
The abbreviation for gram.

gefilte fish
Yiddish for "filled fish." Chopped fish, usually whitefish and pike, mixed with crumbs, egg, and various seasonings, shaped into balls and then cooked in a broth. Usually served cold.

gelatin
A water-soluble incomplete protein with little nutritional value.

gin
An alcoholic beverage distilled from rye or other grains and flavored with juniper berries, it is the basis of martinis, gibsons, and other drinks, and is popular with those who "drink" their lunch. Though containing 70 calories per ounce at 86 proof it carries negligible food value.

COMPOSITION AND NUTRIENT VALUE PER 1 1/2 ounce (42 g)

Protein	0 g	Phosphorous	0 mg
Carbohydrate	Trace g	Potassium	Trace mg
Fat	0 g	Sodium	Trace mg
Saturated Fatty Acids	0 g	Vitamin A	0 I.U.
Oleic Acid	0 g	Vitamin B_1	0 mg
Linoleic Acid	0 g	Vitamin B_2	0 mg
Iron	0 mg	Niacin	0 mg
Calcium	0 mg	Vitamin C	0 mg
		Calories	80 proof 100
			86 proof 105
			90 proof 110
			100 proof 125

glucose
A six-carbon sugar found in animal and plant tissue and derived synthetically from starch. Along with fructose, it is the fastest form of energy, passing directly into the

bloodstream unchanged. A synonym for dextrose and blood sugar.

See Blood Sugar

glucose syrup
A colorless-to-yellowish syrup mixture of dextrose, maltose, and dextrins, containing about 20 percent water. It is widely used in the making of confectioneries.

gluten
The protein fraction of wheat, and the part of the flour that has the elastic properties necessary for bread-making. It is prepared from flour by washing out the starch.

gluten bread
Bread made from flour with a high gluten and low starch content.

glycogen
Also called "animal starch." It is the form in which carbohydrate is stored in the liver and muscles of the body, and is composed of glucose units synthesized from the blood sugar and broken down again into blood sugar as energy demands require.

See Carbohydrates; Starch

goiter
The name used for any swelling of the thyroid gland. It may be caused by a variety of reasons, but when it is endemic to a region, the cause is usually iodine deficiency.* The endemic goiter regions in the United States are mainly in the Canadian border states, particularly the Great Lakes region, and in those states situated between the Rocky Mountains and the Appalachians.

Goiter is more common in women, particularly during puberty and pregnancy. The enlargement of the thyroid gland may not easily be detectable or it may swell enough to be easily identified by the eye. Thyroid cancer is more common among those with goiter and cretinism in children is more frequent in the endemic goiter areas, where it is almost always due to a severe iodine deficiency in the mother. Mental retardation and deaf mutism are more frequently found in children whose mothers suffer from goiter.

See Iodine; Iodized Salt

graham crackers

Crackers made from graham flour, i.e., coarsely ground whole wheat flour.

COMPOSITION AND NUTRIENT VALUE PER 4, 2-1/2" squares (28 g)

Protein	2 g	Phosphorous	112 mg
Carbohydrate	21 g	Potassium	90 mg
Fat	3 g	Sodium	180 mg
Saturated Fatty Acids	— g	Vitamin A	0 I.U.
Oleic Acid	— g	Vitamin B$_1$	0.01 mg
Linoleic Acid	— g	Vitamin B$_2$	0.06 mg
Iron	0.4 mg	Niacin	0.40 mg
Calcium	11 mg	Vitamin C	0 mg
		Calories	110

grain

The generic name of the seed or fruit of plants belonging to the grass family, especially wheat, barley, rice and oats. The seeds consist largely of starch and sugars, but the germ of the grain contains vitamins, minerals, and proteins—as does the outer coating, the bran.

See Flour, Refining and Bleaching

GRAS (generally recognized as safe)

A designation given to food additives which, having been added to foods for many years, were generally recognized as safe by most qualified scientists when used as intended. The additives on the GRAS list were exempt from premarketing clearance from the FDA. The list was established by Congress in 1958 on the basis of information that the critics of the list considered inadequate. At the present time more than 100 of the items on the GRAS list

are being investigated by the FDA as possibly harmful substances.
See Additives

gray hair
It is believed by some researchers that gray hair is the result of deficiency in at least four B vitamins—PABA, folic acid, biotin, and pantothenic acid.

PABA para-aminobenzoic acid was once called the anti-gray-hair vitamin because animals with black hair who lacked it became gray.

half and half
A combination of cream and milk

COMPOSITION AND NUTRIENT VALUE PER Cup (242 g)

Protein	8 g	Phosphorous	90 mg
Carbohydrate	11 g	Potassium	95 mg
Fat	28 g	Sodium	55 mg
Saturated Fatty Acids	15 g	Vitamin A	1160 I.U.
Oleic Acid	9 g	Vitamin B_1	0.07 mg
Linoleic Acid	1 g	Vitamin B_2	0.39 mg
Iron	0.1 mg	Niacin	0.1 mg
Calcium	261 mg	Vitamin C	2 mg
		Calories	325

halibut liver oil
A rich source of vitamin A and D, containing 4,500,000 and 70,000 I.U.'s respectively per ounce.

health foods
See Organic Foods

heart sugar
See Inositol

heat stroke
See Perspiration; Salt

hemoglobin
The oxygen-bearing, iron-containing component of red blood cells.

herbicides
Substances used to destroy weeds and other plants not wanted in cultivated crops. Usually a synthetic chemical.
See Pesticides for a discussion of possible harmful effects

herbs
A name commonly applied to a variety of aromatic plants used as seasonings or for their medicinal qualities, which have fleshy stems (as distinguished from the woody stems of shrubs and trees) and which usually live only one growing season (annuals). Not easily distinguished from spices, except that "herb" usually refers to the whole plant, whereas "spice" refers to only a part of the plant.
See Spices

histidine
One of the amino acids essential to the growing child.
See Amino Acids

homogenization
The process in which heated (pasteurized) milk is forced through small openings in order to break up the milk fat into particles able to remain suspended and evenly distributed throughout the milk. Once homogenized, the cream cannot be separated from the milk.

honey, strained
The syruplike liquid made by bees from the nectar of flowers. Flavor, color and composition depend on the source of the nectar.

COMPOSITION AND NUTRIENT VALUE PER Tablespoon (21 g)

Protein	Trace g	Phosphorous	N.D. mg
Carbohydrate	17 g	Potassium	N.D. mg
Fat	0 g	Sodium	N.D. mg
Saturated Fatty Acids	— g	Vitamin A	0 I.U.
Oleic Acid	— g	Vitamin B_1	Trace mg
Linoleic Acid	— g	Vitamin B_2	0.01 mg
Iron	0.1 mg	Niacin	0.10 mg
Calcium	1 mg	Vitamin C	Trace mg
		Calories	65

humectant

A substance that absorbs moisture and is used to maintain the water content of certain prepared foods, especially in baked goods, where it allows additions of sugar without adding more water and thus aids in preventing the growth of molds.

See Additives; Moisture Control Agents

hydrogenation

The process by which hydrogen is added to an unsaturated organic compound. Most commonly, vegetable oils are condensed to solid fats which can be kept for considerable periods of time without refrigeration. The shortenings used in frying and baking, and the principal ingredient of most margarines are hydrogenated vegetable oils. Unfortunately the hydrogenation process destroys the vitamin and mineral content of the oils. In addition, the protection afforded fat-soluble vitamins by unrefined vegetable oils is lacking in hydrogenated vegetable oils—and the great bulk of vegetable oils available on the American market are hydrogenated.

hydrogen peroxide

A bacteria-killer and preservative used in milk and cheese. Also, a bleaching and oxidizing agent. It is on the FDA list of additives to be studied for short-term mutagenic, teratogenic, subacute, and reproductive effects.

See GRAS

hypoglycemia
An abnormally low level of sugar in the blood, causing symptoms such as constant fatigue, dizziness, nervousness, headaches and even fainting spells. Nutritionally, it has been associated with potassium and pantothenic acid deficiencies.*

ice cream
A smooth, sweet, and cold confection prepared from a frozen mixture of milk products usually containing 10 percent to 14 percent butterfat and an average of 10.5 percent nonfat milk solids, approximately 15 percent sugar, flavoring, and small amounts of colloidal materials and emulsifiers.

COMPOSITION AND NUTRIENT VALUE PER Cup (133 g) of 10 percent fat ice cream

Protein	6 g	Phosphorous	150 mg
Carbohydrate	28 g	Potassium	170 mg
Fat	14 g	Sodium	140 mg
Saturated Fatty Acids	8 g	Vitamin A	590 I.U.
Oleic Acid	5 g	Vitamin B_1	0.05 mg
Linoleic Acid	Trace g	Vitamin B_2	0.28 mg
Iron	0.1 g	Niacin	0.1 mg
Calcium	194 g	Vitamin C	1 mg
		Calories	255

impotence
   See Sex

incomplete proteins
Those proteins which either lack one or more of the essential amino acids or which supply any of them in amounts too small to support good health.
   See Essential Amino Acids; subheading *Sources* under PROTEIN

inositol
  See under Vitamin B Complex

international units (I.U.)
The measure used to indicate the comparative potency of natural substances, such as Vitamin A. When they are obtained in a sufficiently pure state they are measured by grams, e.g. Vitamin B_1.

intestinal juice
The digestive juice produced by the intestinal glands lining the small intestine.

intrinsic factor
Vitamin B_{12} was once known as the "extrinsic factor" and it is now believed that B_{12} cannot be properly absorbed by the body unless an enzyme known as the "intrinsic factor" is present in sufficient quantity. In pernicious anemia, B_{12} is not absorbed due to a deficiency of the intrinsic factor.

iodized salt
Salt to which iodine has been added. Since few foods other than seafoods are reliable sources of iodine, the use of iodized salt is highly recommended by virtually all nutritionists. Unfortunately, the majority of table salt sold in America is not iodized.

The Food and Nutrition Board* has recommended federal legislation which would make mandatory the iodization of all salt sold for human consumption. This recommendation has not been acted upon.

  See Iodine (under Minerals)

irradiation
A process by which food is preserved by exposing it to cobalt-60, a radioactive chemical element. The rays emitted ionize the food atoms, killing various decay-causing microorganisms. Low doses are roughly equivalent to pasteurization. High doses effect complete sterilization,

but also cause changes in flavor, texture, and color. The Food and Drug Administration has approved the irradiation of wheat and wheat flour to eliminate insect infestation and the irradiation of potatoes to prevent sprouting (and thus prolong their storage life). Irradiated food does not become radioactive.

isoleucine
One of the essential amino acids.*

I.U.
International units (I.U.)*

jams
Fruit preserves set to a gel by the combined actions of acid, pectin and added sugar.

COMPOSITION AND NUTRIENT VALUE PER Tablespoon (20 g)

Protein	Trace g	Phosphorous	N.D. mg
Carbohydrate	14 g	Potassium	N.D. mg
Fat	Trace g	Sodium	N.D. mg
Saturated Fatty Acids	— g	Vitamin A	Trace I.U.
Oleic Acid	— g	Vitamin B_1	Trace mg
Linoleic Acid	— g	Vitamin B_2	Trace mg
Iron	0.2 mg	Niacin	Trace mg
Calcium	4 mg	Vitamin C	Trace mg
		Calories	55

jellies
A soft, semisolid food made of fruit juice containing pectin boiled with sugar.

COMPOSITION AND NUTRIENT VALUE PER Tablespoon (18 g)

Protein	Trace g	Phosphorous	N.D. mg
Carbohydrate	13 g	Potassium	N.D. mg
Fat	Trace g	Sodium	N.D. mg

Saturated Fatty Acids	— g	Vitamin A	Trace I.U.
Oleic Acid	— g	Vitamin B$_1$	Trace mg
Linoleic Acid	— g	Vitamin B$_2$	0.01 mg
Iron	0.3 mg	Niacin	Trace mg
Calcium	4 mg	Vitamin C	1 mg
		Calories	50

kelp
The generic name for a variety of large, brown seaweeds, rich in iodine and other minerals. Health food stores sell kelp in tablet and powdered form. By law the tablets cannot contain more than 0.15 milligrams of iodine. Therefore if you wish to take as much iodine in this form as some nutritionists recommend, you have to swallow a lot of tablets.
See Iodine under Minerals

keratomalacia
A disease of the eye leading to blindness and caused by Vitamin A deficiency. It is very rare in the United States but its precursor, xerophthalmia, is less rare.
See Vitamin A; Xerophthalmia

kilocalorie
See Calorie

kosher
Food selected and prepared in accordance with Jewish dietary laws.

kwashiorkor
Severe malnutrition in young children caused by a gross shortage of protein in the diet. Symptoms include anemia, edema, potbelly, muscular atrophy, loss of hair, depigmentation of the skin, and mental apathy. It occurs especially in the underdeveloped countries.

lactalbumin
One of the proteins of milk.
See Cheese; Milk

lactase
Enzyme that splits lactose (milk sugar) into glucose and galactose. Present in the pancreatic juice.

lactic acid
A syrupy liquid present in sour milk, various fruits, molasses, and wines and used as an acidulant, flavoring, and preservative in sugar confectionery, soft drinks, and other foods and beverages.

lactose
Milk sugar. A white crystalline disaccharide made from whey and used in infant foods, bakery products, confections, and pharmaceuticals.

lard
The white, rendered fat of a hog, used as a shortening.*

COMPOSITION AND NUTRIENT VALUE PER Cup (205 g)

Protein	0 g	Phosphorous	0 mg
Carbohydrate	0 g	Potassium	Trace mg
Fat	205 g	Sodium	Trace mg
Saturated Fatty Acids	78 g	Vitamin A	0 I.U.
Oleic Acid	94 g	Vitamin B$_1$	0 mg
Linoleic Acid	20 g	Vitamin B$_2$	0 mg
Iron	0 mg	Niacin	0 mg
Calcium	0 mg	Vitamin C	0 mg
		Calories	1850

laxatives
Any substance that stimulates the evacuation of the bowels. Under normal conditions laxatives are unnecessary if the body is adequately supplied with essential nutrients. In particular, adequate protein and roughage are necessary in the diet if normal digestion is to be maintained.

leavening agents
Substances such as yeast, cream of tartar, or baking soda,

used as an ingredient in doughs to produce fermentation, which in turn produces gas bubbles and allows the dough to rise when baked.

Yeast is a natural substance, but today all commercial food processors use chemical leavening agents—e.g., sodium bicarbonate (baking powder) in combination with an acid salt and starch, sodium aluminum sulfate with calcium phosphate—which in their combinations retain the gas in the dough, allowing it to be refrigerated for future use.

By law, all synthetic leavening agents must be listed on the product's label or package.

See Additives

lecithin
Any of a group of fatty substances found in all plant and animal tissues, made of fat, choline, inositol, and essential fatty acids. The liver normally produces lecithin in a person with an adequate diet. It is produced commercially from soybeans, egg yolk, and corn, and is sold in health food stores.

Lecithin breaks down cholesterol into minute particles which pass easily into the body tissues. When too little lecithin is produced by the liver or too little available in the diet, the cholesterol particles become large and can become trapped in the blood and in the arterial walls.

See Choline; Inositol

legume
A vegetable whose pod splits into two valves, with the seeds attached to one of the valves, such as a pea or bean.

leucine
An essential amino acid.*

levitin
One of the proteins of egg yolk, rich in sulphur. (The other protein is vitellin.)

libido
The psychic and emotional energy associated with the instinctual sexual drives. Many clinical investigations have demonstrated that libido decreases or disappears altogether when nutrition is sufficiently inadequate.

linoleic acid
  See Essential Fatty Acids

lysine
An essential amino acid.*

macrobiotics
A form of diet based on the Zen Buddhist concept that the universe is ordered by the opposing but complementary principles of yin and yang (light and dark, masculine and feminine, and other opposites). All problems are said to flow from the imbalance of yin and yang and thus the most desirable state of affairs is when an equilibrium exists between them. Since everything in the universe is either more yin or more yang, it follows that nutrients are too, and that the proper macrobiotic diet will greatly benefit the balance of yin and yang in mankind which in turn will lead to health, happiness and a long life.

The chief ingredients of the macrobiotic diet are grains and cereals, especially unpolished rice. Certain vegetables, seafood, nuts, and seeds are included according to their yin and yang qualities. Animal products and fruits are usually avoided. Nothing eaten should be processed, refined, or contain additives.

Some persons in this country have apparently thrived on this diet. Others have gotten very sick, and some have died.

malnutrition
A condition resulting from an insufficient intake of food, a poorly balanced diet, defective digestion, or a defective utilization of food.

Some authorities attempt to differentiate between malnutrition and undernourishment, but in general the terms are used interchangeably. The important thing is that poor nutrition is widespread in this country, crossing economic as well as state lines. The poor suffer most, but surprising numbers of the affluent are malnourished. Tooth decay, osteoporosis, heart disease, atherosclerosis, hypertension, and anemia are all associated with poor nutrition.

Dental caries is the most widespread disease in America. In some parts of the country, 90 per cent of the population have serious dental problems. Iron-deficiency anemia is thought to affect 25 per cent of the population; 50 per cent of adults over sixty suffer from osteoporosis; and hypertension, atherosclerosis, and coronary heart disease are responsible for over 50 per cent of the deaths in America.

And poor nutrition is considered largely responsible for the increased severity of infectious diseases among certain groups of children. The mortality rate for measles, for example, is very low among well-nourished children but high among the malnourished.

Severe deficiencies of essential nutrients leading to the classical nutritional diseases such as scurvy, beriberi, pellagra, and xerophthalmia are not common in this country but what little data is available on a national level suggests that the milder forms of deficiency are far more common than one would expect from so rich a society. Estimates vary, but it is thought that from 25,000,000 to 50,000,000 Americans suffer from undernourishment. On the other hand, approximately 50 per cent of Americans are overweight and take in too many calories and too much saturated fat. In short, both obesity and malnutrition are problems in our society.

See also Kwashiorkor; Nutritional Marasmus; Obesity

malpotane
Trade name for a vitamin preparation which is advertised as "The Vitamin for Men," the implication being that the preparation will restore or increase sexual vigor. Whether this be true or not, Malpotane is enjoying very brisk sales. It contains useful amounts of vitamins E, B_1, B_6, C, and nothing else.

See Sex; Vitamin E

malt
A grain, usually barley, that has been allowed to sprout. It is chiefly used in brewing and distilling. Malt contains the sugars, maltose and dextrin, and has a high carbohydrate and protein content.

maltase
An enzyme that converts maltose to glucose, a simple sugar.

malted milk
A soluble powder made of dried milk, malted barley, and wheat flour. When milk, ice cream, and flavoring is added to this powder, the result is a typical American drink.

COMPOSTION AND NUTRIENT VALUE PER 2 cups (540 g), including 1/2 cup of ice cream:

Protein	24 g	Phosphorous	615 mg
Carbohydrate	70 g	Potassium	60 mg
Fat	24 g	Sodium	19 mg
Saturated Fatty Acids	14 g	Vitamin A	670 I.U.
Oleic Acid	8 g	Vitamin B_1	0.3 mg
Linoleic Acid	Trace g	Vitamin B_2	1.1 mg
Iron	0.8 mg	Niacin	0.2 mg
Calcium	270 mg	Vitamin C	2 mg
		Calories	690

Malthus, Thomas R.
An English economist (1776-1834) who noted that while the food supply increased arithmetically, the population increased geometrically, and concluded that in time much of the world's people must starve if the increase in population could not be checked. He was viewed as an alarmist, especially after modern technology dramatically increased crop yields. His conclusion, however, is no longer considered eccentric.

maltose
Also called "malt sugar." Maltose exists in the body tissues
as an intermediate stage during the breakdown of starch
to glucose.

maple sugar candy
A candy made by boiling down maple syrup.

maple syrup
A sweet syrup manufactured from the sap of the sugar
maple.

COMPOSITION AND NUTRIENT VALUE PER 2 Tablespoons
(40 g)

Protein	0 g	Phosphorous	3 mg
Carbohydrate	25 g	Potassium	70 mg
Fat	0 g	Sodium	4 mg
Saturated Fatty Acids	0 g	Vitamin A	0 I.U.
Oleic Acid	0 g	Vitamin B_1	Trace mg
Linoleic Acid	0 g	Vitamin B_2	Trace mg
Iron	0.3 mg	Niacin	Trace mg
Calcium	41 mg	Vitamin C	0 mg
		Calories	100

marasmus, nutritional
The severe wasting away of the body caused by a grossly
inadequate diet. It is frequently found in survivors of concentration camps, famines, and total wars. Like kwashiorkor, it is one of the major problems of infant nutrition in
those areas of the world where food supplies are insufficient for the needs of the population. Symptoms include
muscular atrophy, growth failure and a typically wizened,
monkeylike facial appearance.

margarine
Also known as oleomargarine, and usually made from vegetable oils (chiefly corn, soybean, and cottonseed). The

oils are refined and churned with cultured or skim milk to the consistency of butter. Most brands are "enriched" with vitamin A and D. Brands made from unhydrogenated oils contain nearly twice as many unsaturated fatty acids as butter, but the making of margarine from hydrogenated oils is becoming more and more common.

See Fats; Hydrogenation

COMPOSITION AND NUTRIENT VALUE PER 1/4 pound (113 g), fortified with Vitamin A

Protein	1 g	Phosphorous	16 mg
Carbohydrate	1 g	Potassium	58 mg
Fat	92 g	Sodium	1150 mg
Saturated Fatty Acids	17 g	Vitamin A	3750 I.U.
Oleic Acid	46 g	Vitamin B$_1$	— mg
Linoleic Acid	25 g	Vitamin B$_2$	— mg
Iron	0 mg	Niacin	— mg
Calcium	23 mg	Vitamin C	0 mg
		Calories	815

marmite
The trade name for an English vegetable-flavored yeast extract used as a spread on bread, or any other suitable surface. It is very nutritious.

matzo
A flat piece of unleavened bread, usually rectangular. It is eaten especially during Passover, but many people eat matzos the year around.

mayonnaise
A dressing made from egg yolk, butter, lemon juice and seasonings, or from egg yolk, olive oil, and vinegar.

COMPOSITION AND NUTRIENT VALUE PER Tablespoon (14 g)

Protein	Trace g	Phosphorous	8 mg
Carbohydrate	Trace g	Potassium	3 mg

Fat	11 g	Sodium	85 mg
Saturated Fatty Acids	2 g	Vitamin A	40 I.U.
Oleic Acid	2 g	Vitamin B_1	Trace mg
Linoleic Acid	6 g	Vitamin B_2	0.01 mg
Iron	0.1 mg	Niacin	Trace mg
Calcium	3 mg	Vitamin C	0 mg
		Calories	100

meat

The edible flesh of mammals, such as beef from cattle, pork from pigs, and lamb from young sheep. All meats are good sources of protein and vitamins B_1, B_2, and niacin. They are also good sources of iron and phosphate. In addition, kidney and liver are rich sources of Vitamin A.

See also Poultry

bacon

The salted and smoked meat taken from the back, hindquarters, and sides of a pig.

COMPOSITION AND NUTRIENT VALUE OF 2 slices (15 g), crisp, drained

Protein	5 g	Phosphorous	42 mg
Carbohydrate	1 g	Potassium	65 mg
Fat	8 g	Sodium	600 mg
Saturated Fatty Acids	3 g	Vitamin A	0 I.U.
Oleic Acid	4 g	Vitamin B_1	0.08 mg
Linoleic Acid	1 g	Vitamin B_2	0.05 mg
Iron	0.5 mg	Niacin	0.8 mg
Calcium	2 mg	Vitamin C	0 mg
		Calories	90

beef

The meat of a full-grown steer or cow.

COMPOSITION AND NUTRIENT VALUE PER 3 ounces (85 g), pot-roasted, braised, or simmered

Protein	23 g	Phosphorous	110 mg
Carbohydrate	0 g	Potassium	340 mg
Fat	16 g	Sodium	50 mg
Saturated Fatty Acids	8 g	Vitamin A	30 I.U.
Oleic Acid	7 g	Vitamin B_1	0.04 mg
Linoleic Acid	Trace g	Vitamin B_2	0.18 mg
Iron	2.9 mg	Niacin	3.5 mg
Calcium	10 mg	Vitamin C	0 mg
		Calories	245

beef, hamburger (commercial)

COMPOSITION AND NUTRIENT VALUE PER 3 ounces (85 g)

Protein	21 g	Phosphorous	145 mg
Carbohydrate	0 g	Potassium	320 mg
Fat	17 g	Sodium	100 mg
Saturated Fatty Acids	8 g	Vitamin A	30 I.U.
Oleic Acid	8 g	Vitamin B_1	0.07 mg
Linoleic Acid	Trace g	Vitamin B_2	0.18 mg
Iron	2.7 mg	Niacin	4.6 mg
Calcium	9 mg	Vitamin C	0 mg
		Calories	245

beef, hamburger (lean)

COMPOSITION AND NUTRIENT VALUE PER 3 ounces (85 g)

Protein	23 g	Phosphorous	158 mg
Carbohydrate	0 g	Potassium	340 mg
Fat	10 g	Sodium	110 mg
Saturated Fatty Acids	5 g	Vitamin A	20 I.U.
Oleic Acid	4 g	Vitamin B_1	0.08 mg
Linoleic Acid	Trace g	Vitamin B_2	0.20 mg
Iron	3 mg	Niacin	5.1 mg
Calcium	10 mg	Vitamin C	0 mg
		Calories	185

beef, rib roast (oven-cooked)

COMPOSITION AND NUTRIENT VALUE PER 3 ounces (85 g)

Protein	17 g	Phosphorous	105 mg
Carbohydrate	0 g	Potassium	350 mg
Fat	34 g	Sodium	60 mg
Saturated Fatty Acids	16 g	Vitamin A	70 I.U.
Oleic Acid	15 g	Vitamin B_1	0.05 mg
Linoleic Acid	1 g	Vitamin B_2	0.13 mg
Iron	2.2 mg	Niacin	3.1 mg
Calcium	8 mg	Vitamin C	0 mg
		Calories	375

beef, round steak (broiled)

COMPOSITION AND NUTRIENT VALUE PER 3 ounces (85 g)

Protein	24 g	Phosphorous	180 mg
Carbohydrate	0 g	Potassium	300 mg
Fat	13 g	Sodium	62 mg
Saturated Fatty Acids	6 g	Vitamin A	20 I.U.
Oleic Acid	6 g	Vitamin B_1	0.07 mg
Linoleic Acid	Trace g	Vitamin B_2	0.19 mg
Iron	3 mg	Niacin	4.8 mg
Calcium	10 mg	Vitamin C	0 mg
		Calories	220

beef heart

COMPOSITION AND NUTRIENT VALUE PER 3 ounces (85 g), braised

Protein	27 g	Phosphorous	14 mg
Carbohydrate	1 g	Potassium	203 mg
Fat	5 g	Sodium	190 mg
Saturated Fatty Acids	— g	Vitamin A	20 I.U.
Oleic Acid	— g	Vitamin B_1	0.21 mg

Linoleic Acid	— g	Vitamin B$_2$	1.04 mg
Iron	5 mg	Niacin	6.5 mg
Calcium	5 mg	Vitamin C	1 mg
		Calories	160

beef kidney

COMPOSITION AND NUTRIENT VALUE PER 3.5 ounces (100 g), braised

Protein	33 g	Phosphorous	220 mg
Carbohydrate	1 g	Potassium	320 mg
Fat	7 g	Sodium	250 mg
Saturated Fatty Acids	— g	Vitamin A	1150 I.U.
Oleic Acid	— g	Vitamin B$_1$	0.5 mg
Linoleic Acid	— g	Vitamin B$_2$	4.8 mg
Iron	13.1 mg	Niacin	10.7 mg
Calcium	18 mg	Vitamin C	0 mg
		Calories	230

beef liver

COMPOSITION AND NUTRIENT VALUE PER 2 ounces (57 g), fried

Protein	17 g	Phosphorous	270 mg
Carbohydrate	3 g	Potassium	216 mg
Fat	6 g	Sodium	108 mg
Saturated Fatty Acids	— g	Vitamin A	30,280 I.U.
Oleic Acid	— g	Vitamin B$_1$	0.15 mg
Linoleic Acid	— g	Vitamin B$_2$	2.37 mg
Iron	5 mg	Niacin	9.4 mg
Calcium	6 mg	Vitamin C	15 mg
		Calories	130

calf's liver

COMPOSITION AND NUTRIENT VALUE PER 3.5 ounces (100 g)

Protein	29 g	Phosphorous	537 mg
Carbohydrate	4 g	Potassium	453 mg
Fat	13 g	Sodium	118 mg
Saturated Fatty Acids	— g	Vitamin A	32,000 I.U.
Oleic Acid	— g	Vitamin B_1	0.2 mg
Linoleic Acid	— g	Vitamin B_2	4.2 mg
Iron	14.2 mg	Niacin	16.5 mg
Calcium	13 mg	Vitamin C	37 mg
		Calories	261

beef, sirloin steak (broiled)

COMPOSITION AND NUTRIENT VALUE PER 3 ounces (85 g)

Protein	20 g	Phosphorous	150 mg
Carbohydrate	0 g	Potassium	320 mg
Fat	27 g	Sodium	60 mg
Saturated Fatty Acids	13 g	Vitamin A	50 I.U.
Oleic Acid	12 g	Vitamin B_1	0.05 mg
Linoleic Acid	1 g	Vitamin B_2	0.16 mg
Iron	2.5 mg	Niacin	4 mg
Calcium	9 mg	Vitamin C	0 mg
		Calories	330

beef stew (with vegetables)

COMPOSITION AND NUTRIENT VALUE PER Cup (235 g)

Protein	15 g	Phosphorous	150 mg
Carbohydrate	15 g	Potassium	500 mg
Fat	10 g	Sodium	75 mg
Saturated Fatty Acids	5 g	Vitamin A	2310 I.U.
Oleic Acid	4 g	Vitamin B_1	0.13 mg
Linoleic Acid	Trace g	Vitamin B_2	0.17 mg
Iron	2.8 mg	Niacin	4.4 mg
Calcium	28 mg	Vitamin C	15 mg
		Calories	210

bologna

A seasoned and smoked sausage made from mixed meats.

COMPOSITION AND NUTRIENT VALUE PER 2 slices (26 g)

Protein	3 g	Phosphorous	27 mg
Carbohydrate	Trace g	Potassium	55 mg
Fat	7 g	Sodium	275 mg
Saturated Fatty Acids	— g	Vitamin A	— I.U.
Oleic Acid	— g	Vitamin B$_1$	0.04 mg
Linoleic Acid	— g	Vitamin B$_2$	0.06 mg
Iron	0.5 mg	Niacin	0.7 mg
Calcium	2 mg	Vitamin C	0 mg
		Calories	80

brains (beef, calf, pork, sheep)

COMPOSITION AND NUTRIENT VALUE PER 3.5 ounces (100 g)

Protein	10 g	Phosphorous	312 mg
Carbohydrate	0 g	Potassium	219 mg
Fat	8 g	Sodium	125 mg
Saturated Fatty Acids	— g	Vitamin A	0 I.U.
Oleic Acid	— g	Vitamin B$_1$	0.2 mg
Linoleic Acid	— g	Vitamin B$_2$	0.2 mg
Iron	2.4 mg	Niacin	4.4 mg
Calcium	10 mg	Vitamin C	0 mg
		Calories	125

chipped or dried beef

COMPOSITION AND NUTRIENT VALUE PER 2 ounces (57 g)

Protein	19 g	Phosphorous	60 mg
Carbohydrate	0 g	Potassium	190 mg
Fat	4 g	Sodium	30 mg
Saturated Fatty Acids	2 g	Vitamin A	— I.U.
Oleic Acid	2 g	Vitamin B$_1$	0.04 mg
Linoleic Acid	Trace g	Vitamin B$_2$	0.18 mg
Iron	2.9 mg	Niacin	2.2 mg
Calcium	11 mg	Vitamin C	0 mg
		Calories	115

corned beef

COMPOSITION AND NUTRIENT VALUE PER 3 ounces (85 g)

Protein	22 g	Phosphorous	100 mg
Carbohydrate	0 g	Potassium	60 mg
Fat	10 g	Sodium	1200 mg
Saturated Fatty Acids	5 g	Vitamin A	20 I.U.
Oleic Acid	4 g	Vitamin B_1	0.01 mg
Linoleic Acid	Trace g	Vitamin B_2	0.20 mg
Iron	3.7 mg	Niacin	2.9 mg
Calcium	17 mg	Vitamin C	0 mg
		Calories	185

corned beef hash (canned)

COMPOSITION AND NUTRIENT VALUE PER 3 ounces (85 g)

Protein	7 g	Phosphorous	125 mg
Carbohydrate	9 g	Potassium	180 mg
Fat	10 g	Sodium	540 mg
Saturated Fatty Acids	5 g	Vitamin A	— I.U.
Oleic Acid	4 g	Vitamin B_1	0.01 mg
Linoleic Acid	Trace g	Vitamin B_2	0.08 mg
Iron	1.7 mg	Niacin	1.8 mg
Calcium	11 mg	Vitamin C	0 mg
		Calories	155

frankfurter

Or hot dog. A smoked sausage made from beef or a mixture of beef and pork.

COMPOSITION AND NUTRIENT VALUE PER 1 (56 g)

Protein	7 g	Phosphorous	25 mg
Carbohydrate	1 g	Potassium	105 mg
Fat	15 g	Sodium	550 mg

Saturated Fatty Acids	— g	Vitamin A	— I.U.
Oleic Acid	— g	Vitamin B$_1$	0.02 mg
Linoleic Acid	— g	Vitamin B$_2$	0.01 mg
Iron	0.8 mg	Niacin	0.2 mg
Calcium	3 mg	Vitamin C	0 mg
		Calories	170

ham

The meat from the thigh of a hog, usually cured by smoking or drying. The flavor varies according to the particular way in which these processes are carried out.

COMPOSITION AND NUTRIENT VALUE PER 3 ounces (85 g)

Protein	18 g	Phosphorous	240 mg
Carbohydrate	0 g	Potassium	270 mg
Fat	9 g	Sodium	1000 mg
Saturated Fatty Acids	7 g	Vitamin A	— I.U.
Oleic Acid	8 g	Vitamin B$_1$	0.4 mg
Linoleic Acid	2 g	Vitamin B$_2$	0.16 mg
Iron	2.2 mg	Niacin	3.1 mg
Calcium	8 mg	Vitamin C	0 mg
		Calories	245

ham, boiled (luncheon meat)

The boiled meat of the thigh of a hog.

COMPOSITION AND NUTRIENT VALUE PER 2 ounces (57 g)

Protein	11 g	Phosphorous	170 mg
Carbohydrate	0 g	Potassium	290 mg
Fat	10 g	Sodium	700 mg
Saturated Fatty Acids	4 g	Vitamin A	— I.U.
Oleic Acid	4 g	Vitamin B$_1$	0.25 mg
Linoleic Acid	1 g	Vitamin B$_2$	0.09 mg
Iron	1.6 mg	Niacin	1.5 mg
Calcium	6 mg	Vitamin C	0 mg
		Calories	135

lamb

The meat of a young sheep, usually less than twelve to fourteen months.

lamb chop (broiled)

COMPOSITION AND NUTRIENT VALUE PER 4 ounces (112 g)

Protein	25 g	Phosphorous	140 mg
Carbohydrate	0 g	Potassium	275 mg
Fat	33 g	Sodium	75 mg
Saturated Fatty Acids	18 g	Vitamin A	— I.U.
Oleic Acid	12 g	Vitamin B_1	0.14 mg
Linoleic Acid	1 g	Vitamin B_2	0.25 mg
Iron	1.5 mg	Niacin	5.6 mg
Calcium	10 mg	Vitamin C	0 mg
		Calories	400

lamb, leg of (roasted)

COMPOSITION AND NUTRIENT VALUE PER 3 ounces (85 g)

Protein	22 g	Phosphorous	190 mg
Carbohydrate	0 g	Potassium	270 mg
Fat	16 g	Sodium	70 mg
Saturated Fatty Acids	9 g	Vitamin A	— I.U.
Oleic Acid	6 g	Vitamin B_1	0.13 mg
Linoleic Acid	Trace g	Vitamin B_2	0.23 mg
Iron	1.4 mg	Niacin	4.7 mg
Calcium	9 mg	Vitamin C	0 mg
		Calories	235

lamb, shoulder of (roasted)

COMPOSITION AND NUTRIENT VALUE PER 3 ounces (85 g)

Protein	18 g	Phosphorous	170 mg
Carbohydrate	0 g	Potassium	260 mg

Fat	23 g	Sodium	60 mg
Saturated Fatty Acids	13 g	Vitamin A	— I.U.
Oleic Acid	8 g	Vitamin B_1	0.11 mg
Linoleic Acid	1 g	Vitamin B_2	0.20 mg
Iron	1 mg	Niacin	4 mg
Calcium	9 mg	Vitamin C	0 mg
		Calories	285

liverwurst

A sausage made from or containing ground liver.

COMPOSITION AND NUTRIENT VALUE PER 2 ounces (85 g)

Protein	8 g	Phosphorous	120 mg
Carbohydrate	1 g	Potassium	75 mg
Fat	11 g	Sodium	450 mg
Saturated Fatty Acids	— g	Vitamin A	2860 I.U.
Oleic Acid	— g	Vitamin B_1	0.2 mg
Linoleic Acid	— g	Vitamin B_2	0.6 mg
Iron	2.8 mg	Niacin	2.3 mg
Calcium	4 mg	Vitamin C	0 mg
		Calories	132

pork

The meat of a pig.

COMPOSITION AND NUTRIENT VALUE PER 1 chop, thick, 3.5 ounces, (100 g)

Protein	16 g	Phosphorous	250 mg
Carbohydrate	0 g	Potassium	390 mg
Fat	21 g	Sodium	30 mg
Saturated Fatty Acids	8 g	Vitamin A	0 I.U.
Oleic Acid	9 g	Vitamin B_1	0.63 mg
Linoleic Acid	2 g	Vitamin B_2	0.18 mg
Iron	2.2 mg	Niacin	3.8 mg
Calcium	8 mg	Vitamin C	0 mg
		Calories	260

pork roast

COMPOSITION AND NUTRIENT VALUE PER 3 ounces (85 g)

Protein	21 g	Phosphorous	240 mg
Carbohydrate	0 g	Potassium	360 mg
Fat	24 g	Sodium	40 mg
Saturated Fatty Acids	9 g	Vitamin A	0 I.U.
Oleic Acid	10 g	Vitamin B$_1$	0.78 mg
Linoleic Acid	2 g	Vitamin B$_2$	0.22 mg
Iron	2.7 mg	Niacin	4.7 mg
Calcium	9 mg	Vitamin C	0 mg
		Calories	310

pork sausage

COMPOSITION AND NUTRIENT VALUE PER 2 links (26 g)

Protein	8 g	Phosphorous	120 mg
Carbohydrate	Trace g	Potassium	75 mg
Fat	11 g	Sodium	450 mg
Saturated Fatty Acids	— g	Vitamin A	2860 I.U.
Oleic Acid	— g	Vitamin B$_1$	0.2 mg
Linoleic Acid	— g	Vitamin B$_2$	0.6 mg
Iron	2.8 mg	Niacin	2.3 mg
Calcium	4 mg	Vitamin C	0 mg
		Calories	132

sweetbreads, calf
The thymus gland of a calf, used as food.

COMPOSITION AND NUTRIENT VALUE PER 3.5 ounces (100 g), braised

Protein	18 g	Phosphorous	360 mg
Carbohydrate	Trace g	Potassium	244 mg
Fat	3 g	Sodium	116 mg

Saturated Fatty Acids	— g	Vitamin A	0 I.U.
Oleic Acid	— g	Vitamin B$_1$	0.1 mg
Linoleic Acid	— g	Vitamin B$_2$	0.3 mg
Iron	0.8 mg	Niacin	5 mg
Calcium	7 mg	Vitamin C	0 mg
		Calories	170

tongue, beef

COMPOSITION AND NUTRIENT VALUE PER 3 ounces (85 g)

Protein	18 g	Phosphorous	180 mg
Carbohydrate	Trace g	Potassium	240 mg
Fat	14 g	Sodium	90 mg
Saturated Fatty Acids	7 g	Vitamin A	0 I.U.
Oleic Acid	7 g	Vitamin B$_1$	Trace mg
Linoleic Acid	Trace g	Vitamin B$_2$	0.3 mg
Iron	2.5 mg	Niacin	0.3 mg
Calcium	7 mg	Vitamin C	0 mg
		Calories	205

veal

The meat of a young calf. Most of the veal now sold 's from older, rather than younger calves.

COMPOSITION AND NUTRIENT VALUE PER 3-ounce cutlet (85 g), broiled

Protein	23 g	Phosphorous	230 mg
Carbohydrate	— g	Potassium	400 mg
Fat	9 g	Sodium	70 mg
Saturated Fatty Acids	5 g	Vitamin A	— I.U.
Oleic Acid	4 g	Vitamin B$_1$	0.06 mg
Linoleic Acid	Trace g	Vitamin B$_2$	0.21 mg
Iron	2.7 mg	Niacin	4.6 mg
Calcium	9 mg	Vitamin C	0 mg
		Calories	185

veal, roasted

COMPOSITION AND NUTRIENT VALUE PER 3 ounces (85 g)

Protein	23 g	Phosphorous	200 mg
Carbohydrate	0 g	Potassium	390 mg
Fat	14 g	Sodium	70 mg
Saturated Fatty Acids	7 g	Vitamin A	— I.U.
Oleic Acid	6 g	Vitamin B_1	0.11 mg
Linoleic Acid	Trace g	Vitamin B_2	0.26 mg
Iron	2.9 mg	Niacin	6.6 mg
Calcium	10 mg	Vitamin C	0 mg
		Calories	230

metabolic rate
The rate of utilization of energy.
    See Basal Metabolic Rate

metabolism
The sum of all the chemical processes involved in the maintenance of life and especially the growth of new tissues, the repair of tissues, the breakdown and elimination of old tissues, and the production of energy.
    See Basal Metabolic Rate

methionine
An essential amino acid.*

Metrecal
Trade name for a preparation containing the dietary "essentials" and used as an aid in losing weight. Four portions contain 900 calories.

mg
The abbreviation for milligram, 1/1,000 of a gram.

milk
A liquid secreted from the mammary glands of a variety

of mammals and consumed as a food in most parts of the world. (Cow's milk is the most widely consumed.) It is a major source of complete protein, Vitamins A and B_2, and calcium and phosphorus. Some milk in America has 400 I.U. of Vitamin D added to it per quart, and most of it is pasteurized* and homogenized.*

See Buttermilk; Certified Raw Milk

milk, evaporated

Milk that has been concentrated by evaporation to approximately 45 per cent of original volume.

COMPOSITION AND NUTRIENT VALUE PER Cup (252 g)

Protein	18 g	Phosphorous	465 mg
Carbohydrate	24 g	Potassium	102 mg
Fat	20 g	Sodium	38 mg
Saturated Fatty Acids	11g	Vitamin A	810 I.U.
Oleic Acid	7 g	Vitamin B_1	0.1 mg
Linoleic Acid	1 g	Vitamin B_2	0.86 mg
Iron	0.3 mg	Niacin	0.5 mg
Calcium	635 mg	Vitamin C	3 mg
		Calories	345

milk, skim

Milk from which the cream has been removed.

COMPOSITION AND NUTRIENT VALUE PER Cup (245 g)

Protein	9 g	Phosphorous	235 mg
Carbohydrate	12 g	Potassium	54 mg
Fat	Trace g	Sodium	19.5 mg
Saturated Fatty Acids	Trace g	Vitamin A	10 I.U.
Oleic Acid	Trace g	Vitamin B_1	0.09 mg
Linoleic Acid	0 g	Vitamin B_2	0.44 mg
Iron	0.1 mg	Niacin	0.2 mg
Calcium	296 mg	Vitamin C	2 mg
		Calories	90

milk, whole

COMPOSITION AND NUTRIENT VALUE PER Cup (244 g)

Protein	9 g	Phosphorous	232 mg
Carbohydrate	12 g	Potassium	52 mg
Fat	9 g	Sodium	19 mg
Saturated Fatty Acids	5 g	Vitamin A	350 I.U.
Oleic Acid	3 g	Vitamin B_1	0.07 mg
Linoleic Acid	Trace g	Vitamin B_2	0.41 mg
Iron	0.1 mg	Niacin	0.2 mg
Calcium	288 mg	Vitamin C	2 mg
		Calories	160

milk, condensed
Milk that has been evaporated to less than one-third of its original volume and to which sugar has been added as a preservative.

milk, dried
Milk that has been reduced to a powder by an evaporation process.

milk, homogenized
Milk in which the fat globules have been broken into minute droplets and evenly distributed throughout the milk, thus leaving no layer of cream on top. The process is done after pasteurization.

milk, nonfat
Skim milk.

milk custard
A baked dessert made from milk, eggs, sugar, and flavoring.

COMPOSITION AND NUTRIENT VALUE PER Cup (265 g)

Protein	14 g	Phosphorous	150 mg
Carbohydrate	29 g	Potassium	170 mg
Fat	15 g	Sodium	140 mg
Saturated Fatty Acids	7 g	Vitamin A	930 I.U.
Oleic Acid	5 g	Vitamin B_1	0.11 mg
Linoleic Acid	1 g	Vitamin B_2	0.50 mg
Iron	1.1 mg	Niacin	0.3 mg
Calcium	297 mg	Vitamin C	1 mg
		Calories	305

mineral salts

The inorganic salts of such elements as calcium, potassium, sodium, and the like; most commonly, sodium chloride, table salt.

minerals, general

In nutrition, those inorganic substances which are part of the body's composition and which the body needs to enable it to grow and function properly. The minerals and the other nutrients required by the body interact, and an inadequate intake of minerals disturbs this interaction. Recommended daily allowances (RDA) have been established for some of the minerals but many nutritionists believe that the amounts recommended are too low for the maintenance of good health.

bromide

A binary compound of bromine, a nonmetallic element, which is found in human blood and is therefore required by humans in some small amount. How much is not known.

See Soil; Trace Elements for sources

calcium

A metallic element present in most animal and vegetable matter, and the most abundant mineral in the human body. The body of a healthy adult contains about 1250 grams, 99 per cent of which is in the bones and teeth, and which is essential to their formation and maintenance.

The remaining 1 per cent circulating in the blood and soft tissues is of vital importance to the metabolic processes, the heartbeat, the excitability of muscles and nerves, and is necessary for the clotting of blood.

The absorption of calcium into the body depends on several factors of which Vitamin D is probably the most important. A person whose intake of calcium is adequate will nevertheless be deficient in calcium if Vitamin D is undersupplied. Also, if the diet is too high in phosphorus —a common problem in America—large amounts of calcium are lost through the urine.

It should be remembered that the bones are not lifeless structures erected during the growth period, but rather are living entities especially dependent on an adequate supply of calcium for their maintenance and repair.

SOURCES

The richest sources are milk and milk products such as yogurt, cheese, and cultured buttermilk. Soybeans, mustard and turnip greens have appreciable amounts of calcium, but vegetables and fruit are generally poor in calcium.

REQUIREMENTS

The recommended dietary allowance (RDA) is 0.8 grams for adults and 1.2 grams for adolescents. An additional 0.4 grams is recommended for pregnant or lactating women.

Some nutritionists recommend additional calcium during menstruation and menopause. The blood calcium drops drastically during the week prior to menstruation, often resulting in irritability and nervous tension. It drops even further at the onset of menstruation, causing the cramps associated with menstruation. Additional calcium usually relieves these symptoms. At menopause, the lack of hormones from the ovaries causes a severe deficiency of calcium, resulting in the hot flashes, leg cramps, irritability, and mental depression so common to that period. Sufficient additional calcium usually reduces or relieves these symptoms. (One cup of milk contains 288 milligrams of calcium, one cup of yogurt 294 milligrams.)

DEFICIENCIES

Calcium deficiency is more widespread than that of any other nutrient. Mild deficiencies of the blood calcium lead to nervousness, irritability, insomnia, backache, and muscle cramps, especially in the leg or foot. When the blood calcium is extremely low, the increased sensitivity of the motor nerves to stimuli can result in convulsions, a condition known as tetany.

Deficiencies of the bone calcium result in susceptibility to tooth decay and the demineralization of the bones (osteoporosis and osteomalacia). In the cases of osteoporosis and osteomalacia, however, it is thought that a deficiency of Vitamin D is the most important factor.

EXCESS AND TOXICITY

In some cultures, people take in as much as 2,000 mg. of calcium per day. This has not been shown to have any deleterious effects. In certain medical conditions excessive calcium is found in the urine, serum, or soft tissues but there are no data to prove that high calcium intakes are responsible for these conditions.

See Phosphorus; Tetany; Vitamin D

chlorine

A nonmetallic element which the body requires in fairly large amounts. Along with potassium and sodium, chlorine aids in maintaining the water balance in the body. It is also used to stimulate the production of hydrochloric acid and other digestive juices in the stomach, and plays a role in the waste removal processes and in the distribution of hormones.

Chlorine is amply supplied in the average diet by table salt (sodium chloride). Other sources include green leafy vegetables, raw meat, beets, and radishes.

chromium

A metallic element which may be required by humans in small amounts. Some authorities believe that it is essential to the proper utilization of sugars; others feel that the evidence is vague.

See Soil; Trace Elements for sources

cobalt

A metallic element which forms part of vitamin B_{12} and is therefore required by humans in some small amount. How much is not known.

See Soil; Trace Elements for sources

copper

A metallic element essential for the formation of hemoglobin (which carries oxygen throughout the body in the red blood cells) and the production of ribonucleic acid (RNA, which is part of the nucleus of every cell). It is therefore required by humans in small amounts. How much is not known.

Some authorities say that there is no evidence of ill health due to a dietary deficiency of copper. Others dispute this, claiming that a deficiency decreases the absorption of iron and thus may lead to anemia. They further point out that copper deficiencies in test animals lead to porous bones, loss of hair, skin rash, and heart damage.

Copper is supplied by a wide variety of foods, but the best sources are green leafy vegetables, seafood, liver, whole-grain breads and cereals, kidney, dried fruits, and egg yolk.

EXCESS AND TOXICITY

In some medical conditions excessive copper accumulates in the tissues. It is probably due to a genetic absence of a liver enzyme.

See Soil; Trace Elements

fluoride

Defined as any binary compound of fluorine with another element, it is now considered by some authorities a mineral nutrient essential for optimum health, inasmuch as traces of this mineral in the teeth help to protect them against dental caries. (Other authorities, however, disagree, and the disagreement goes beyond the paranoid suggestion that adding fluoride to drinking water is a communist plot. Among other things, they cite studies indicating that in some localities, tooth decay increased after the drinking water supply was fluoridated; that an excess of fluoride discolors the teeth, interferes with some of the body's enzyme systems, and increases the brittleness of the teeth and other bones.)

Nevertheless, it is widely accepted that the protective effects of fluoride occur when the teeth are developing, an effect which carries over into adult life when one drinks fluoridated water. It is also thought to strengthen the bones and that it may be an important factor in reducing the chances of osteoporosis* in the elderly.

The main source of fluoride is treated drinking water. At a concentration of one part per million, it supplies enough fluoride to adequately protect against tooth decay. One to two milligrams per day is deemed adequate and this amount can be obtained by drinking normal amounts of fluoridated water and beverages made with this water.

EXCESS AND TOXICITY
Very high intake of fluoride during childhood results in mottled, discolored teeth, and very high intake at any time in life can result in increased brittleness of bones. These possibilities arise when the drinking water contains 10 to 45 parts per million of fluoride.
See Trace Elements

fluorine
See Fluoride

iodine
A nonmetallic element essential for the formation of thyroxine and triiodothyronine, the hormones secreted by the thyroid gland. Since the thyroid gland controls the basal metabolism of the body, an undersupply of the thyroid hormones leads to fatigue, slowed pulse, low blood pressure, and a tendency to gain weight even though the calorie intake is small.

Iodine is found in minute amounts in all parts of the

body, but it is particularly concentrated in the thyroid gland. (The body of the average adult contains about 40 milligrams of iodine, half of which is present in the thyroid gland.)

SOURCES

Much of the iodine once present in rocks and soil has been washed into the ocean. Consequently the only reliable sources of iodine are seafood and iodized salt.* Dairy products, eggs, and some vegetables may be good sources, but they are undependable since the amount of iodine they contain varies with the amount of iodine in the soil from which they grow or from which the food they eat grows.

REQUIREMENTS

The recommended dietary allowance (RDA) for adults is approximately two micrograms (2/1,000,000 of a gram) per kilogram (2.2 lbs.) of body weight. For example a 128 lb. woman (58 kilograms) should have 100 micrograms of iodine per day and a 154 lb. man (70 kilograms) should have 130 micrograms. Growing children and pregnant or lactating women need somewhat more than 2 micrograms per kilogram of body weight. Many nutritionists recommend a daily intake much greater than the RDA, on the theory that iodine deficiency is not worth chancing. Adelle Davis, for example, recommends at least 3 milligrams (1/1000 of a gram) per day. Since the body eliminates unused iodine, no harm will result from following her advice.

Iodized salt,* if used throughout life, will supply all the iodine necessary for good health.

DEFICIENCIES

Small deficiencies result in lethargy, fatigue, decreased sexual interest, slowed pulse, low blood pressure, and a tendency to gain weight. Larger deficiencies cause goiter,* the enlargement of the thyroid gland. This enlargement occurs because when iodine is deficient in the diet, the gland expands in order to more efficiently use this limited supply to produce the thyroid hormones.

Goiter caused by iodine deficiency is therefore really a defense mechanism designed to help the thyroid hormones at the proper level. Due to our laxness in using iodized salt, iodine deficiency is a major public health problem in America. Endemic goiter exists in the states bordering on Canada and in those between the Rocky Mountains and the Appalachians. Cretinism can also result from a dietary deficiency of iodine.

EXCESS AND TOXICITY

The body eliminates unused iodine.

See Cretinism; Goiter; Trace Elements

iron

A metallic element essential to the biological processes of most animals and many plants. The body of a healthy adult contains about 4 grams, about two-thirds of which is present in the blood as hemoglobin. The majority of the remainder is stored in the liver, spleen, bone marrow, and muscles.

Iron is an essential component of hemoglobin, the pigment in the red blood cells which carries oxygen from the lungs to all the cells of the body. Without oxygen the cells die. Iron is also an important element in many enzyme systems and is present as myoglobin in the muscles where it accepts the oxygen carried by the hemoglobin.

SOURCES

Meat, especially pork and beef liver, egg yolk, wheat germ, brewer's yeast, apricots, beans and peas are rich sources of iron. Whole grains, green leafy vegetables, and fish are good sources.

REQUIREMENTS

The recommended dietary allowance (RDA) is 10 milligrams per day for men and postmenopausal women; 18 milligrams per day for adolescents and women of childbearing age; 10 milligrams per day for one- to six-month-old infants; 15 milligrams per day for six-month to twelve-month-old infants; 15 milligrams per day for children from one to three years of age; and 10 milligrams per day for children from four to ten years of age. These requirements are approximately 10 times the body's physiologic needs and are made necessary by the fact that healthy people absorb only about 10 per cent of the iron in their foods. Iron-deficient persons absorb about twice this amount. Ascorbic acid (vitamin C) promotes iron absorption, and refined carbohydrates decrease absorption. (Two ounces of beef liver contain 5 milligrams of iron, two eggs 1.8 milligrams, and one cup of navy beans 5.1 milligrams.)

DEFICIENCY

The most common result of iron deficiency is iron-deficiency anemia. This anemia is common among women, adolescent boys and girls, and children, but is rare in men. Given the requirements for iron and the iron content of commonly eaten foods one would think that iron-deficiency anemia would be rare except during pregnancy and lactation, but iron loss occurs whenever blood is lost and a very common cause of iron-deficiency anemia is a chronic loss of blood about which the loser is unaware or unconcerned: bleeding gums, hemorrhoids, mild peptic ulcer, blood donations.

It should also be noted that the refined breads and cereals commonly eaten have had much of their iron content either removed or destroyed in the refining process, and only a small amount is replaced in the "enriched" or fortified breads and cereals.

EXCESS AND TOXICITY

Excessive accumulations of iron, resulting in siderosis, can occur through a number of causes. Among these are frequent blood transfusions, and the excessive ingestion of therapeutic doses of iron. As a result of advertising promoting iron as a tonic and body strengthener it is not uncommon for people to be consuming much more iron than is healthful for them.

See Anemia

magnesium

A metallic element which is an essential constituent of all soft tissue and bone in humans, 70 per cent of which is found in the bones. It is essential for the synthesis of protein, the utilization of fats and carbohydrates, and for many enzyme systems involved in energy production.

SOURCES

Most foods of vegetable origin contain magnesium. Whole grains, nuts, soybeans, and cooked green leafy vegetables are especially good sources. Magnesium is lost, however, if soaked or boiled in water and the water discarded. Moreover, foods grown in chemically fertilized soil have their magnesium content greatly reduced because chemical fertilizers inhibit the absorption of magnesium by the soil and the plants. Thus many American diets are at best marginal in their magnesium content. For this reason, a growing number of nutritionists strongly recommend the use of a magnesium supplement.

REQUIREMENTS

The recommended dietary allowance (RDA) is 300-400 milligrams per day for normal adults, 450 milligrams per day during pregnancy and lactation, and 60-70 milligrams per day for infants. Some nutritionists consider the RDA grossly inadequate and recommend 500 milligrams per day for infants, children and women, and 800 milligrams per day for adolescents, men and pregnant women. (According to some nutritionists, magnesium and Vitamin B_6 are interdependent, and thus must be supplied in adequate amounts at the same time if either is to perform its functions.)

DEFICIENCY

Slight magnesium deficiency produces symptoms of irritability, apprehension, and belligerence. Prolonged deficiency produces twitching, tremors, irregular pulse, muscle weakness, foot and leg cramps. In severe deficiency the brain is especially affected, with symptoms of confusion, disorientation, depression, and sometimes delirium tremens.

(Alcoholics, for example, usually have a very low serum magnesium level.) Due to the extra loss of calcium via the urine when magnesium is undersupplied, magnesium deficiency can indirectly be responsible for degenerative diseases of the bones and teeth.

In experimental animals, magnesium deficiency leads to soft tissue calcification, convulsions, kidney damage, and heart disease. It is reported that in groups of people whose diets are rich in magnesium, heart attacks and arteriosclerosis are rare.

EXCESS AND TOXICITY
Neither are known to occur.
See Calcium; Soil

manganese

A metallic element considered a dietary essential because it aids the utilization of fats, milk production in females, the proper functioning of the liver, pancreas, and adrenal glands, and appears necessary for reproduction.

Deficiencies in test animals result in retarded growth, hyperactivity, abnormal bone structure, sterility in females, and impotence in males. The eggs of hens fed a manganese-free diet do not hatch.

Good sources of manganese are: green leafy vegetables, wheat germ, whole-grain breads and cereals, nuts, beans, and liver.
See Soil; Trace Elements

molybdenum

A metallic element that is part of the enzyme xanthine oxidase and therefore required by humans in some small amount. How much is not known.
See Soil; Trace Elements for sources

phosphorus

A nonmetallic element present in the tissues of all animals and plants. In biological tissues it is present in the form of phosphate. In humans 80 per cent of it is present in the skeleton and teeth, about 10 per cent in the muscles, and 1 per cent in the nervous system. It is of vital importance in metabolism; acts as a hardening agent in the bones and teeth; and is necessary for the proper functioning of the muscles and nerves.

Phosphorus and calcium, though not chemically related, occur together in the body in an almost constant ratio of 1.5 to 1 (calcium to phosphorus). But if the diet is too high in phosphorus in relation to calcium intake—and in many American diets this is the case—calcium is lost through the urine. And if the intake of calcium is inadequate, phosphorus is not properly absorbed and used. Moreover, both can only be properly absorbed when adequate amounts of Vitamin D are present.

Since phosphorus is ubiquitous in the American diet and calcium often deficient and the proper balance between the two is vitally necessary, it is suggested by most nutritionists that one obtain one's phosphorus from the calcium-rich foods: milk, cheese, nuts and the like. A sufficient intake of protein foods usually supplies the necessary amount of phosphorus. Dietary deficiencies in phosphorus per se are rare, occurring in almost all cases because of the imbalance between calcium and phosphorus, and the lack of Vitamin D. The symptoms of deficiency are therefore similar to those of calcium deficiency: rickets, brittle bones, susceptibility to tooth decay, and retarded growth.

EXCESS AND TOXICITY
A marked excess of phosphorus leads to calcium deficiency and its attendant problems.
See Calcium; Vitamin D

potassium
A metallic element necessary to the human diet. Without it glucose cannot be utilized for energy nor glycogen stored for future energy needs, with the result that the muscles are unable to contract and partial or complete paralysis results. It also functions, along with sodium, in maintaining the balance between the extra- and intracellular fluid

compartments of the body. In addition it aids, along with phosphorus, the carrying of oxygen to the brain cells, and it is an important element in the proper functioning of the cardiovascular system.

SOURCES
Potassium is present in most commonly eaten foods: vegetables, fruits, whole grains, meats and nuts, for example.

REQUIREMENTS
Allowances for potassium have not been established by the Food and Nutrition Board, but it is believed that the minimum need is between 0.8 and 1.3 grams per day. Some authorities vehemently dispute this figure. They cite the need for maintaining a proper sodium-potassium balance* and the fact that the typical American diet provides proportionally a good deal more sodium than potassium. They claim that 5 grams of potassium are required if the salt intake (the major source of sodium) is no more than 4 grams (1 teaspoon), and that for each additional teaspoon of salt an additional 5 grams of potassium should be taken. The average intake of sodium in America is almost 5 grams per day per person and by the reasoning just cited, the potassium requirement should be a little more than 6 grams. (One cup of soybeans contains 1080 milligrams of potassium; one fresh medium-sized orange, 300 milligrams; two ounces of boiled ham, 290 milligrams.)

DEFICIENCIES
Potassium deficiency leads to a general weakening of the muscles; the most important muscle it affects is the heart. Heart attacks are frequently associated with low potassium intake and it is possible that the lack of potassium in the coronary muscles is a major factor in death from heart disease. Low blood sugar, hypoglycemia, is also associated with potassium deficiency. When the cells are low in potassium, they are also low in blood sugar.

Weakness in the muscles of the intestinal walls is very

commonly experienced, which results in indigestion and gas pains.

Edema, or water retention, is also a common symptom of potassium deficiency. (When the sodium-potassium balance is disturbed by insufficient potassium, sodium and water enter the cells.)

Some persons have a high hereditary requirement for potassium. When they do not receive sufficient amounts of it, they often suffer a temporary paralysis—a condition which can be quickly corrected by the administration of potassium.

EXCESS AND TOXICITY
Neither are known to occur.
    See Sodium; Sodium-Potassium Balance

sodium

A metallic element essential in the human diet. Its functions include maintaining the equilibrium between the extra and intracellular fluid compartments of the body, maintaining the pH level of the blood, and the conduction of nerve impulses.

SOURCES
In American diets most sodium is supplied by the table salt added to food either during cooking or after. Salt is added as a preservative in the manufacture and processing of many foods such as bacon, sausage, ham, butter, and bread. In addition, the use of monosodium glutamate (MSG)* as a flavor enhancer has provided an additional, if perhaps dubious, source of sodium.

REQUIREMENTS
Official daily requirements have not been established, but it is believed that one (1) gram per day is needed. The average intake in the United States is approximately five (5) grams per day.

DEFICIENCY
Sodium being oversupplied in the American diet, defi-

ciencies occur only when great amounts of it are lost through profuse sweating. When this happens, dizziness, nausea, lethargy, exhaustion, and cramps result. Vomiting and respiratory failure can occur in severe cases. All these symptoms can be avoided by adding more salt to the diet in hot weather, or, in extreme cases, by taking salt tablets.

Sodium deficiency, via depletion can also result from severe vomiting or diarrhea.

EXCESS AND TOXICITY

Many studies show the relationship between excessive sodium intake and high blood pressure: the greater the intake of sodium, the more numerous are the deaths caused by hypertension. And some scientists postulate that the oversalted prepared baby foods may cause dangerously high blood pressure in later life. An additional harm done by an excessive intake of sodium is that it causes a serious loss of potassium from the body.

See Perspiration; Potassium; Salt; Salt-Free Diets; Sodium-Potassium Balance

sulphur

A nonmetallic element present in all protein material. In humans it is present chiefly in two sulphur-containing amino acids (methionine and cystine) and in the Vitamins B (thiamine) and biotin.

Sulphur is needed for healthy skin, hair, and nails. It aids the metabolism of other minerals by the liver and helps in the secretion of bile.

The best sources are the protein foods, wheat germ, brussels sprouts, lentils, and onions.

Very little is known about either the sulphur requirements or sulphur deficiencies of man.

zinc

A metallic element necessary for the synthesis of body protein, for the action of a large number of the enzymes, and probably for the production of male hormones. It is therefore considered a dietary essential for humans, and it has been estimated that 15 milligrams per day is the minimum amount required by adults.

Zinc deficiencies induced in laboratory animals result in low resistance to infections, skin abnormalities, low fertility, and slow healing. In addition the offspring of such animals frequently have abnormalities of the bones, eyes, kidney and brain. It appears that like deficiencies in man produce similar effects.

Good sources of zinc are: green leafy vegetables and nuts if grown in soil with adequate zinc deposits, shellfish, liver, and kidney.

See Soil; Trace Elements; RDA chart in front of book.

minimum daily requirements
An attempt by the Food and Drug Administration to set forth the minimal nutritional needs of the people of the United States. According to many establishment nutritionists the data on which they are based is out of date and there is no evidence to justify their continued use. The FDA still uses the MDR, as does the food and vitamin industry. Most nutritionists, however, now use the Recommended Dietary Allowances,* compiled by the Food and Nutrition Board, National Academy of Sciences—National Research Council of the United States.*

moisture-control agents
Also known as humectants, they are substances which when added to foods absorb moisture and thus maintain their water content, thereby preventing the product from drying out. They are especially prevalent in baked goods and candy. Glycerine, sorbitol, and propylene glycol are some of those in common use. By law all such substances must be listed on the product's label or package.

See Additives; Anticaking Agents; Oxidation

monosodium glutamate (MSG)
The monosodium salt of glutamic acid, occurring naturally in soybeans, seaweed, and sugar beets. Used as a "flavor enhancer" on meat, in soups, baked goods, and many other things. In laboratory animals, MSG has caused brain

damage effects. It is believed responsible for what has been termed the "Chinese Restaurant Syndrome."* MSG is no longer added to baby foods.

MSG is still on the GRAS list* but is also on the FDA list of additives needing further study.

mushrooms

Any of a variety of nonpoisonous and hence edible fungi, especially the common field mushroom, Agraricus campestis. (The hunting of edible mushrooms is an activity engaged in by a goodly number of persons. There is much literature on the subject and a number of reference books with illustrations of the poisonous and non-poisonous types. Nevertheless, it should be kept in mind that a surprising number of those who die after eating poisonous mushrooms were considered most knowledgeable on the subject.)

COMPOSITION AND NUTRIENT VALUE PER Cup (244 g), cooked or canned.

Protein	5 g	Phosphorous	210 mg
Carbohydrate	6 g	Potassium	360 mg
Fat	Trace g	Sodium	N.D. mg
Saturated Fatty Acids	— g	Vitamin A	Trace I.U.
Oleic Acid	— g	Vitamin B_1	0.04 mg
Linoleic Acid	— g	Vitamin B_2	0.60 mg
Iron	1.2 mg	Niacin	4.80 mg
Calcium	15 mg	Vitamin C	4 mg
		Calories	40

natural foods

Those foods that retain their nutrients and are free of chemical additives. Synonyms: Health Foods, Organic Foods, Whole Foods.

See Organic Foods

niacin

See under Vitamin B Complex

nicotinic acid
Alternate name for niacin.*

night blindness
The inability to see well in dim light caused by a Vitamin A deficiency. Night blindness is the first indication of such a deficiency.
   See Dark Adaptation; Vitamin A

nitrous oxide
The gas used in pressurized containers that aids the ejection of the contents. Those who are willing to do anything to feel good have been known to inhale this gas. Also known as laughing gas and also used by the more humanitarian dentists as an anesthetic.

nonessential amino acids
   See Amino Acid

nucleic acids
There are two chief kinds of nucleic acid—RNA and DNA—which in combination with proteins form the nucleo-proteins (the protein occurring in all cell nuclei). They are believed to play a key role in the synthesis of protein in the body and in the transmission of hereditary characteristics.

nutrient
An ingredient in food that provides nourishment for the body and plays a role in the metabolic process, for example, protein, vitamins, minerals, and the essential fatty acids.

nutrition
The study of foods as related to the growth and maintenance of living organisms.

nutritionist
One who applies the science of nutrition.

nutrition supplements
   See Enriched or Fortified Foods; Food Supplements

nuts
Botanically, one-seeded fruits (e.g., acorns, chestnuts, hazelnuts) but commonly the name for a wide variety of fruits which have edible kernels, or edible seeds, enclosed in shells. Most of the "nuts" we eat are not true nuts: the walnut, pecan, and coconut are fruits; the cashew and pistachio are seeds; and the peanut is a legume.
   All nuts are a good source of incomplete protein,* and the unsaturated fatty acids.
   See Protein

almonds

COMPOSITION AND NUTRIENT VALUE PER Cup, shelled (142 g)

Protein	26 g	Phosphorous	706 mg
Carbohydrate	28 g	Potassium	1082 mg
Fat	77 g	Sodium	4 mg
Saturated Fatty Acids	6 g	Vitamin A	0 I.U.
Oleic Acid	52 g	Vitamin B_1	0.34 mg
Linoleic Acid	15 g	Vitamin B_2	1.31 mg
Iron	6.7 mg	Niacin	5 mg
Calcium	332 mg	Vitamin C	Trace mg
		Calories	850

cashew nuts

COMPOSITION AND NUTRIENT VALUE PER Cup (140 g), roasted

Protein	24 g	Phosphorous	484 mg
Carbohydrate	41 g	Potassium	650 mg
Fat	64 g	Sodium	80 mg
Saturated Fatty Acids	11 g	Vitamin A	140 I.U.

Oleic Acid	45 g	Vitamin B_1	0.60 mg
Linoleic Acid	4 g	Vitamin B_2	0.35 mg
Iron	5.3 mg	Niacin	2.50 mg
Calcium	484 mg	Vitamin C	0 mg
		Calories	785

coconut

COMPOSITION AND NUTRIENT VALUE PER piece 2″x2″x 1/2″ (45 g)

Protein	2 g	Phosphorous	N.D. mg
Carbohydrate	4 g	Potassium	N.D. mg
Fat	16 g	Sodium	N.D. mg
Saturated Fatty Acids	14 g	Vitamin A	0 I.U.
Oleic Acid	1 g	Vitamin B_1	0.02 mg
Linoleic Acid	Trace g	Vitamin B_2	0.01 mg
Iron	0.8 mg	Niacin	0.20 mg
Calcium	6 mg	Vitamin C	1 mg
		Calories	155

peanuts, roasted and salted

COMPOSITION AND NUTRIENT VALUE PER Cup (144 g)

Protein	37 g	Phosphorous	600 mg
Carbohydrate	37 g	Potassium	1091 mg
Fat	72 g	Sodium	606 mg
Saturated Fatty Acids	16 g	Vitamin A	— I.U.
Oleic Acid	31 g	Vitamin B_1	0.46 mg
Linoleic Acid	21 g	Vitamin B_2	0.19 mg
Iron	3 mg	Niacin	24.7 mg
Calcium	107 mg	Vitamin C	0 mg
		Calories	840

peanut butter, commercial

COMPOSITION AND NUTRIENT VALUE PER Tablespoon (16 g)

Protein	4 g	Phosphorous	450 mg
Carbohydrate	3 g	Potassium	930 mg
Fat	8 g	Sodium	900 mg
Saturated Fatty Acids	2 g	Vitamin A	— I.U.
Oleic Acid	4 g	Vitamin B_1	0.02 mg
Linoleic Acid	2 g	Vitamin B_2	0.02 mg
Iron	0.3 mg	Niacin	2.40 mg
Calcium	9 mg	Vitamin C	0 mg
		Calories	95

pecans

COMPOSITION AND NUTRIENT VALUE PER Cup (108 g), raw

Protein	10 g	Phosphorous	N.D. mg
Carbohydrate	16 g	Potassium	N.D. mg
Fat	77 g	Sodium	N.D. mg
Saturated Fatty Acids	5 g	Vitamin A	140 I.U.
Oleic Acid	48 g	Vitamin B_1	0.93 mg
Linoleic Acid	15 g	Vitamin B_2	0.14 mg
Iron	2.6 mg	Niacin	1.0 mg
Calcium	79 mg	Vitamin C	2 mg
		Calories	740

walnuts

COMPOSITION AND NUTRIENT VALUE PER Cup (126 g), raw

Protein	26 g	Phosphorous	N.D. mg
Carbohydrate	19 g	Potassium	N.D. mg
Fat	75 g	Sodium	N.D. mg
Saturated Fatty Acids	4 g	Vitamin A	380 I.U.
Oleic Acid	26 g	Vitamin B_1	0.28 mg
Linoleic Acid	36 g	Vitamin B_2	0.14 mg
Iron	7.6 mg	Niacin	0.90 mg
Calcium	Trace mg	Vitamin C	— mg
		Calories	790

nyctalopia
  See Night Blindness

obesity
The condition of being very fat, as opposed to being merely overweight. The majority of doctors consider obesity a disease insofar as it generally shortens the lifespan. And certainly obesity is associated with, though not shown to be the direct cause of, a number of diseases. There is a higher incidence of hypertension, cardiovascular and pulmonary diseases, and diabetes among obese persons than among any other group. And quite apart from the medical problems associated with obesity, the obese person usually encounters social and psychological difficulties simply as a result of his condition. In addition, the obese person's general sense of well-being is severely tested on a daily basis. Some notion of the severity of this testing can be gained by healthy people of normal weight if they imagine strapping fifty pounds of weights to themselves and going about their daily chores. Obese persons are in this situation day after day, carrying much more weight than their bone and muscle structures were designed for.

Overeating is the usual cause of obesity and the treatment for it is dieting and exercise. The prognosis is so dim, however—obese persons usually quickly gain back the weight they lose dieting—that most physicians believe that the prevention of obesity by sensible eating habits and regular exercise is the best answer to the problem.
  See Weight Watchers

obesity drugs
  See Amphetamines

oleomargarine
  See Margarine

olives
The fruit of the oldest fruit tree known to man, and the longest-living fruit tree. Olives have been grown for some

4,000 years and some trees bearing fruit are over 1,000 years old.

olives, green (canned)

COMPOSITION AND NUTRIENT VALUE PER 10 large (65 g)

Protein	1 g	Phosphorous	13 mg
Carbohydrate	3 g	Potassium	45 mg
Fat	10 g	Sodium	1400 mg
Saturated Fatty Acids	— g	Vitamin A	200 I.U.
Oleic Acid	— g	Vitamin B$_1$	Trace mg
Linoleic Acid	Trace g	Vitamin B$_2$	0 mg
Iron	1.2 mg	Niacin	0 mg
Calcium	65 mg	Vitamin C	0 mg
		Calories	72

olives, ripe (canned)

COMPOSITION AND NUTRIENT VALUE PER 10 large (65 g)

Protein	1 g	Phosphorous	11 mg
Carbohydrate	1 g	Potassium	23 mg
Fat	13 g	Sodium	650 mg
Saturated Fatty Acids	— g	Vitamin A	60 I.U.
Oleic Acid	— g	Vitamin B$_1$	Trace mg
Linoleic Acid	Trace g	Vitamin B$_2$	Trace mg
Iron	1.1 mg	Niacin	0 mg
Calcium	56 mg	Vitamin C	0 mg
		Calories	105

olive oil
The oil pressed from olives.

COMPOSITION AND NUTRIENT VALUE PER tablespoon (14 g)

Protein	0 g	Phosphorous	0 mg
Carbohydrate	14 g	Potassium	0 mg
Fat	0 g	Sodium	0 mg

Saturated Fatty Acids	2 g	Vitamin A	— I.U.
Oleic Acid	11 g	Vitamin B_1	0 mg
Linoleic Acid	1 g	Vitamin B_2	0 mg
Iron	0 mg	Niacin	0 mg
Calcium	0 mg	Vitamin C	0 mg
		Calories	125

opsomania
The craving for special foods. A common source for comedians' jokes about pregnant women. More seriously, it is quite common for persons suffering a particular nutrient deficiency to crave foods high in that nutrient, e.g., someone deficient in vitamin C might crave oranges or someone deficient in protein intake, meat.

organic
Substances of animal and vegetable origin are organic, minerals are inorganic.

organic farming
A system of farming (or gardening) that uses fertilizers and mulches consisting only of animal and vegetable matter rather than the synthetic chemicals generally used, and in which the crops are not sprayed with chemical pesticides and herbicides. In short, the growing of crops and raising of livestock and poultry in an atmosphere as free of synthetic chemicals as possible.

Before the introduction of chemical fertilizers, all farming was organic in the sense just described. And it was the fear of some agronomists that chemical fertilizers would adversely affect the soil and the nutritive values of the crops grown in it that led to a movement to return to the old ways.

In this country this movement was led by the late J. I. Rodale who started his experiments in organic farming in the early 1940s. Mr. Rodale and other advocates of organic farming have claimed that foods grown on organic farms are nutritionally superior to those grown with chemical fertilizers. This claim has not been substantiated by the available data. Most people agree, however, that organic foods are superior in taste. Moreover, organically grown foods do reduce the amount of possibly injurious substances one takes in on a daily basis. There is little or no data available on the long-term effects on humans of the ingesting of chemical fertilizers, pesticides, and the like, but no one claims that they are likely to prove beneficial.

See Pesticides; Soil

organic foods
Generally any vegetable or fruit grown in soil fertilized with natural compost as opposed to chemical fertilizers and not exposed to chemical pesticides or herbicides. Also, the meat of animals raised on grasses and grains not exposed to pesticides and herbicides, and not subjected to various drugs and chemicals used to promote growth. There has been no substantiation of the claims that organic foods have greater nutritive value than other foods, but they certainly taste better and undoubtedly contain substantially fewer possibly harmful chemicals than the typical commercial product. Unfortunately, they are considerably more expensive too.

osteomalacia
Literally "bad bones," caused by the inadequate absorption of calcium and loss of calcium from the bones, occasioned by a serious Vitamin D deficiency.

osteoporosis
Literally "porous bones," from the same causes as in osteomalacia.*

overweight
Exceeding the ideal weight for your age and frame, a condition afflicting 50 percent of the U. S. population.
See Obesity; Weight Watchers

oxidation
The combination of a substance with oxygen. Oxidation of foods causes losses in nutritive value, bad odor, discoloration, and decay. Animal fats and oils become rancid,

vegetables and fruits become discolored and soft. Chemical antioxidants are added to a great number of commercially processed foods to retard spoilage.

See Additives; Preservatives

pancakes (made from mix with egg and milk)

COMPOSITION AND NUTRIENT VALUE PER cake (27 g)

Protein	2 g	Phosphorous	— mg
Carbohydrate	9 g	Potassium	— mg
Fat	2 g	Sodium	— mg
Saturated Fatty Acids	1 g	Vitamin A	70 I.U.
Oleic Acid	1 g	Vitamin B_1	0.04 mg
Linoleic Acid	Trace g	Vitamin B_2	0.06 mg
Iron	0.3 mg	Niacin	0.20 mg
Calcium	58 mg	Vitamin C	Trace mg
		Calories	60

pancakes, buckwheat (made from mix with egg and milk)

COMPOSITION AND NUTRIENT VALUE PER cake (27 g)

Protein	2 g	Phosphorous	N.D. mg
Carbohydrate	6 g	Potassium	N.D. mg
Fat	2 g	Sodium	N.D. mg
Saturated Fatty Acids	1 g	Vitamin A	60 I.U.
Oleic Acid	1 g	Vitamin B_1	0.03 mg
Linoleic Acid	Trace g	Vitamin B_2	0.04 mg
Iron	0.4 mg	Niacin	0.20 mg
Calcium	59 mg	Vitamin C	Trace mg
		Calories	55

pancreas
A gland located in the abdomen which secretes the hormone insulin and pancreatic juice.

pancreatic juice
The digestive juice produced by the pancreas. It contains

the following enzymes: aminopeptidase, amylase, carboxy-peptidase, chymotrypsinogen, lactase, lipase, maltase, nuclease, sucrase, and trypsinogen, which further break down proteins, amino acids, sugars, fats and starches.

panic
A mental condition manifested by volunteers in whom biotin deficiencies were induced.
See Biotin

pantothenic acid
See under Vitamin B Complex

papain
The proleolytic enzyme from the juice of the papaya, a tropical fruit. It is often added to enriched farina to reduce cooking time but its best-known use is as a meat-tenderizer. These are marketed under a variety of trade-names, but all work in the same way: the papain when applied to raw meat is absorbed into the connective tissues and tenderizes the meat by breaking down (pre-digesting) the proteins. Some people have allergic reactions to papain.

para-aminobenzoic acid
See under Vitamin B Complex

paralysis
Some persons have a high hereditary requirement for potassium; if they fail to receive large enough amounts they often suffer a paralysis which starts in the legs and moves upwards. The condition can be immediately relieved by a sufficient dose of potassium. Pernicious anemia, a result of a prolonged deficiency of the B vitamins which in turn prevents the production of an enzyme known as the intrinsic factor, can also lead to paralysis.
See Intrinsic Factor; Pernicious Anemia; Potassium; Vitamin B_{12}

pasta
Doughs, shaped and dried, made from semolina or wheat flour with water, and sometimes egg and milk.

egg noodles ("enriched")
A pasta*

COMPOSITION AND NUTRIENT VALUE PER cup, cooked (160 g)

Protein	7 g	Phosphorous	52 mg
Carbohydrate	37 g	Potassium	— mg
Fat	2 g	Sodium	— mg
Saturated Fatty Acids	1 g	Vitamin A	110 I.U.
Oleic Acid	1 g	Vitamin B_1	0.22 mg
Linoleic Acid	Trace g	Vitamin B_2	0.13 mg
Iron	1.4 mg	Niacin	1.90 mg
Calcium	16 mg	Vitamin C	0 mg
		Calories	200

egg noodles (unenriched)
A pasta.*

COMPOSITION AND NUTRIENT VALUE PER cup (160 g), cooked

Protein	7 g	Phosphorous	52 mg
Carbohydrate	37 g	Potassium	— mg
Fat	2 g	Sodium	— mg
Saturated Fatty Acids	1 g	Vitamin A	110 I.U.
Oleic Acid	1 g	Vitamin B_1	0.05 mg
Linoleic Acid	Trace g	Vitamin B_2	0.03 mg
Iron	1.0 mg	Niacin	0.60 mg
Calcium	16 mg	Vitamin C	0 mg
		Calories	200

macaroni
A pasta*

COMPOSITION AND NUTRIENT VALUE PER Cup (140 g), cooked until tender

Protein	5 g	Phosphorous	82 mg
Carbohydrate	32 g	Potassium	276 mg
Fat	1 g	Sodium	1 mg
Saturated Fatty Acids	— g	Vitamin A	0 I.U.
Oleic Acid	— g	Vitamin B$_1$	0.01 mg
Linoleic Acid	— g	Vitamin B$_2$	0.01 mg
Iron	0.6 mg	Niacin	0.40 mg
Calcium	11 mg	Vitamin C	0 mg
		Calories	155

macaroni ("enriched")
A pasta*

COMPOSITION AND NUTRIENT VALUE PER Cup (140 g), cooked until tender

Protein	5 g	Phosphorous	N.D. mg
Carbohydrate	32 g	Potassium	N.D. mg
Fat	1 g	Sodium	N.D. mg
Saturated Fatty Acids	— g	Vitamin A	0 I.U.
Oleic Acid	— g	Vitamin B$_1$	0.20 mg
Linoleic Acid	— g	Vitamin B$_2$	0.11 mg
Iron	1.3 mg	Niacin	1.50 mg
Calcium	11 mg	Vitamin C	0 mg
		Calories	155

macaroni ("enriched") and cheese
A pasta*

COMPOSITION AND NUTRIENT VALUE PER Cup (200 g) baked

Protein	17 g	Phosphorous	363 mg
Carbohydrate	40 g	Potassium	132 mg
Fat	22 g	Sodium	1192 mg
Saturated Fatty Acids	10 g	Vitamin A	860 I.U.

Oleic Acid	9 g	Vitamin B_1	0.20 mg
Linoleic Acid	2 g	Vitamin B_2	0.40 mg
Iron	1.8 mg	Niacin	1.8 mg
Calcium	362 mg	Vitamin C	0 mg
		Calories	430

spaghetti ("enriched")
A pasta*

COMPOSITION AND NUTRIENT VALUE PER Cup (140 g), cooked

Protein	5 g	Phosphorous	N.D. mg
Carbohydrate	32 g	Potassium	N.D. mg
Fat	1 g	Sodium	N.D. mg
Saturated Fatty Acids	— g	Vitamin A	0 I.U.
Oleic Acid	— g	Vitamin B_1	0.20 mg
Linoleic Acid	— g	Vitamin B_2	0.11 mg
Iron	1.3 mg	Niacin	1.50 mg
Calcium	11 mg	Vitamin C	0 mg
		Calories	155

spaghetti (with meatballs and tomato sauce)
A pasta*

COMPOSITION AND NUTRIENT VALUE PER Cup (248 g)

Protein	19 g	Phosphorous	N.D. mg
Carbohydrate	39 g	Potassium	N.D. mg
Fat	12 g	Sodium	N.D. mg
Saturated Fatty Acids	4 g	Vitamin A	1590 I.U.
Oleic Acid	6 g	Vitamin B_1	0.25 mg
Linoleic Acid	1 g	Vitamin B_2	0.30 mg
Iron	3.7 mg	Niacin	4 mg
Calcium	124 mg	Vitamin C	22 mg
		Calories	330

spaghetti (with tomato sauce and cheese)
A pasta*

COMPOSITION AND NUTRIENT VALUE PER Cup (250 g)

Protein	9 g	Phosphorous	N.D. mg
Carbohydrate	37 g	Potassium	N.D. mg
Fat	9 g	Sodium	N.D. mg
Saturated Fatty Acids	2 g	Vitamin A	1080 I.U.
Oleic Acid	5 g	Vitamin B_1	0.25 mg
Linoleic Acid	1 g	Vitamin B_2	0.18 mg
Iron	2.3 mg	Niacin	2.3 mg
Calcium	80 mg	Vitamin C	13 mg
		Calories	260

pasteurization

The heating of food at relatively mild temperatures to kill the vegetative forms of many bacteria. The complete destruction of all bacteria and spores—sterilization—demands higher temperatures and usually destroys the product in the process. Pasteurization prolongs the storage life of foods but not for any extended period.

By law the pasteurization of milk requires a temperature of 145°-150°F for 30 minutes followed by a temperature of 161°F for 15 seconds, followed by immediate cooling.

pathogens

Disease-causing bacteria. The pasteurization of milk, e.g., destroys all the pathogens but not all the other harmless bacteria in milk.

pectin

Plant tissues contain protopectins which hold the cell walls together, which in ripe fruit break down to pectin. (In overripe and then in rotten fruits the pectin in turn breaks down into pectinic acid and pectic acid respectively.) The richest source of pectin is orange or lemon rind, but the commercial source of pectin is usually apple pulp and orange pith. It is used as the setting agent for jams, and as an emulsifier and stabilizer in a wide variety of products, including ice cream, soft drinks, french dressing, syrups, confections, jellies, and preserves. It has no known toxicity.

pectins, low-methoxyl
Pectins able to form gels with little or no sugar and consequently used in low-calorie products.

pellagra
A chronic disease caused by niacin deficiency,* and characterized by skin eruptions, mental disturbances, digestive disorders, and eventually mental deterioration. Unfortunately it is still seen in the rural South.

pernicious anemia
    See Anemia

personality
Since all that touches us contributes in some manner to our personality, it follows that the nutrients we ingest or fail to ingest affect it also. The subject being so complex, measurements of the degree to which minor deficiencies of essential nutrients affect our character is probably impossible but studies have shown definite personality changes in subjects suffering major deficiencies of iron or niacin or vitamin B_1.

Iron deficiency leads to chronic fatigue. Persons suffering niacin deficiency become grumpy, emotionally unstable, paranoid, forgetful and the like. Such symptoms are often eliminated a few hours after the administration of niacinamide. Even schizophrenics have been helped by massive doses of niacinamide. Vitamin B_1 deficiencies often result in irritability, quarrelsomeness, forgetfulness, depression and a greatly reduced ability to do work. Sufficient doses of B_1 remove these symptoms in such cases.
    See Iron; Niacin; Vitamin B_1

perspiration
Under normal conditions a healthy person is unlikely to be deficient in sodium and chlorine but in extremely hot

weather where one sweats excessively, the loss of salt (table salt, sodium chloride) from the body can be great enough to cause death. Sunstroke and heatstroke have similar symptoms, and both are due largely to the loss of salt from the body through perspiration. Symptoms are nausea, exhaustion, dizziness and cramps.

See Salt for treatment of sunstroke or heatstroke

pesticides
Any chemical used to kill pests, especially those insects which infest crops, and a topic of heated debate between ecologists and food producers.

The extensive and, frequently, overuse of pesticides (and herbicides) undoubtedly disturbs the balance of nature as well as does injury to all of us who eat the food saved from pests in this manner. On the other hand, there is little question that the world's population is so great that there is no hope of feeding it if pesticides are eliminated. The answer to this dilemma lies in the proper and controlled use of pesticides, an answer upon which there has been little agreement as to particulars.

phagocytes
White blood cells which engulf and digest microorganisms or other foreign bodies in the blood stream and tissues. One of the major mechanisms which helps to protect the body against infections. As with antibodies, the production of phagocytes is dependent on an adequate intake of protein.

See Antibodies; Protein

phenylalanine
An essential amino acid.*

See Amino Acids; Protein

photosynthesis
The process by which the chlorophyll-containing cells in green plants convert sunlight into chemical energy and manufacture complex foods (especially carbohydrates)

from simple salts and carbon dioxide, with the simultaneous release of oxygen. Most of the oxygen we breathe comes from this source, and the respiratory processes of humans and animals in turn release the carbon dioxide necessary for photosynthesis. Photosynthesis is the ultimate source of all food since all that we eat is taken either directly or indirectly from these plants, and consequently the ultimate source of all energy for living beings.

See Chlorophyll

pica

A craving for unnatural foods such as earth, paper, clay, lead paint and the like. Often found in malnourished women during pregnancy, and malnourished young children.

pie

A baked food consisting of a pastry shell filled with fruit, meat, or other ingredients and sometimes covered with a pastry crust. (The piecrust of the pies listed below are made with unenriched flour.)

apple pie

COMPOSITION AND NUTRIENT VALUE PER Slice, 1/7 of 9-inch diam. pie (135 g)

Protein	3 g	Phosphorous	29 mg
Carbohydrate	51 g	Potassium	106 mg
Fat	15 g	Sodium	400 mg
Saturated Fatty Acids	4 g	Vitamin A	40 I.U.
Oleic Acid	7 g	Vitamin B_1	0.03 mg
Linoleic Acid	3 g	Vitamin B_2	0.03 mg
Iron	0.4 mg	Niacin	0.50 mg
Calcium	11 mg	Vitamin C	1 mg
		Calories	350

cherry pie

COMPOSITION AND NUTRIENT VALUE PER Slice (135 g)

Protein	4 g	Phosphorous	33 mg
Carbohydrate	52 g	Potassium	140 mg
Fat	15 g	Sodium	405 mg
Saturated Fatty Acids	4 g	Vitamin A	590 I.U.
Oleic Acid	7 g	Vitamin B_1	0.03 mg
Linoleic Acid	3 g	Vitamin B_2	0.03 mg
Iron	0.4 mg	Niacin	0.70 mg
Calcium	11 mg	Vitamin C	1 mg
		Calories	350

custard pie

COMPOSITION AND NUTRIENT VALUE PER Slice (130 g)

Protein	8 g	Phosphorous	151 mg
Carbohydrate	30 g	Potassium	182 mg
Fat	14 g	Sodium	405 mg
Saturated Fatty Acids	5 g	Vitamin A	300 I.U.
Oleic Acid	6 g	Vitamin B_1	0.07 mg
Linoleic Acid	2 g	Vitamin B_2	0.21 mg
Iron	0.8 mg	Niacin	0.40 mg
Calcium	125 mg	Vitamin C	0 mg
		Calories	285

lemon meringue pie

COMPOSITION AND NUTRIENT VALUE PER Slice (120 g)

Protein	4 g	Phosphorous	65 mg
Carbohydrate	45 g	Potassium	66 mg
Fat	12 g	Sodium	337 mg
Saturated Fatty Acids	4 g	Vitamin A	200 I.U.
Oleic Acid	6 g	Vitamin B_1	0.04 mg
Linoleic Acid	2 g	Vitamin B_2	0.10 mg
Iron	0.6 mg	Niacin	0.20 mg
Calcium	17 mg	Vitamin C	4 mg
		Calories	305

mince pie

COMPOSITION AND NUTRIENT VALUE PER Slice (135 g)

Protein	3 g	Phosphorous	N.D. mg
Carbohydrate	56 g	Potassium	N.D. mg
Fat	16 g	Sodium	N.D. mg
Saturated Fatty Acids	4 g	Vitamin A	Trace I.U.
Oleic Acid	8 g	Vitamin B_1	0.09 mg
Linoleic Acid	3 g	Vitamin B_2	0.05 mg
Iron	1.4 mg	Niacin	0.50 mg
Calcium	38 mg	Vitamin C	1 mg
		Calories	365

pecan pie

COMPOSITION AND NUTRIENT VALUE PER Slice (118 g)

Protein	6 g	Phosphorous	N.D. mg
Carbohydrate	60 g	Potassium	N.D. mg
Fat	27 g	Sodium	N.D. mg
Saturated Fatty Acids	4 g	Vitamin A	190 I.U.
Oleic Acid	16 g	Vitamin B_1	0.19 mg
Linoleic Acid	5 g	Vitamin B_2	0.08 mg
Iron	3.3 mg	Niacin	0.40 mg
Calcium	55 mg	Vitamin C	Trace mg
		Calories	490

pumpkin pie

COMPOSITION AND NUTRIENT VALUE PER Slice (130 g)

Protein	5 g	Phosphorous	N.D. mg
Carbohydrate	32 g	Potassium	N.D. mg
Fat	15 g	Sodium	N.D. mg
Saturated Fatty Acids	5 g	Vitamin A	3210 I.U.
Oleic Acid	6 g	Vitamin B_1	0.04 mg

Linoleic Acid	2 g	Vitamin B$_2$	0.13 mg
Iron	0.7 mg	Niacin	0.70 mg
Calcium	66 mg	Vitamin C	Trace mg
		Calories	275

pigment
A substance producing a characteristic color in plant and animal tissues, such as chlorophyll in plants and hemoglobin in animals.

A deficiency in Vitamin E* produces a ceroid pigmentation in many parts of the body which is thought to be a negative factor in heart disease, varicose veins, and phlebitis. And some authorities believe that the brown spots, often called "liver spots," frequently found on the backs of the hands of older persons are the result of Vitamin E deficiency.

pizza (cheese)
COMPOSITION AND NUTRIENT VALUE PER slice 1/8, of 14" diam. pie (75 g)

Protein	7 g	Phosphorous	N.D. mg
Carbohydrate	27 g	Potassium	N.D. mg
Fat	6 g	Sodium	N.D. mg
Saturated Fatty Acids	2 g	Vitamin A	290 I.U.
Oleic Acid	3 g	Vitamin B$_1$	0.04 mg
Linoleic Acid	Trace g	Vitamin B$_2$	0.12 mg
Iron	0.7 mg	Niacin	0.70 mg
Calcium	107 mg	Vitamin C	4 mg
		Calories	185

polyunsaturates
Name sometimes given to the essential fatty acids.*

popcorn

COMPOSITION AND NUTRIENT VALUE PER Cup (9 g), with oil and salt

Protein	1 g	Phosphorous	N.D. mg
Carbohydrate	5 g	Potassium	N.D. mg
Fat	2 g	Sodium	N.D. mg
Saturated Fatty Acids	1 g	Vitamin A	— I.U.
Oleic Acid	Trace g	Vitamin B_1	— mg
Linoleic Acid	Trace g	Vitamin B_2	0.01 mg
Iron	0.2 mg	Niacin	0.20 mg
Calcium	1 mg	Vitamin C	0 mg
		Calories	40

potato chips
Thin slices of potato fried in deep fat until crisp, and then salted, packaged, and in America consumed in large quantities.

COMPOSITION AND NUTRIENT VALUE PER 10 medium (20 g)

Protein	1 g	Phosphorous	38 mg
Carbohydrate	10 g	Potassium	210 mg
Fat	8 g	Sodium	200 mg
Saturated Fatty Acids	2 g	Vitamin A	Trace I.U.
Oleic Acid	2 g	Vitamin B_1	0.04 mg
Linoleic Acid	4 g	Vitamin B_2	0.01 mg
Iron	0.4 mg	Niacin	1 mg
Calcium	8 mg	Vitamin C	3 mg
		Calories	115

poultry
Domesticated fowl, such as chicken, turkey, duck, or goose, raised for their meat and eggs. The meat of poultry is a good source of complete protein, minerals, and many of the B-vitamin complex. In addition, poultry contains more unsaturated fatty acids than meat, and less saturated ones.

chicken breast (fried)

COMPOSITION AND NUTRIENT VALUE PER 1/2 breast (94 g)

Protein	25 g	Phosphorous	218 mg
Carbohydrate	1 g	Potassium	320 mg
Fat	5 g	Sodium	50 mg
Saturated Fatty Acids	1 g	Vitamin A	70 I.U.
Oleic Acid	2 g	Vitamin B_1	0.04 mg
Linoleic Acid	1 g	Vitamin B_2	0.17 mg
Iron	1.3 mg	Niacin	11.2 mg
Calcium	9 mg	Vitamin C	— mg
		Calories	155

chicken, broiled

COMPOSITION AND NUTRIENT VALUE PER 3 ounces (85 g)

Protein	20 g	Phosphorous	250 mg
Carbohydrate	0 g	Potassium	350 mg
Fat	3 g	Sodium	50 mg
Saturated Fatty Acids	1 g	Vitamin A	80 I.U.
Oleic Acid	1 g	Vitamin B_1	0.05 mg
Iron	1.4 mg	Vitamin B_2	0.16 mg
Calcium	8 mg	Niacin	7.4 mg
Linoleic Acid	1 g	Vitamin C	— mg
		Calories	115

chicken, drumstick (fried)

COMPOSITION AND NUTRIENT VALUE PER 2.1 ounces (59 g)

Protein	12 g	Phosphorous	148.0 mg
Carbohydrate	Trace g	Potassium	220.0 mg
Fat	4 g	Sodium	35.0 mg
Saturated Fatty Acids	1 g	Vitamin A	50 I.U.
Oleic Acid	2 g	Vitamin B_1	0.03 mg
Linoleic Acid	1 g	Vitamin B_2	0.15 mg
Iron	0.9 mg	Niacin	2.7 mg
Calcium	6 mg	Vitamin C	— mg
		Calories	90

chicken livers (fried)

COMPOSITION AND NUTRIENT VALUE PER 3 medium (100 grams)

Protein	22 g	Phosphorous	240 mg
Carbohydrate	2.3 g	Potassium	160 mg
Fat	14 g	Sodium	51 mg
Saturated Fatty Acids	6 g	Vitamin A	32,200 I.U.
Oleic Acid	6 g	Vitamin B$_1$	0.2 mg
Linoleic Acid	2 g	Vitamin B$_2$	2.4 mg
Iron	7.4 mg	Niacin	11.8 mg
Calcium	16 mg	Vitamin C	20 mg
		Calories	140

turkey

COMPOSITION AND NUTRIENT VALUE PER 3.5 oz. (100 g), roasted

Protein	27 g	Phosphorous	320 mg
Carbohydrate	0 g	Potassium	320 mg
Fat	15 g	Sodium	60 mg
Saturated Fatty Acids	— g	Vitamin A	0 I.U.
Oleic Acid	— g	Vitamin B$_1$	Trace mg
Linoleic Acid	— g	Vitamin B$_2$	0.1 mg
Iron	3.8 mg	Niacin	8 mg
Calcium	23 mg	Vitamin C	0 mg
		Calories	265

ppm
Part per million. Used to describe small amounts of one substance in another. Usually the substance so described is a food additive which when the allowed concentration (PPM) is exceeded, is considered toxic to the eater.

preservation
Foods deteriorate when stored, chiefly through microor-

ganisms, oxidation, and their own enzymes. Refrigeration, dehydration, chemicals and sterilization control deterioration in varying degrees for relatively long periods. Pasteurization, smoking, pickling, and salting are short-term methods of preservation. Most preservation methods destroy some of the vitamin and mineral content of the foods.

preservatives, chemical
Substances used to retard or arrest the chemical deterioration or the bacterial spoilage of foods.
—Antioxidants are used to retard or prevent the rancidity caused by the oxidation of fats. For example, BHA (Butylated hydroxyanisole) is used for this purpose in shortenings, lard, potato chips, soda crackers, and the like.
—Fungicides are used to retard or prevent the growth of mold and fungus on citrus fruits.
—Sequestrants, which combine with metal ions or acid radicals, and render them inactive, are used in such things as soft drinks and dairy products EDTA (Ethylenediaminetetracetic acid) for example, is used to prevent the metal ions from giving the beverage a "cloudy" appearance.
—Mold and rope (a type of bacteria) inhibitors such as sodium propionate and sodium diacetate are used in bread manufacturing.
—Sulphur dioxide gas is used to dehydrate grapes (raisins), plums (prunes) and other fruits and thus preserve them.
Not all of these are harmless and many which individually may not produce any observable deleterious effects on humans, may in combination with others do precisely that. (*See* Additives for a fuller discussion of this topic.)
By law, all preservatives must be listed on the product's label or package.
See also Dried Fruits; Oxidation; Preservation

preserves
Fruit cooked with sugar.

COMPOSITION AND NUTRIENT VALUE PER Tablespoon (20 g)

Protein	Trace g	Phosphorous	N.D. mg
Carbohydrate	14 g	Potassium	N.D. mg
Fat	Trace g	Sodium	N.D. mg
Saturated Fatty Acids	— g	Vitamin A	Trace I.U.
Oleic Acid	— g	Vitamin B_1	Trace mg
Linoleic Acid	— g	Vitamin B_2	0.01 mg
Iron	0.02 mg	Niacin	Trace mg
Calcium	4 mg	Vitamin C	Trace mg
		Calories	55

proline
A nonessential amino acid.
See Amino Acids; Protein

propionate
Salts of propionic acid, used as mold inhibitors.

proteins

DESCRIPTION
The essential constituent of all living matter and distinguished from fats and carbohydrates in that they contain nitrogen. All proteins are made up of large combinations of amino acids containing carbon, hydrogen, oxygen, nitrogen, sulphur and sometimes phosphorus, iron and iodine, twenty-two of which have been identified as necessary to biological growth and survival. The human body is capable of manufacturing fourteen of these amino acids, (which are termed "nonessential," because they need not be obtained from specific dietary sources). Eight can be obtained only from food sources and are thus termed the "essential" amino acids.* In addition, two other amino acids, histidine and arginine, might also be called essential particularly in growing children, insofar as the body does not appear able to produce them fast enough to ensure an adequate supply. Proteins which supply an adequate

amount of the essential amino acids are called "complete"; those which either lack one or more of the essential amino acids or which supply any of them in amounts too small to support health are called "incomplete."

PROPERTIES AND FUNCTIONS

Protein is the chief and often the only source of nitrogen, an element necessary for the growth and repair of the body tissues. For this reason if no other it is considered the most important of all nutrients. But protein serves a large number of functions, more probably than have as yet been clearly recognized and described. Protein is known to be a very important source of energy; an essential element for resistance to disease and infection; an essential element in proper digestion; and an essential element in proper elimination of waste materials.

Energy is the product of the oxidization of sugar or the oxidization of a combination of sugar and fat. The amount of sugar in the blood plasma (the blood-sugar level) determines how much is available to each cell and only if the blood-sugar level is adequate can each cell take the quantity it needs. Not only does the breakdown of protein in the digestive process provide a percentage of this sugar, but a meal with adequate protein slows down the digestive process so that sugar enters the blood slowly, providing a sustained level of energy. Many studies of the breakfast habits of Americans have proved that the level of well-being felt and the level of energy are directly related to the amount of protein eaten. Indeed it appears that the more protein eaten at any meal the greater the energy produced and the longer it is maintained. These studies showed that a breakfast containing 55 grams of protein provided a high level of energy for six hours after the meal. (The typical urban American breakfast of orange juice, packaged cereal, pancakes, coffee cake, toast, jam, and coffee is very high in carbohydrates and provides quick energy. The energy, however, is short-lived and the result is mid-morning fatigue.)

Protein is also essential to the digestive process. The enzymes which break down food are made of protein; if the diet provides inadequate protein, digestion is incomplete and so is the production of energy. Incomplete digestion which results from inadequate protein also results from a flabby condition of the muscles of the stomach and intestines, muscles which work with the enzymes to digest food. And because flabby muscles cannot push waste material from the body, constipation results. Laxatives are then resorted to, further robbing the body of protein since they force food through the body before the protein can be fully digested.

An adequate protein intake also helps provide the body with high resistance to disease and infection. Two of the many mechanisms which aid the body to fight infection are especially dependent on protein: antibodies and white blood cells.

SOURCES

The richest sources of protein are those containing the eight essential amino acids, the complete proteins, in the greatest amounts—egg yolk, fresh milk, liver and kidney. Muscle meats (roasts, steaks, and chops) seafood, and cheese provide complete protein but contain a smaller amount of some of the essential amino acids than those cited above. Protein from brewer's yeast, wheat germ, soybeans and certain nuts are also complete proteins.

Peas, most kinds of beans, cereals, lentils and processed flour provide incomplete protein. When two or more incomplete proteins are eaten at the same time, they may together provide the essential amino acids. But if for example baked beans were eaten at 6 P.M. and cornbread at 7 P.M. the two, which if eaten together would have allowed the body to form complete protein by combining their essential amino acids, no longer can. The liver, it seems, stores only complete proteins. In short, animal proteins (meat, fish and dairy products) provide the essential amino acids in greater amounts than do vegetable proteins.

REQUIREMENTS

The recommended dietary allowance (RDA) is 23 to 36 grams per day for children, 44 to 54 grams for adolescents, 48 to 56 grams for adults, an additional 30 grams for pregnant women and an additional 20 grams for lactating women. Most nutritionists feel that at least two-thirds of this should come from animal sources and many nutritionists feel that the Food and Nutrition Board protein recommendation is inadequate and recommend twice this amount. (Three ounces of lean hamburger provides 23 grams of protein; two eggs, 12 grams; one cup of milk, 9 grams.)

DEFICIENCIES

In America, severe protein deficiency resulting in kwashiorkor* or nutritional marasmus* is not nearly so common as it is in many of the underdeveloped countries, but it does occur. Mild to moderate protein deficiency, however, is far more common than one would expect in a nation with so high a general living standard. Growth and development patterns falling below the norm are usually signs of protein deficiency and are generally classed as cases of malnutrition. Children who suffer protein-calorie malnutrition early in life pay a heavy price: permanent stunting of physical growth, failure to reach full intellectual development, and susceptibility to infectious disease.

A great volume of research has and is being done on the specific ills resulting from amino acid deficiencies. A few of the highlights are as follows:

—when the diets of babies and test animals lack isoleucine, tryptophane, or methionine, the liver is unable to produce albumin and globulin, and urine is not collected normally. The result is edema and an increased susceptibility to infectious disease.

—a lack of methionine or tryptophane causes the hair to fall out of test animals.

—a lack of arginine results in sterility in test animals.

—a lack of tryptophane causes pregnant female test animals to miscarry.

—children with chronic rheumatic fever show signs of being particularly deficient in methionine.

See RDA chart in front of book.

psoriasis
A chronic, noncontagious skin disease characterized by inflammation and scaly patches. Like many other skin diseases it may have many causes, but it is often completely cured by better nutrition. Salad oils and lecithin* seem particularly helpful.

ptomaine poisoning
Food poisoning caused by the toxins produced in the putrefaction and decomposition of protein.

puberty
The stage of growth where an individual becomes physiologically capable of sexual reproduction. It is also a time when the body has especially high requirements for calcium, magnesium, and iodine.

pyorrhea
The inflammation of the gum and of the tooth sockets leading to the loosening of the teeth. Vitamin C and D deficiencies are considered the chief nutritional causes of pyorrhea.

pyridoxine
Vitamin B_6.*

pyruvic acid
A fundamental intermediate in metabolism of carbohydrates. Pyruvic and lactic acids are formed during the breakdown of sugar, and then further broken down by enzymes containing Vitamin B -pyruvic acid into carbon dioxide and water, lactic acid into glycogen. If Vitamin B is deficient in the diet, these changes do not take place and the acids accumulate in the blood. The production of energy from sugar is thus reduced, with ensuing fatigue and a general feeling of lassitude.
   See Vitamin B_1

RDA
See Recommended Dietary Allowances

recommended dietary allowances (RDA)

A report by the Food and Nutrition Board, National Academy of Sciences—National Research Council of the United States setting forth daily dietary allowances which are designed, in the words of the introduction to the seventh Edition:

> "to afford a margin of sufficiency above average physiological requirements to cover variations among essentially all individuals in the general population. They provide a buffer against the increased needs during common stresses and permit full realization of growth and productive potential: but they are not to be considered adequate to meet additional requirements of persons depleted by disease or traumatic stresses."

The RDA in the various editions are not the same, each edition attempting to update the data in accord with the latest accepted findings.

It should be noted that the Food and Nutrition Board, National Academy of Sciences—National Research Council of the United States is not a government organization but a private one, supported by industry. It also should be noted that some authorities, e.g., Adelle Davis, doubt that the RDA are sufficient to maintain health.

See RDA chart in front of book.

reducing

Being overweight is a condition affecting many sedentary Americans. The eating of large quantities of refined foods which lack the nutrients able to supply the energy needed for exercise and which leave the body so starved for these nutrients that we perhaps unconsciously gorge ourselves in the attempt to supply them is undoubtedly a contributing factor to overweight. Few persons who maintain sound, nutritious diets have problems with undue gains of weight. Eating properly and exercising properly is probably the best way to maintain correct weight or to shed excess weight for those not suffering from glandular or other disturbances requiring a physician. It should be noted that many physicians consider the constant gaining and losing of weight—the up-and-down cycle so familiar to those who diet—as injurious to health as is overweight itself.

See Obesity; Weight Watchers

refined foods

A large part of the typical American's diet is composed of refined and/or processed foods. With the exception of fresh vegetables, and dairy and meat products, there is little in your supermarket that is not refined and/or processed. In a large, technological society this is probably inevitable. The problems of food storage and transportation are enormous and feeding the inhabitants of great urban centers on unrefined and highly perishable foods probably even greater. Unfortunately, refined foods have been stripped of a great portion of their nutrients and those who subsist on them are deprived of essential vitamins, amino acids, and minerals. It has been estimated that two-thirds of the calories ingested by the average American come from refined or processed foods from which the original nutrients have been either largely or wholly discarded. Bread, for example, was once the staff of life but for those who now buy the typical commercial loaf it is a very thin reed indeed. Modern methods of refining grain discard or destroy most of the nutrients available in whole wheat. So-called "enriched" bread, i.e., bread made from refined flour to which is added Vitamin B_1, niacin, and iron, is a very poor substitute for whole-grain bread.

And it is not only in bread that we lose nutrients essential to our good health—virtually everything made from refined grains presents the same loss. These include noodles, spaghetti, macaroni, cookies, cakes, crackers, breakfast cereals, and baked goods of every description, to name but a few. In addition, the supermarket is now crowded with a bewildering variety of synthetic foods which contain few or no nutrients. Gelatin desserts, soft drinks, imitation fruit juices are but a few of the items on this long list.

See Additives; Flour, Refining and Bleaching

respiratory quotient

The ratio of the volume of carbon dioxide produced when a substance (e.g., fat, protein, carbohydrate) is oxidized, to the volume of oxygen used.

Respiratory-quotient studies have shown that a person whose diet is deficient in the essential fatty acids changes sugar to fat far more rapidly than normal. As a result, the blood sugar drops quickly and one feels starved, causing overeating and the ensuing gain in weight.

See Essential Fatty Acids; Salad Oils

retinol

Alternative name for Vitamin A.*

riboflavin

Vitamin B_2.*

rice

A grain, the seeds of which form the basic food for nearly half the world's population. The nutritional value of rice lies chiefly in the various inner layers of its bran.

The white rice of commerce is rice in which the bran layers and germ are removed by the milling process. Brown rice is that in which only the outer fibrous husk has been removed.

See Beriberi

rice, brown (cooked)

COMPOSITION AND NUTRIENT VALUE PER Cup (208 g), measured before cooking

Protein	15 g	Phosphorous	608 mg
Carbohydrate	154 g	Potassium	310 mg
Fat	3 g	Sodium	18 mg
Saturated Fatty Acids	— g	Vitamin A	0 I.U.
Oleic Acid	— g	Vitamin B_1	0.6 mg
Linoleic Acid	— g	Vitamin B_2	0.1 mg
Iron	4 mg	Niacin	9.20 mg
Calcium	78 mg	Vitamin C	0 mg
		Calories	748

rice, white ("enriched," cooked)

COMPOSITION AND NUTRIENT VALUE PER Cup (205 g), measured before cooking

Protein	4 g	Phosphorous	N.D. mg
Carbohydrate	50 g	Potassium	N.D. mg
Fat	Trace g	Sodium	N.D. mg
Saturated Fatty Acids	— g	Vitamin A	0 I.U.
Oleic Acid	— g	Vitamin B_1	0.23 mg
Linoleic Acid	— g	Vitamin B_2	0.02 mg
Iron	1.8 mg	Niacin	2.10 mg
Calcium	21 mg	Vitamin C	0 mg
		Calories	225

rice polish
The removed and separated inner layers of the rice bran.

COMPOSITION AND NUTRIENT VALUE PER 1/2 cup (50 g)

Protein	6 g	Phosphorous	553 mg
Carbohydrate	28 g	Potassium	357 mg
Fat	6 g	Sodium	Trace mg
Saturated Fatty Acids	N.D. g	Vitamin A	0 I.U.
Oleic Acid	N.D. g	Vitamin B_1	0.9 mg
Linoleic Acid	N.D. g	Vitamin B_2	0.2 mg
Iron	8 mg	Niacin	14 mg
Calcium	35 mg	Vitamin C	0 mg
		Calories	132

rickets
A disease characterized by defective bone growth and caused by Vitamin D deficiency.
   See Vitamin D

RNA
Ribonucleic acid.
   See Nucleic Acids

rolls, "enriched," hamburger and frankfurter

COMPOSITION AND NUTRIENT VALUE PER roll (40 g)

Protein	3 g	Phosphorous	N.D. mg
Carbohydrate	21 g	Potassium	N.D. mg
Fat	3 g	Sodium	N.D. mg
Saturated Fatty Acids	1 g	Vitamin A	Trace I.U.
Oleic Acid	1 g	Vitamin B_1	0.11 mg
Linoleic Acid	1 g	Vitamin B_2	0.07 mg
Iron	0.8 mg	Niacin	0.90 mg
Calcium	30 mg	Vitamin C	Trace mg
		Calories	120

rose hips
The fruit of the rose—an especially rich source of Vitamin C.

roughage
The undigestible fibers of raw plants, especially fruits and vegetables. Since they are not digested they pass through the intestines unchanged, but by giving a soft bulkiness to other foods in the digestive tract, they promote intestinal motility, the absorption of nutrients, and the elimination of waste materials. A certain amount of roughage is considered necessary to the maintenance of normal good health.

royal jelly
Bee larvae which develop into queen bees are fed on this

food. It is the richest-known source of pantothenic acid. Some hopeful people, a class which includes some who sell the product, assert that it has a rejuvenating effect on humans, a claim that has not been substantiated by research.

rum

An alcoholic beverage distilled from fermented sugar cane or molasses.

COMPOSITION AND NUTRIENT VALUES PER 1 1/2 fl. ounce (42 g)

Protein	0 g	Phosphorous	0 mg
Carbohydrate	Trace g	Potassium	Trace mg
Fat	0 g	Sodium	Trace mg
Saturated Fatty Acids	0 g	Vitamin A	0 I.U.
Oleic Acid	0 g	Vitamin B_1	0 mg
Linoleic Acid	0 g	Vitamin B_2	0 mg
Iron	0 mg	Niacin	0 mg
Calcium	0 mg	Vitamin C	0 mg
		Calories	80 proof 100
			86 proof 105
			90 proof 110
			100 proof 125

saccharin

Benzoic sulphimide, an artificial sweetener over 500 times as sweet as sugar and of no food value. On the FDA top priority list to retest for mutagenic, teratogenic, subacute, and reproductive effects.

safflower oil

From the seeds of herb safflower. Very rich in linoleic acid, an essential fatty acid.* Used in cooking and baking.
    See Fats

salmonellae

A genus of bacteria which is one of the common causes of food poisoning.*

salt

Any compound of acid and alkali is a salt but in a nutritional context "salt" usually refers to common table salt —sodium chloride—whose two principal components, sodium and chlorine, are essential elements in the body.

Salt deficiency results in undue fatigue and exhaustion. Low blood pressure is often a sign of a deficiency in salt.

Profuse sweating in hot weather from heavy exercise or from any other cause leads to much salt being lost from the body. If only water is drunk, the salt is not replaced and salt depletion occurs causing dizziness, nausea, exhaustion, muscular cramps and in extreme cases heatstroke and even death. During very hot weather, therefore, it is advisable to add more salt than usual to one's food and when working or exercising under such conditions to take a salt tablet with each drink of water.

See Chlorine; Iodine; Monosodium Glutamate (MSG); Salt-Free Diets; Sodium; Sodium-Potassium Balance

salt-free diets

More properly diets that are low in sodium, but since most required sodium is supplied by sodium chloride (common table salt) they are called salt-free diets. Sodium controls fluid retention and some conditions requiring low-retention, e.g., hypertension, are aided by low-sodium diets.

In a nutritional context low-sodium diets make it difficult for the dieter to acquire sufficient iodine in the manner usually supplied, i.e., through the intake of iodized salt. Thus an iodine supplement must be used.

saltines

Salted soda crackers.

COMPOSITION AND NUTRIENT VALUE PER 4 (11 g)

Protein	1 g	Phosphorous	19 mg
Carbohydrate	8 g	Potassium	12 mg
Fat	1 g	Sodium	110 mg
Saturated Fatty Acids	— g	Vitamin A	0 I.U.

Oleic Acid	— g	Vitamin B_1	Trace mg
Linoleic Acid	1 g	Vitamin B_2	Trace mg
Iron	0.1 mg	Niacin	0.1 mg
Calcium	2 mg	Vitamin C	0 mg
		Calories	50

saltpeter

Potassium nitrate or sodium nitrate. Used as a color fixative in cured meats, chopped meats, frankfurters, bacon, bologna, spiced ham, and meat spreads, poultry, and baby foods among other things. And once a popular food additive in establishments which confined males (boarding schools, prisons, the military)—the idea being that saltpeter reduced the sexual urge. The FDA is testing nitrates for their possible cancer-causing and other harmful side effects.

saturated fatty acids
See Fats

schizophrenia
See Niacin—Deficiency

scurvy

A disease characterized by spongy and bleeding gums, bleeding under the skin, and extreme muscular weakness. It is caused by Vitamin C deficiency but usually only after a relatively long period of time on a diet containing very little fresh food. Today scurvy is a rare disease.
See Vitamin C

sea salt

Common table salt—sodium chloride—obtained from the evaporation of sea water. Unlike mined salt, however, it contains iodine,* an essential nutrient, and many other trace minerals.

semolina

The flour made from the coarse particles (containing the bran and other nutrients) of durum wheat after the finer flour has passed through the bolting machine. It too, however, is usually refined and bleached. Used chiefly in the manufacture of pasta.

See Flour, Refining and Bleaching

sequestrants
Substances such as citrates, tartrates, phosphates, and ethylenediamine tetra-acetate (EDA) which render metal ions or acid radicals inactive by absorbing them. They are added to foods and beverages for this purpose.

See Additives

serine
A nonessential amino acid.

See Amino Acids

sesame seeds, dry

COMPOSITION AND NUTRIENT VALUE PER 1/2 cup (50 g)

Protein	9 g	Phosphorous	308 mg
Carbohydrate	10 g	Potassium	360 mg
Fat	24 g	Sodium	30 mg
Saturated Fatty Acids	8 g	Vitamin A	15 I.U.
Oleic Acid	5 g	Vitamin B_1	0.4 mg
Linoleic Acid	10 g	Vitamin B_2	0.4 mg
Iron	5.2 mg	Niacin	2.7 mg
Calcium	580 mg	Vitamin C	0 mg
		Calories	280

sex
A term with several meanings but which here refers only to sexual intercourse, of which the inability to have, whether caused by impotency or frigidity, has led many persons to seek aid in the form of aphrodisiacs and certain vitamins.

There is no reliable evidence indicating that aphrodisiacs produce the desired results. Nor is there any generally accepted evidence that Vitamin E does.

In the absence of organic malfunction or serious psychological problems, the most likely cause of a marked decrease in sexual desire or vigor is the serious lack of one or more of the essential nutrients. In such cases the proper cure is a sound diet.

See Aphrodisiacs; Malpotane; Vitamin E

shellfish
Any of a variety of fresh or salt-water animals such as mollusks (clams, oysters, scallops) and crustaceans (crabs, lobsters, shrimp).

clams
Any of the edible varieties of marine and fresh water bivalve mollusks of the class *Pelecypoda*.

COMPOSITION AND NUTRIENT VALUE PER 3 ounces (85 g), steamed or canned

Protein	7 g	Phosphorous	110 mg
Carbohydrate	2 g	Potassium	230 mg
Fat	1 g	Sodium	170 mg
Saturated Fatty Acids	— g	Vitamin A	— I.U.
Oleic Acid	— g	Vitamin B$_1$	0.01 mg
Linoleic Acid	— g	Vitamin B$_2$	0.09 mg
Iron	3.5 mg	Niacin	0.9 mg
Calcium	47 mg	Vitamin C	— mg
		Calories	45

crabmeat
The meat from marine crustaceans of the suborder *Brachyura* of the order *Decapoda*.

COMPOSITION AND NUTRIENT VALUE PER 3 ounces (85 g), canned

Protein	15 g	Phosphorous	170 mg
Carbohydrate	1 g	Potassium	100 mg
Fat	2 g	Sodium	900 mg
Saturated Fatty Acids	— g	Vitamin A	— I.U.
Oleic Acid	— g	Vitamin B$_1$	0.07 mg

Linoleic Acid	— g	Vitamin B$_2$	0.07 mg
Iron	0.07 mg	Niacin	1.6 mg
Calcium	38 mg	Vitamin C	— mg
		Calories	85

lobster
Any of several marine crustaceans of the genus *Homarus*.

COMPOSITION AND NUTRIENT VALUE PER 1/2 (100 g), steamed

Protein	18 g	Phosphorous	192 mg
Carbohydrate	Trace g	Potassium	180 mg
Fat	1 g	Sodium	210 mg
Saturated Fatty Acids	0 g	Vitamin A	0 I.U.
Oleic Acid	0 g	Vitamin B$_1$	0.1 mg
Linoleic Acid	0 g	Vitamin B$_2$	Trace mg
Iron	0.6 mg	Niacin	1.9 mg
Calcium	65 mg	Vitamin C	0 mg
		Calories	92

oysters
Any of a variety of edible bivalve mollusks of the genus *Ostrea*.

COMPOSITION AND NUTRIENT VALUE PER Cup (240 g), raw

Protein	20 g	Phosphorous	300 mg
Carbohydrate	8 g	Potassium	240 mg
Fat	4 g	Sodium	160 mg
Saturated Fatty Acids	— g	Vitamin A	740 I.U.
Oleic Acid	— g	Vitamin B$_1$	0.33 mg
Linoleic Acid	— g	Vitamin B$_2$	0.43 mg
Iron	13.2 mg	Niacin	6 mg
Calcium	226 mg	Vitamin C	— mg
		Calories	160

scallops
The edible meat of a bivalve mollusk.

COMPOSITION AND NUTRIENT VALUE PER 3.5 ounces (100 g), breaded, fried

Protein	18 g	Phosphorous	338 mg
Carbohydrate	10 g	Potassium	470 mg
Fat	8 g	Sodium	265 mg
Saturated Fatty Acids	— g	Vitamin A	0 I.U.
Oleic Acid	— g	Vitamin B$_1$	Trace mg
Linoleic Acid	— g	Vitamin B$_2$	0.1 mg
Iron	1.4 mg	Niacin	1.4 mg
Calcium	110 mg	Vitamin C	0 mg
		Calories	194

shrimp

Any of a variety of edible marine decapod crustaceans of the suborder *Natantia*.

COMPOSITION AND NUTRIENT VALUE PER 3 ounces (85 g), steamed

Protein	21 g	Phosphorous	250 mg
Carbohydrate	1 g	Potassium	205 mg
Fat	1 g	Sodium	130 mg
Saturated Fatty Acids	— g	Vitamin A	50 I.U.
Oleic Acid	— g	Vitamin B$_1$	0.01 mg
Linoleic Acid	— g	Vitamin B$_2$	0.03 mg
Iron	2.6 mg	Niacin	1.5 mg
Calcium	98 mg	Vitamin C	— mg
		Calories	100

shortening

A fat usually made from vegetable oils and used in baking, frying, and cooking. Vegetable oils are hydrogenated, a process which not only condenses them into a semihard state and makes them less susceptible to rancidity, but also destroys much of their nutritive value.

See Hydrogenation

siderosis

A usually fatal disease, in which excessive iron is held in the body.

skim milk

Milk from which the fat content has been removed. Most of the vitamin A is removed with the cream, but all other nutrients remain.

sodium bicarbonate

Baking soda. The major ingredient in baking powder.*

sodium chloride

Common table salt.*

sodium-potassium balance

The human body contains about three times as much potassium as sodium and good health requires that this balance be maintained. An excess of sodium causes potassium to be lost through the urine and an excess of potassium causes sodium to be lost.

Since the average diet is usually proportionally richer in sodium (e.g., from table salt) an excess of sodium is far more common.

See Potassium; Sodium, for symptoms of deficiencies

soft drinks

Nonalcoholic beverages, usually carbonated, and usually containing a good deal of sugar which is already oversupplied in the American diet. There are a staggering variety of them but generally they can be divided into two groups; those containing extracts from kola nuts and coca leaves, and those containing natural or artificial fruit flavorings. Synthetic Vitamin C is sometimes added to the latter, but neither variety offers much, if any, nutritional value.

soil

The top layer of the earth's surface in which plants grow. All that we eat, other than seafood, comes from the soil.

Fruits, vegetables, and grains come directly, and meat as the product of animals who feed on them comes indirectly. And just as we, if we are to be healthy, require the nutrients provided by the food grown in the soil, it, in turn, requires the nutrients in the soil to be healthy. If the soil is deficient, the plants grown in it, the animals which eat them, and the people who eat both, are all shortchanged. The proper care of the land, therefore, is essential to a nation's well-being.

Allowing fields to lie fallow, crop rotation, and the addition of fertilizers are all practices introduced to conserve and replenish the strength of the soil. But the widespread use of synthetic fertilizers (as opposed to organic manure), has given rise to a controversy. Proponents of organic farming claim that the nitrogen, phosphorus, and potassium of synthetic fertilizers are so soluble that they saturate the soil solution making it very difficult or impossible for essential minerals such as iron, copper, magnesium, zinc and others to stay in the soil solution and be absorbed by the plants. Whether this is so or not, the results of several experiments on the relative nutritional values of plants grown with synthetic fertilizers and those grown organically, have not shown that organically grown plants are superior in nutritional value to those grown with synthetic fertilizers.

The use of compost (decayed or partially decayed vegetable matter) in organic farming does seem to have a benefit not available to farming which relies on synthetic fertilizers. Compost or humus promotes the growth of soil molds which in turn produce natural antibiotics that deter the various insects and pests which destroy plants. When the soil lacks sufficient humus, the molds do not manufacture enough antibiotics to deter insects. Farmers using such soil must use pesticides and herbicides to protect their crops. And we who eat their crops must also eat the pesticides and herbicides used to protect them. Moreover, the soil in which heavily sprayed crops are grown becomes saturated with poisons, as does the surrounding soil and water.

See Herbicides; Organic Farming; Pesticides

sorbic acid
A white, crystalline solid obtained from the berries of the mountain ash and also manufactured synthetically. It is used as a mold- and yeast-inhibitor in a wide variety of products including soft drinks, baked goods, packaged cheeses, and artificially sweetened jellies and preserves, and is on the GRAS list.

soup
A liquid food made from vegetables, meat, or fish stock with various other ingredients added. Sometimes combined with a milk or cream sauce. Served either hot or cold.

(The composition and nutrient values of soups listed below are for canned, condensed, ready-to-serve soups.)

soup, beef bouillon, (consomme)

COMPOSITION AND NUTRIENT VALUE PER Cup (240 g), prepared with water

Protein	5 g	Phosphorous	N.D. mg
Carbohydrate	3 g	Potassium	N.D. mg
Fat	0 g	Sodium	N.D. mg
Saturated Fatty Acids	— g	Vitamin A	Trace I.U.
Oleic Acid	— g	Vitamin B_1	Trace mg
Linoleic Acid	— g	Vitamin B_2	0.02 mg
Iron	0.5 mg	Niacin	1.20 mg
Calcium	Trace mg	Vitamin C	0 mg
		Calories	30

soup, chicken noodle (dehydrated, dry form)

COMPOSITION AND NUTRIENT VALUE PER 2 oz. package (57 g)

Protein	8 g	Phosphorous	N.D. mg
Carbohydrate	33 g	Potassium	N.D. mg
Fat	6 g	Sodium	N.D. mg

Saturated Fatty Acids	2 g	Vitamin A	190 I.U.
Oleic Acid	3 g	Vitamin B_1	0.30 mg
Linoleic Acid	1 g	Vitamin B_2	0.15 mg
Iron	1.4 mg	Niacin	2.4 mg
Calcium	34 mg	Vitamin C	3 mg
		Calories	220

soup, clam chowder (Manhattan)

COMPOSITION AND NUTRIENT VALUE PER Cup (245 g), prepared with an equal volume of water

Protein	2 g	Phosphorous	49 mg
Carbohydrate	12 g	Potassium	225 mg
Fat	3 g	Sodium	1099 mg
Saturated Fatty Acids	— g	Vitamin A	880 I.U.
Oleic Acid	— g	Vitamin B_1	0.02 mg
Linoleic Acid	— g	Vitamin B_2	0.02 mg
Iron	1 mg	Niacin	1 mg
Calcium	34 mg	Vitamin C	0 mg
		Calories	80

soup, clam chowder (New England, frozen, condensed)

COMPOSITION AND NUTRIENT VALUE PER Cup (245 g), prepared with an equal volume of milk

Protein	9 g	Phosphorous	N.D. mg
Carbohydrate	16 g	Potassium	N.D. mg
Fat	12 g	Sodium	N.D. mg
Saturated Fatty Acids	— g	Vitamin A	250 I.U.
Oleic Acid	— g	Vitamin B_1	0.07 mg
Linoleic Acid	— g	Vitamin B_2	0.29 mg
Iron	1 mg	Niacin	0.50 mg
Calcium	240 mg	Vitamin C	Trace mg
		Calories	210

soup, cream of chicken

COMPOSITION AND NUTRIENT VALUE PER Cup (245 g), prepared with an equal volume of milk

Protein	7 g	Phosphorous	— mg
Carbohydrate	15 g	Potassium	— mg
Fat	10 g	Sodium	— mg
Saturated Fatty Acids	3 g	Vitamin A	610 I.U.
Oleic Acid	3 g	Vitamin B_1	0.05 mg
Linoleic Acid	3 g	Vitamin B_2	0.27 mg
Iron	0.5 mg	Niacin	0.70 mg
Calcium	172 mg	Vitamin C	2 mg
		Calories	180

soup, cream of mushroom

COMPOSITION AND NUTRIENT VALUE PER Cup (245 g), prepared with an equal volume of milk

Protein	7 g	Phosphorous	N.D. mg
Carbohydrate	16 g	Potassium	N.D. mg
Fat	14 g	Sodium	N.D. mg
Saturated Fatty Acids	4 g	Vitamin A	250 I.U.
Oleic Acid	4 g	Vitamin B_1	0.05 mg
Linoleic Acid	5 g	Vitamin B_2	0.34 mg
Iron	0.5 mg	Niacin	0.70 mg
Calcium	191 mg	Vitamin C	1 mg
		Calories	215

soup, onion (dehydrated, dry form)

COMPOSITION AND NUTRIENT VALUE PER 1.5 oz. pkg. (43 g)

Protein	6 g	Phosphorous	N.D. mg
Carbohydrate	23 g	Potassium	N.D. mg
Fat	5 g	Sodium	N.D. mg
Saturated Fatty Acid	1 g	Vitamin A	30 I.U.

Oleic Acid	2 g	Vitamin B$_1$	0.05 mg
Linoleic Acid	1 g	Vitamin B$_2$	0.03 mg
Iron	0.6 mg	Niacin	0.30 mg
Calcium	42 mg	Vitamin C	6 mg
		Calories	150

soup, split pea

COMPOSITION AND NUTRIENT VALUE PER Cup (245 g), prepared with an equal volume of water

Protein	9 g	Phosphorous	152 mg
Carbohydrate	21 g	Potassium	275 mg
Fat	3 g	Sodium	959 mg
Saturated Fatty Acids	1 g	Vitamin A	440 I.U.
Oleic Acid	2 g	Vitamin B$_1$	0.25 mg
Linoleic Acid	Trace g	Vitamin B$_2$	0.15 mg
Iron	1.5 mg	Niacin	1.50 mg
Calcium	29 mg	Vitamin C	1 mg
		Calories	145

soup, tomato

COMPOSITION AND NUTRIENT VALUE PER Cup (245 g), prepared with an equal volume of water

Protein	2 g	Phosphorous	N.D. mg
Carbohydrate	16 g	Potassium	N.D. mg
Fat	3 g	Sodium	N.D. mg
Saturated Fatty Acids	Trace g	Vitamin A	1000 I.U.
Oleic Acid	1 g	Vitamin B$_1$	0.05 mg
Linoleic Acid	1 g	Vitamin B$_2$	0.05 mg
Iron	0.7 mg	Niacin	1.20 mg
Calcium	15 mg	Vitamin C	12 mg
		Calories	90

soup, tomato

COMPOSITION AND NUTRIENT VALUE PER Cup (250 g), prepared with an equal volume of milk

Protein	7 g	Phosphorous	155 mg
Carbohydrate	23 g	Potassium	417 mg
Fat	7 g	Sodium	1055 mg
Saturated Fatty Acids	3 g	Vitamin A	1200 I.U.
Oleic Acid	2 g	Vitamin B_1	0.10 mg
Linoleic Acid	1 g	Vitamin B_2	0.25 mg
Iron	0.8 mg	Niacin	1.30 mg
Calcium	168 mg	Vitamin C	15 mg
		Calories	175

soup, vegetable (vegetarian)

COMPOSITION AND NUTRIENT VALUE PER Cup (245 g), prepared with an equal volume of water

Protein	2 g	Phosphorous	40 mg
Carbohydrate	13 g	Potassium	170 mg
Fat	2 g	Sodium	855 mg
Saturated Fatty Acids	— g	Vitamin A	2940 I.U.
Oleic Acid	— g	Vitamin B_1	0.05 mg
Linoleic Acid	— g	Vitamin B_2	0.05 mg
Iron	1 mg	Niacin	1 mg
Calcium	20 mg	Vitamin C	— mg
		Calories	80

soup, vegetable beef

COMPOSITION AND NUTRIENT VALUES PER Cup (245 g), prepared with an equal volume of water

Protein	5 g	Phosphorous	50 mg
Carbohydrate	10 g	Potassium	165 mg
Fat	2 g	Sodium	1067 mg
Saturated Fatty Acids	— g	Vitamin A	2700 I.U.
Oleic Acid	— g	Vitamin B_1	0.05 mg
Linoleic Acid	— g	Vitamin B_2	0.05 mg
Iron	0.7 mg	Niacin	1 mg
Calcium	12 mg	Vitamin C	— mg
		Calories	80

soybean

A bean, originally a native of China where it has been cultivated for some five thousand years but now widely cultivated in Europe and North America. It is a good source of complete protein* and unsaturated fatty acids.*

soy flour (full fat)

COMPOSITION AND NUTRIENT VALUE PER Cup (110 g)

Protein	39 g	Phosphorous	613 mg
Carbohydrate	33 g	Potassium	1826 mg
Fat	22 g	Sodium	1 mg
Saturated Fatty Acids	— g	Vitamin A	121 I.U.
Oleic Acid	— g	Vitamin B_1	0.9 mg
Linoleic Acid	11 g	Vitamin B_2	0.3 mg
Iron	8.8 mg	Niacin	2.3 mg
Calcium	218 mg	Vitamin C	0 mg
		Calories	460

spices

The oldest food additive, distinguished from herbs in that only a part, (seed, root, stem, bark, and so on) of the whole aromatic plant is meant. For example, cinnamon as a spice refers only to the bark of the plant. Originally, spices were used to mask the odor of decaying foods, especially meats, in times prior to the invention of refrigeration. Some were also used chiefly for the preservative effects of their essential oils: e.g., cloves and cinnamon. Now they are chiefly used as flavoring agents. Generally they are employed in quantities too small to provide any nutritional values.

See Flavoring Agents; Herbs

stabilizers and thickeners

Substances used to stabilize (bind together) emulsions of fat and water or to add body (thickness) to foods and drinks. The majority of stabilizers and thickeners are extracted from natural sources, from seaweed, trees, and seeds; some are chemically modified versions of these, and a few are entirely synthetic. Such products as ice cream, frozen and canned desserts, puddings, artificially sweetened soft drinks, soups and sauces, cheese spreads, and the like, have such additives. By law, all such agents, whether natural or synthetic, must be listed on the product's label or package.

See Additives; Emulsifiers; Firming Agents

starch

A carbohydrate nutrient found in abundance in all grains (e.g., wheat), tubers (e.g., potatoes), and dried legumes (e.g., peas). As the principal carbohydrate of the diet, it is the chief source of energy for man.

The digestive process converts starch first to maltose, then glucose, which supplies energy. The bulk of unused sugar is stored in the liver as glycogen* which can be used for future energy needs. An excessive accumulation, however, soon leads to weight gain.

sterols

Unsaturated solid alcohols of the steroid group occurring in the fatty tissues of plants and animals. Cholesterol and ergosterol are sterols.

struvite

Crystals of magnesium ammonium phosphate resembling broken glass which sometimes form in canned seafood and which EDTA is used to prevent. Unsightly, but not poisonous.

sucrose

A crystalline disaccharide carbohydrate found chiefly in cane sugar and beet sugar—both of which in their refined state are almost pure sucrose.

See Sugar

sugar

A white, crystalline refined carbohydrate substance obtained mainly from two plants, sugar cane and sugar beet.

The extraction and refining process for both is similar, and both in their refined states are pure sucrose, containing neither vitamins nor minerals.

Raw, unrefined sugar, does retain some small amount of nutrients but one does not gain much by substitution of it for white sugar. The nutritive values are negligible.

Natural sugars, such as those occurring in fruits, grains, milk and honey, normally provide all the sugar the body requires for energy and the typical American overconsumption of refined sugar does not benefit health. Among other things, an excessive indulgence in soft drinks, bakery goods, and candies increases the need for vitamins, and elevates the blood-sugar level—an elevation usually followed by a sudden drop to a low-blood-sugar level which can result in fatigue, blackouts and fainting. It also leads to a feeling of great hunger, ensuing overeating and unwanted weight gain.

See Blood Sugar; Carbohydrates; Proteins; Starch

sugar, brown

COMPOSITION AND NUTRIENT VALUE PER Cup (220 g)

Protein	0 g	Phosphorous	38 mg
Carbohydrate	212 g	Potassium	688 mg
Fat	0 g	Sodium	390 mg
Saturated Fatty Acids	0 g	Vitamin A	0 I.U.
Oleic Acid	0 g	Vitamin B_1	0.02 mg
Linoleic Acid	0 g	Vitamin B_2	0.07 mg
Iron	7.5 mg	Niacin	0.40 mg
Calcium	187 mg	Vitamin C	0 mg
		Calories	820
			(50 per tablespoon)

sugar, white

COMPOSITION AND NUTRIENT VALUE PER Cup (200 g)

Protein	0 g	Phosphorous	0 mg
Carbohydrate	199 g	Potassium	0 mg

Fat	0 g	Sodium	0 mg
Saturated Fatty Acids	0 g	Vitamin A	0 I.U.
Oleic Acid	0 g	Vitamin B_1	0 mg
Linoleic Acid	0 g	Vitamin B_2	0 mg
Iron	0.2 mg	Niacin	0 mg
Calcium	0 mg	Vitamin C	0 mg
		Calories	770

(48 per tablespoon)

sunflower seeds

COMPOSITION AND NUTRIENT VALUE PER 1/2 cup (50 g)

Protein	12 g	Phosphorous	418 mg
Carbohydrate	10 g	Potassium	460 mg
Fat	26 g	Sodium	15 mg
Saturated Fatty Acids	4 g	Vitamin A	0 I.U.
Oleic Acid	3 g	Vitamin B_1	1.8 mg
Linoleic Acid	15 g	Vitamin B_2	0.2 mg
Iron	3.5 mg	Niacin	13.6 mg
Calcium	60 mg	Vitamin C	0 mg
		Calories	280

sunstroke
See Perspiration; and salt for treatment of condition.

surface active agents
See Emulsifiers

sweat
See Perspiration

synthetic vitamins
Vitamins which are not extracted from plants or animals but which are produced by chemical synthesis. For the most part synthetic vitamins are identical to those occurring in nature. All the synthetic B vitamins, for example, are chemically identical to their natural counterparts. Synthetic Vitamin C, however, usually lacks the bioflavonoids that protect it from oxidation in the body. And Vitamin A

from fish-liver oils and Vitamin E from soy oil are said to be more effective than their synthetic counterparts.

Since the differences between natural and synthetic vitamins are usually slight and in some cases nonexistent, and since it is frequently difficult to obtain adequate quantities of certain vitamins from natural sources, it seems unwise to refuse—as some enthusiasts do—to use synthetic vitamins.

See Vitamins for new FDA regulations pertaining to the labeling and sale of vitamins and minerals, especially of vitamins A and D.

tapioca

A starchy food prepared from the root of the cassava plant.

COMPOSITION AND NUTRIENT VALUE PER Cup (152 g), quick cooking, dry

Protein	1 g	Phosphorous	N.D. mg
Carbohydrate	131 g	Potassium	N.D. mg
Fat	Trace g	Sodium	N.D. mg
Saturated Fatty Acids	— g	Vitamin A	0 I.U.
Oleic Acid	— g	Vitamin B$_1$	0 mg
Linoleic Acid	— g	Vitamin B$_2$	0 mg
Iron	0.6 mg	Niacin	0 mg
Calcium	15 mg	Vitamin C	0 mg
		Calories	535

tartar sauce

Mayonnaise mixed with chopped onion, pickles, olives, and capers. Usually served with fish.

COMPOSITION AND NUTRIENT VALUE PER Tablespoon (14 g)

Protein	Trace g	Phosphorous	N.D. mg
Carbohydrate	1 g	Potassium	N.D. mg
Fat	8 g	Sodium	N.D. mg
Saturated Fatty Acids	1 g	Vitamin A	30 I.U.

Oleic Acid	1 g	Vitamin B_1	Trace mg
Linoleic Acid	4 g	Vitamin B_2	Trace mg
Iron	0.1 mg	Niacin	Trace mg
Calcium	3 mg	Vitamin C	Trace mg
		Calories	75

taste
Bitter and sweet, acid and salt are the only four tastes which can be distinguished on the tongue. All others are detected by smell—which is why foods taste flat and subtleties bypass us when we have colds.

tea
The dried leaves of the shrub *Thea sinensis* or *Camellia sinensis* made into a beverage by steeping in hot water. Contains only slightly less caffeine than coffee.
    (*See* Coffee for the effect of tea drinking on the loss of B vitamins.)

COMPOSITION AND NUTRIENT VALUE PER Cup (230 g), clear, unsweetened

Protein	0 g	Phosphorous	Trace mg
Carbohydrate	1 g	Potassium	58 mg
Fat	Trace g	Sodium	Trace mg
Saturated Fatty Acids	0 g	Vitamin A	0 I.U.
Oleic Acid	0 g	Vitamin B_1	0 mg
Linoleic Acid	0 g	Vitamin B_2	Trace mg
Iron	Trace mg	Niacin	Trace mg
Calcium	Trace mg	Vitamin C	0 mg
		Calories	4

tenderizer
With reference to the tenderizing of meats, the term usually refers to papain.*

tetany
The oversensitivity of the motor nerves to stimuli caused by an extremely low level of blood calcium which par-

ticularly affects the hands, feet, and face. This condition often accompanies severe rickets.

See Calcium

texturizer
Any chemical used to improve the texture of foods. Many canned foods have a tendency to become soft and fall apart. Canned tomatoes and canned potatoes become soft unless calcium chloride is added.

See Additives; Firming Agents

thiamine
Vitamin B_1.*

thousand island dressing
A salad dressing.

COMPOSITION AND NUTRIENT VALUE PER Tablespoon (16 g)

Protein	Trace g	Phosphorous	Trace mg
Carbohydrate	3 g	Potassium	— mg
Fat	8 g	Sodium	— mg
Saturated Fatty Acids	1 g	Vitamin A	50 I.U.
Oleic Acid	2 g	Vitamin B_1	Trace mg
Linoleic Acid	4 g	Vitamin B_2	Trace mg
Iron	0.1 mg	Niacin	Trace mg
Calcium	2 mg	Vitamin C	Trace mg
		Calories	80

threonine
An essential amino acid.

See Amino Acids

thyroid gland
Endocrine gland located in the neck, which controls the basal metabolism of the body. The metabolism is slowed down when the activity of the thyroid is deficient and speeded up when it is excessive.

See Cretinism; Goiter

thyroxin
A hormone containing iodine, produced by the thyroid
gland to regulate the metabolism. Thyroxin can be produced in the necessary amounts only if iodine is supplied
in the diet in adequate amounts.
    See Iodine

tomato catsup
A preparation made from tomato purée, vinegar, salt,
sugar, and spices.

COMPOSITION AND NUTRIENT VALUE PER Tablespoon
(15 g)

Protein	Trace g	Phosphorous	3 mg
Carbohydrate	4 g	Potassium	160 mg
Fat	Trace g	Sodium	260 mg
Saturated Fatty Acids	— g	Vitamin A	210 I.U.
Oleic Acid	— g	Vitamin B$_1$	0.01 mg
Linoleic Acid	— g	Vitamin B$_2$	0.01 mg
Iron	0.1 mg	Niacin	0.2 mg
Calcium	3 mg	Vitamin C	2 mg
		Calories	15

torula
A yeast preparation.
    See Brewer's Yeast

toxins
Poisonous substances, secreted by certain organisms, usually bacteria. When introduced into the body they can make
you sick, sometimes fatally so.

trace elements
Those minerals the body requires in very small amounts,
as opposed to those it requires in much larger amounts.
    It is generally supposed that the trace elements, with
the exception of iodine, are all supplied in adequate
amounts by normal diets and that the chances of deficiency

are therefore very slight. Some authorities dispute this general view.

Green leafy vegetables, whole grain breads and cereals, seafood, liver and kidney are good sources of most of the trace elements.

See Minerals: Bromide; Chromium; Cobalt; Copper; Fluoride; Iodine; Manganese; Molybdenum; and Zinc. *See also* Soil

trichinosis

A disease resulting from infection caused by a parasitic worm which inhabits pork muscle. The worm is destroyed by heat and freezing and consequently one can be infected by trichinosis by eating undercooked pork. A meat thermometer reading of 160° should be achieved if you wish to be sure your pork is not undercooked.

tryptophane

An essential amino acid* which the body is able to convert into the B vitamin niacin.*

See Amino Acids

tyrosine

A nonessential amino acid.

See Amino Acids

ulcers

An inflammatory, frequently suppurating lesion on the skin or on an internal mucous surface of the body resulting in the death of living tissue.

Severe vitamin A deficiency may result in corneal ulcers, and skin and mucous membrane ulcers.

See Vitamin A

unsaturated fatty acids

See Fats

vegetables

Plants cultivated for food or the edible parts of such plants.

Some "vegetables" are botanically fruits (e.g., tomatoes), some are seeds (peas and beans), and some (mushrooms) are fungi.

Consisting mainly of water, starches, and sugar, vegetables are principally carbohydrate foods with little protein except in the case of the dried legumes such as beans and peas. These contain a large amount of proteins, but with the exception of the soybean they do not possess all the essential amino acids and thus provide only incomplete protein.

Vegetables are the main source of many necessary vitamins and minerals. The indigestible fibers of vegetables are important to the proper function of the intestines.

Cooking destroys or seriously depletes many of the nutrients available from vegetables (especially the water-soluble vitamins) and thus it is a good practice to include raw vegetables in the diet.

See Individual vegetable entries (e.g., carrots) for composition and nutrient value.

asparagus, green

COMPOSITION AND NUTRIENT VALUE PER 4 spears, (60 g) cooked, drained

Protein	1 g	Phosphorous	28 mg
Carbohydrate	2 g	Potassium	90 mg
Fat	Trace g	Sodium	1 mg
Saturated Fatty Acids	— g	Vitamin A	540 I.U.
Oleic Acid	— g	Vitamin B_1	0.10 mg
Linoleic Acid	— g	Vitamin B_2	0.11 mg
Iron	0.4 mg	Niacin	0.8 mg
Calcium	13 mg	Vitamin C	16 mg
		Calories	10

beans, green snap

COMPOSITION AND NUTRIENT VALUE PER Cup, (125 g) cooked, drained

Protein	2 g	Phosphorous	20 mg
Carbohydrate	7 g	Potassium	204 mg
Fat	Trace g	Sodium	2 mg
Saturated Fatty Acids	— g	Vitamin A	680 I.U.
Oleic Acid	— g	Vitamin B_1	0.09 mg
Linoleic Acid	— g	Vitamin B_2	0.11 mg
Iron	0.8 mg	Niacin	0.6 mg
Calcium	63 mg	Vitamin C	15 mg
		Calories	30

beans, lima

COMPOSITION AND NUTRIENT VALUE PER Cup, (170 g) cooked, drained

Protein	13 g	Phosphorous	105 mg
Carbohydrate	34 g	Potassium	320 mg
Fat	1 g	Sodium	2 mg
Saturated Fatty Acids	— g	Vitamin A	480 I.U.
Oleic Acid	— g	Vitamin B_1	0.31 mg
Linoleic Acid	— g	Vitamin B_2	0.17 mg
Iron	4.3 mg	Niacin	2.2 mg
Calcium	80 mg	Vitamin C	29 mg
		Calories	190

beans, navy (pea)

COMPOSITION AND NUTRIENT VALUE PER Cup, (190 g) cooked, drained

Protein	15 g	Phosphorous	N.D. mg
Carbohydrate	40 g	Potassium	N.D. mg
Fat	1 g	Sodium	N.D. mg
Saturated Fatty Acids	— g	Vitamin A	0 I.U.
Oleic Acid	— g	Vitamin B_1	0.27 mg
Linoleic Acid	— g	Vitamin B_2	0.13 mg
Iron	5.1 mg	Niacin	1.30 mg
Calcium	95 mg	Vitamin C	0 mg
		Calories	225

beans, red kidney (canned)

COMPOSITION AND NUTRIENT VALUE PER Cup (255 g)

Protein	15 g	Phosphorous	350 mg
Carbohydrate	42 g	Potassium	750 mg
Fat	1 g	Sodium	6 mg
Saturated Fatty Acids	— g	Vitamin A	10 I.U.
Oleic Acid	— g	Vitamin B$_1$	0.13 mg
Linoleic Acid	— g	Vitamin B$_2$	0.10 mg
Iron	4.6 mg	Niacin	1.50 mg
Calcium	74 mg	Vitamin C	0 mg
		Calories	230

beans, yellow or wax

COMPOSITION AND NUTRIENT VALUE PER Cup (125 g)
cooked, drained

Protein	2 g	Phosphorous	N.D. mg
Carbohydrate	6 g	Potassium	N.D. mg
Fat	Trace g	Sodium	N.D. mg
Saturated Fatty Acids	— g	Vitamin A	290 I.U.
Oleic Acid	— g	Vitamin B$_1$	0.09 mg
Linoleic Acid	— g	Vitamin B$_2$	0.11 mg
Iron	0.8 mg	Niacin	0.06 mg
Calcium	63 mg	Vitamin C	16 mg
		Calories	30

bean sprouts

COMPOSITION AND NUTRIENT VALUE PER Cup, (50 g)
uncooked

Protein	1 g	Phosphorous	170 mg
Carbohydrate	3 g	Potassium	514 mg
Fat	Trace g	Sodium	3 mg
Saturated Fatty Acids	0 g	Vitamin A	40 I.U.
Oleic Acid	0 g	Vitamin B$_1$	0.2 mg

Linoleic Acid	Trace g	Vitamin B_2	0.1 mg
Iron	3.8 mg	Niacin	1.3 mg
Calcium	19 mg	Vitamin C	Trace mg
		Calories	17

beets

COMPOSITION AND NUTRIENT VALUE PER Cup, (170 g) cooked, drained

Protein	2 g	Phosphorous	44 mg
Carbohydrate	12 g	Potassium	324 mg
Fat	Trace g	Sodium	64 mg
Saturated Fatty Acids	— g	Vitamin A	30 I.U.
Oleic Acid	— g	Vitamin B_1	0.05 mg
Linoleic Acid	— g	Vitamin B_2	0.07 mg
Iron	0.9 mg	Niacin	0.5 mg
Calcium	24 mg	Vitamin C	10 mg
		Calories	55

beet greens

COMPOSITION AND NUTRIENT VALUE PER Cup, (145 g) cooked, drained

Protein	3 g	Phosphorous	56 mg
Carbohydrate	5 g	Potassium	412 mg
Fat	Trace g	Sodium	102 mg
Saturated Fatty Acids	— g	Vitamin A	7400 I.U.
Oleic Acid	— g	Vitamin B_1	0.10 mg
Linoleic Acid	— g	Vitamin B_2	0.22 mg
Iron	2.8 mg	Niacin	0.4 mg
Calcium	144 mg	Vitamin C	22 mg
		Calories	25

broccoli

COMPOSITION AND NUTRIENT VALUE PER Cup, (155 g) cooked, drained

Protein	5 g	Phosphorous	100 mg
Carbohydrate	7 g	Potassium	405 mg
Fat	1 g	Sodium	15 mg
Saturated Fatty Acids	— g	Vitamin A	3880 I.U.
Oleic Acid	— g	Vitamin B$_1$	0.14 mg
Linoleic Acid	— g	Vitamin B$_2$	0.31 mg
Iron	1.2 mg	Niacin	1.2 mg
Calcium	136 mg	Vitamin C	140 mg
		Calories	40

brussels sprouts

COMPOSITION AND NUTRIENT VALUE PER Cup, (155 g) cooked

Protein	7 g	Phosphorous	95 mg
Carbohydrate	10 g	Potassium	400 mg
Fat	1 g	Sodium	14 mg
Saturated Fatty Acids	— g	Vitamin A	810 I.U.
Oleic Acid	— g	Vitamin B$_1$	0.12 mg
Linoleic Acid	— g	Vitamin B$_2$	0.22 mg
Iron	1.7 mg	Niacin	1.2 mg
Calcium	50 mg	Vitamin C	135 mg
		Calories	55

cabbage

COMPOSITION AND NUTRIENT VALUE PER Cup, (145 g) cooked

Protein	2 g	Phosphorous	50 mg
Carbohydrate	64 g	Potassium	240 mg
Fat	Trace g	Sodium	23 mg
Saturated Fatty Acids	— g	Vitamin A	190 I.U.
Oleic Acid	— g	Vitamin B$_1$	0.06 mg
Linoleic Acid	— g	Vitamin B$_2$	0.06 mg
Iron	0.4 mg	Niacin	0.40 mg
Calcium	64 mg	Vitamin C	48 mg
		Calories	30

carrots

COMPOSITION AND NUTRIENT VALUE PER 1, (50 g), raw

Protein	1 g	Phosphorous	19 mg
Carbohydrate	5 g	Potassium	205 mg
Fat	Trace g	Sodium	25 mg
Saturated Fatty Acids	— g	Vitamin A	5500 I.U.
Oleic Acid	— g	Vitamin B_1	0.03 mg
Linoleic Acid	— g	Vitamin B_2	0.03 mg
Iron	0.4 mg	Niacin	0.30 mg
Calcium	18 mg	Vitamin C	4 mg
		Calories	20

carrots

COMPOSITION AND NUTRIENT VALUE PER Cup, (145 g) cooked

Protein	1 g	Phosphorous	55 mg
Carbohydrate	10 g	Potassium	600 mg
Fat	Trace g	Sodium	75 mg
Saturated Fatty Acids	— g	Vitamin A	15,220 I.U.
Oleic Acid	— g	Vitamin B_1	0.08 mg
Linoleic Acid	— g	Vitamin B_2	0.07 mg
Iron	0.9 mg	Niacin	0.70 mg
Calcium	48 mg	Vitamin C	9 mg
		Calories	45

cauliflower

COMPOSITION AND NUTRIENT VALUE PER Cup, (120 g) cooked

Protein	3 g	Phosphorous	84 mg
Carbohydrate	5 g	Potassium	220 mg
Fat	Trace g	Sodium	11 mg
Saturated Fatty Acids	— g	Vitamin A	70 I.U.
Oleic Acid	— g	Vitamin B_1	0.11 mg

Linoleic Acid	— g	Vitamin B$_2$	0.10 mg
Iron	0.8 mg	Niacin	0.70 mg
Calcium	25 mg	Vitamin C	66 mg
		Calories	25

celery

COMPOSITION AND NUTRIENT VALUE PER Stalk, (40 g) raw

Protein	Trace g	Phosphorous	18 mg
Carbohydrate	2 g	Potassium	130 mg
Fat	Trace g	Sodium	30 mg
Saturated Fatty Acids	— g	Vitamin A	100 I.U.
Oleic Acid	— g	Vitamin B$_1$	0.01 mg
Linoleic Acid	— g	Vitamin B$_2$	0.01 mg
Iron	0.1 mg	Niacin	0.10 mg
Calcium	16 mg	Vitamin C	4 mg
		Calories	5

chard

COMPOSITION AND NUTRIENT VALUE PER Cup, (150 g) steamed

Protein	2 g	Phosphorous	54 mg
Carbohydrate	7 g	Potassium	475 mg
Fat	Trace g	Sodium	120 mg
Saturated Fatty Acids	0 g	Vitamin A	8100 I.U.
Oleic Acid	0 g	Vitamin B$_1$	Trace mg
Linoleic Acid	Trace g	Vitamin B$_2$	0.1 mg
Iron	3.6 mg	Niacin	0.1 mg
Calcium	155 mg	Vitamin C	17 mg
		Calories	30

collards

COMPOSITION AND NUTRIENT VALUE PER Cup, (190 g) cooked

Protein	5 g	Phosphorous	75 mg
Carbohydrate	9 g	Potassium	393 mg
Fat	1 g	Sodium	40 mg
Saturated Fatty Acids	— g	Vitamin A	10,260 I.U.
Oleic Acid	— g	Vitamin B_1	0.27 mg
Linoleic Acid	— g	Vitamin B_2	0.37 mg
Iron	1.1 mg	Niacin	2.4 mg
Calcium	289 mg	Vitamin C	87 mg
		Calories	55

corn, canned

COMPOSITION AND NUTRIENT VALUE PER Cup, (256 g)

Protein	5 g	Phosphorous	102 mg
Carbohydrate	40 g	Potassium	400 mg
Fat	2 g	Sodium	472 mg (salted)
Saturated Fatty Acids	— g	Vitamin A	690 I.U.
Oleic Acid	— g	Vitamin B_1	0.07 mg
Linoleic Acid	— g	Vitamin B_2	0.12 mg
Iron	1 mg	Niacin	2.30 mg
Calcium	10 mg	Vitamin C	13 mg
		Calories	170

corn, sweet

COMPOSITION AND NUTRIENT VALUE PER Ear, (140 g) cooked

Protein	3 g	Phosphorous	120 mg
Carbohydrate	16 g	Potassium	300 mg
Fat	1 g	Sodium	Trace mg
Saturated Fatty Acids	— g	Vitamin A	310 I.U.
Oleic Acid	— g	Vitamin B_1	0.09 mg
Linoleic Acid	— g	Vitamin B_2	0.08 mg
Iron	0.5 mg	Niacin	1 mg
Calcium	2 mg	Vitamin C	7 mg
		Calories	70

corn grits

Coarsely ground corn.

COMPOSITION AND NUTRIENT VALUE PER Cup, (245 g)
cooked, refined from yellow corn

Protein	3 g	Phosphorous	24 mg
Carbohydrate	27 g	Potassium	200 mg
Fat	Trace g	Sodium	2 mg
Saturated Fatty Acids	— g	Vitamin A	150 I.U.
Oleic Acid	— g	Vitamin B_1	0.05 mg
Linoleic Acid	— g	Vitamin B_2	0.02 mg
Iron	0.2 mg	Niacin	0.50 mg
Calcium	2 mg	Vitamin C	0 mg
		Calories	125

cornmeal (yellow)

COMPOSITION AND NUTRIENT VALUE PER Cup, (122 g)
whole-ground, dry

Protein	11 g	Phosphorous	N.D. mg
Carbohydrate	90 g	Potassium	N.D. mg
Fat	5 g	Sodium	N.D. mg
Saturated Fatty Acids	1 g	Vitamin A	620 I.U.
Oleic Acid	2 g	Vitamin B_1	0.46 mg
Linoleic Acid	2 g	Vitamin B_2	0.13 mg
Iron	2.9 mg	Niacin	2.40 mg
Calcium	24 mg	Vitamin C	0 mg
		Calories	435

cucumber

COMPOSITION AND NUTRIENT VALUE PER 6 1/8-inch slices
(50g)

Protein	Trace g	Phosphorous	9 mg
Carbohydrate	2 g	Potassium	80 mg
Fat	Trace g	Sodium	3 mg

Saturated Fatty Acids	— g	Vitamin A	Trace I.U.
Oleic Acid	— g	Vitamin B_1	0.02 mg
Linoleic Acid	— g	Vitamin B_2	0.02 mg
Iron	0.2 mg	Niacin	0.10 mg
Calcium	8 mg	Vitamin C	6 mg
		Calories	5

dandelion greens

COMPOSITION AND NUTRIENT VALUE PER Cup, (180 g) cooked

Protein	4 g	Phosphorous	126 mg
Carbohydrate	12 g	Potassium	760 mg
Fat	1 g	Sodium	130 mg
Saturated Fatty Acids	— g	Vitamin A	21,060 I.U.
Oleic Acid	— g	Vitamin B_1	0.24 mg
Linoleic Acid	— g	Vitamin B_2	0.29 mg
Iron	3.2 mg	Niacin	— mg
Calcium	252 mg	Vitamin C	32 mg
		Calories	60

eggplant

COMPOSITION AND NUTRIENT VALUE PER Cup (180 g), steamed

Protein	2 g	Phosphorous	60 mg
Carbohydrate	9 g	Potassium	390 mg
Fat	Trace g	Sodium	2 mg
Saturated Fatty Acids	— g	Vitamin A	10 I.U.
Oleic Acid	— g	Vitamin B_1	Trace mg
Linoleic Acid	Trace g	Vitamin B_2	Trace mg
Iron	0.9 mg	Niacin	0.9 mg
Calcium	17 mg	Vitamin C	8 mg
		Calories	30

endive

COMPOSITION AND NUTRIENT VALUE PER 2 ounces (57 g)

Protein	1 g	Phosphorous	28 mg
Carbohydrate	2 g	Potassium	215 mg
Fat	Trace g	Sodium	9 mg
Saturated Fatty Acids	— g	Vitamin A	1870 I.U.
Oleic Acid	— g	Vitamin B$_1$	0.04 mg
Linoleic Acid	— g	Vitamin B$_2$	0.08 mg
Iron	1 mg	Niacin	0.30 mg
Calcium	46 mg	Vitamin C	6 mg
		Calories	10

kale

COMPOSITION AND NUTRIENT VALUE PER Cup, (110 g) cooked

Protein	4 g	Phosphorous	57 mg
Carbohydrate	4 g	Potassium	260 mg
Fat	1 g	Sodium	29 mg
Saturated Fatty Acids	— g	Vitamin A	8140 I.U.
Oleic Acid	— g	Vitamin B$_1$	— mg
Linoleic Acid	— g	Vitamin B$_2$	— mg
Iron	1.3 mg	Niacin	— mg
Calcium	147 mg	Vitamin C	68 mg
		Calories	30

lettuce, Boston

COMPOSITION AND NUTRIENT VALUE PER head (220 g)

Protein	3 g	Phosphorous	N.D. mg
Carbohydrate	6 g	Potassium	N.D. mg
Fat	Trace g	Sodium	N.D. mg
Saturated Fatty Acids	— g	Vitamin A	2130 I.U.
Oleic Acid	— g	Vitamin B$_1$	0.14 mg

Linoleic Acid	— g	Vitamin B$_2$	0.13 mg
Iron	4.4 mg	Niacin	0.60 mg
Calcium	77 mg	Vitamin C	18 mg
		Calories	30

lettuce, Iceberg

COMPOSITION AND NUTRIENT VALUE PER head (454 g)

Protein	4 g	Phosphorous	88 mg
Carbohydrate	13 g	Potassium	700 mg
Fat	Trace g	Sodium	36 mg
Saturated Fatty Acids	— g	Vitamin A	1500 I.U.
Oleic Acid	— g	Vitamin B$_1$	0.29 mg
Linoleic Acid	— g	Vitamin B$_2$	0.27 mg
Iron	2.3 mg	Niacin	1.30 mg
Calcium	91 mg	Vitamin C	29 mg
		Calories	60

lettuce, Romaine

COMPOSITION AND NUTRIENT VALUE PER 2 large leaves (50 g)

Protein	1 g	Phosphorous	26 mg
Carbohydrate	2 g	Potassium	260 mg
Fat	Trace g	Sodium	9 mg
Saturated Fatty Acids	— g	Vitamin A	950 I.U.
Oleic Acid	— g	Vitamin B$_1$	0.03 mg
Linoleic Acid	— g	Vitamin B$_2$	0.04 mg
Iron	0.7 mg	Niacin	0.20 mg
Calcium	34 mg	Vitamin C	9 mg
		Calories	10

mustard greens

COMPOSITION AND NUTRIENT VALUE PER Cup, (140 g) cooked

Protein	3 g	Phosphorous	60 mg
Carbohydrate	6 g	Potassium	510 mg
Fat	1 g	Sodium	68 mg
Saturated Fatty Acids	— g	Vitamin A	8120 I.U.
Oleic Acid	— g	Vitamin B_1	0.11 mg
Linoleic Acid	— g	Vitamin B_2	0.90 mg
Iron	2.5 mg	Niacin	0.90 mg
Calcium	193 mg	Vitamin C	68 mg
		Calories	35

onions, green (scallions)

COMPOSITION AND NUTRIENT VALUE PER 6 (50 g), raw, without tops

Protein	1 g	Phosphorous	12 mg
Carbohydrate	5 g	Potassium	115 mg
Fat	Trace g	Sodium	2 mg
Saturated Fatty Acids	— g	Vitamin A	Trace I.U.
Oleic Acid	— g	Vitamin B_1	0.02 mg
Linoleic Acid	— g	Vitamin B_2	0.02 mg
Iron	0.3 mg	Niacin	0.20 mg
Calcium	20 mg	Vitamin C	12 mg
		Calories	20

onions, mature

COMPOSITION AND NUTRIENT VALUE PER Onion (110 g), raw

Protein	2 g	Phosphorous	44 mg
Carbohydrate	10 g	Potassium	155 mg
Fat	Trace g	Sodium	7 mg
Saturated Fatty Acids	— g	Vitamin A	40.0 I.U.
Oleic Acid	— g	Vitamin B_1	0.04 mg
Linoleic Acid	— g	Vitamin B_2	0.04 mg
Iron	0.6 mg	Niacin	0.20 mg
Calcium	30 mg	Vitamin C	11 mg
		Calories	40

onions, mature

COMPOSITION AND NUTRIENT VALUE PER Cup (210 g), cooked

Protein	3 g	Phosphorous	88 mg
Carbohydrate	14 g	Potassium	315 mg
Fat	Trace g	Sodium	14 mg
Saturated Fatty Acids	— g	Vitamin A	80 I.U.
Oleic Acid	— g	Vitamin B_1	0.06 mg
Linoleic Acid	— g	Vitamin B_2	0.06 mg
Iron	0.8 mg	Niacin	0.40 mg
Calcium	50 mg	Vitamin C	14 mg
		Calories	60

parsley

COMPOSITION AND NUTRIENT VALUE PER Tablespoon, (4 g) chopped

Protein	Trace g	Phosphorous	4 mg
Carbohydrate	Trace g	Potassium	40 mg
Fat	Trace g	Sodium	1 mg
Saturated Fatty Acids	— g	Vitamin A	340 I.U.
Oleic Acid	— g	Vitamin B_1	Trace mg
Linoleic Acid	— g	Vitamin B_2	0.01 mg
Iron	0.2 mg	Niacin	Trace mg
Calcium	8 mg	Vitamin C	7 mg
		Calories	Trace

parsnips

COMPOSITION AND NUTRIENT VALUE PER Cup, (155 g) cooked

Protein	2 g	Phosphorous	120 mg
Carbohydrate	23 g	Potassium	570 mg
Fat	1 g	Sodium	11 mg
Saturated Fatty Acids	— g	Vitamin A	50 I.U.

Oleic Acid	— g	Vitamin B$_1$	0.11 mg
Linoleic Acid	— g	Vitamin B$_2$	0.12 mg
Iron	0.9 mg	Niacin	0.20 mg
Calcium	70 mg	Vitamin C	16 mg
		Calories	100

peas

COMPOSITION AND NUTRIENT VALUE PER Cup, (160 g) cooked

Protein	9 g	Phosphorous	190 mg
Carbohydrate	19 g	Potassium	310 mg
Fat	Trace g	Sodium	1.6 mg
Saturated Fatty Acids	— g	Vitamin A	860 I.U.
Oleic Acid	— g	Vitamin B$_1$	0.44 mg
Linoleic Acid	— g	Vitamin B$_2$	0.17 mg
Iron	2.9 mg	Niacin	3.70 mg
Calcium	37 mg	Vitamin C	33 mg
		Calories	115

potato, baked

COMPOSITION AND NUTRIENT VALUE PER 1 medium (99 g), peeled after baking

Protein	3 g	Phosphorous	66 mg
Carbohydrate	21 g	Potassium	500 mg
Fat	Trace g	Sodium	4 mg
Saturated Fatty Acids	— g	Vitamin A	Trace I.U.
Oleic Acid	— g	Vitamin B$_1$	0.10 mg
Linoleic Acid	— g	Vitamin B$_2$	0.04 mg
Iron	0.7 mg	Niacin	1.70 mg
Calcium	9 mg	Vitamin C	20 mg
		Calories	90

potatoes, french fried

COMPOSITION AND NUTRIENT VALUE PER 10 pieces (57 g), cooked in oil

Protein	2 g	Phosphorous	6 mg
Carbohydrate	20 g	Potassium	510 mg
Fat	7 g	Sodium	6 mg
Saturated Fatty Acids	2 g	Vitamin A	Trace I.U.
Oleic Acid	2 g	Vitamin B_1	0.07 mg
Linoleic Acid	4 g	Vitamin B_2	0.04 mg
Iron	0.7 mg	Niacin	1.80 mg
Calcium	9 mg	Vitamin C	12 mg
		Calories	155

potatoes, mashed

COMPOSITION AND NUTRIENT VALUE PER Cup, (195 g) milk and butter added

Protein	4 g	Phosphorous	150 mg
Carbohydrate	24 g	Potassium	654 mg
Fat	8 g	Sodium	660 mg
Saturated Fatty Acids	4 g	Vitamin A	330 I.U.
Oleic Acid	3 g	Vitamin B_1	0.16 mg
Linoleic Acid	Trace g	Vitamin B_2	0.10 mg
Iron	0.8 mg	Niacin	1.90 mg
Calcium	47 mg	Vitamin C	18 mg
		Calories	185

potatoes, pan fried

COMPOSITION AND NUTRIENT VALUE PER 3/4 Cup, (100 g) cooked in oil

Protein	4 g	Phosphorous	100 mg
Carbohydrate	33 g	Potassium	775 mg
Fat	14 g	Sodium	225 mg
Saturated Fatty Acids	3 g	Vitamin A	— I.U.
Oleic Acid	3 g	Vitamin B_1	0.1 mg
Linoleic Acid	8 g	Vitamin B_2	Trace mg
Iron	1.1 mg	Niacin	2.8 mg
Calcium	15 mg	Vitamin C	20 mg
		Calories	268

radish

COMPOSITION AND NUTRIENT VALUE PER 4 small (40 g)

Protein	Trace g	Phosphorous	40 mg
Carbohydrate	1 g	Potassium	105 mg
Fat	Trace g	Sodium	3 mg
Saturated Fatty Acids	— g	Vitamin A	Trace I.U.
Oleic Acid	— g	Vitamin B_1	0.01 mg
Linoleic Acid	— g	Vitamin B_2	0.01 mg
Iron	0.4 mg	Niacin	0.10 mg
Calcium	12 mg	Vitamin C	10 mg
		Calories	5

soybeans

COMPOSITION AND NUTRIENT VALUE PER Cup (200 g)

Protein	22 g	Phosphorous	360 mg
Carbohydrate	20 g	Potassium	1080 mg
Fat	11 g	Sodium	4 mg
Saturated Fatty Acids	— g	Vitamin A	60 I.U.
Oleic Acid	— g	Vitamin B_1	0.4 mg
Linoleic Acid	7 g	Vitamin B_2	0.1 mg
Iron	5.4 g	Niacin	1.2 mg
Calcium	150 mg	Vitamin C	0 mg
		Calories	260

spinach

COMPOSITION AND NUTRIENT VALUE PER Cup (180 g), cooked

Protein	5 g	Phosphorous	N.D. mg
Carbohydrate	6 g	Potassium	N.D. mg
Fat	1 g	Sodium	N.D. mg
Saturated Fatty Acids	— g	Vitamin A	14,580 I.U.
Oleic Acid	— g	Vitamin B_1	0.13 mg

Linoleic Acid	— g	Vitamin B_2	0.25 mg
Iron	4 mg	Niacin	1 mg
Calcium	167 mg	Vitamin C	50 mg
		Calories	40

squash, summer

COMPOSITION AND NUTRIENT VALUE PER Cup (210 g), cooked

Protein	2 g	Phosphorous	32 mg
Carbohydrate	7 g	Potassium	480 mg
Fat	Trace g	Sodium	8 mg
Saturated Fatty Acids	— g	Vitamin A	820 I.U.
Oleic Acid	— g	Vitamin B_1	0.10 mg
Linoleic Acid	— g	Vitamin B_2	0.16 mg
Iron	0.8 mg	Niacin	1.60 mg
Calcium	52 mg	Vitamin C	21 mg
		Calories	30

squash, winter

COMPOSITION AND NUTRIENT VALUE PER Cup (205 g), cooked

Protein	4 g	Phosphorous	49 mg
Carbohydrate	32 g	Potassium	510 mg
Fat	1 g	Sodium	2 mg
Saturated Fatty Acids	— g	Vitamin A	8610 I.U.
Oleic Acid	— g	Vitamin B_1	0.10 mg
Linoleic Acid	— g	Vitamin B_2	0.27 mg
Iron	1.6 mg	Niacin	1.40 mg
Calcium	57 mg	Vitamin C	27 mg
		Calories	130

sweet potatoes

COMPOSITION AND NUTRIENT VALUE PER 1, medium (110 g), baked

Protein	2 g	Phosphorous	58 mg
Carbohydrate	36 g	Potassium	300 mg
Fat	1 g	Sodium	12 mg
Saturated Fatty Acids	— g	Vitamin A	8910 I.U.
Oleic Acid	— g	Vitamin B_1	0.10 mg
Linoleic Acid	— g	Vitamin B_2	0.07 mg
Iron	1 mg	Niacin	0.70 mg
Calcium	44 mg	Vitamin C	24 mg
		Calories	155

sweet potatoes, candied

COMPOSITION AND NUTRIENT VALUE PER 1, medium (175 g)

Protein	2 g	Phosphorous	70 mg
Carbohydrate	60 g	Potassium	360 mg
Fat	6 g	Sodium	18 mg
Saturated Fatty Acids	2 g	Vitamin A	11,030 I.U.
Oleic Acid	3 g	Vitamin B_1	0.10 mg
Linoleic Acid	1 g	Vitamin B_2	0.08 mg
Iron	1.6 mg	Niacin	0.80 mg
Calcium	45 mg	Vitamin C	17 mg
		Calories	295

tomato

COMPOSITION AND NUTRIENT VALUE PER 1, raw (200 g)

Protein	2 g	Phosphorous	53 mg
Carbohydrate	9 g	Potassium	480 mg
Fat	Trace g	Sodium	7 mg
Saturated Fatty Acids	— g	Vitamin A	1640 I.U.
Oleic Acid	— g	Vitamin B_1	0.11 mg
Linoleic Acid	— g	Vitamin B_2	0.07 mg
Iron	0.9 mg	Niacin	1.30 mg
Calcium	24 mg	Vitamin C	42 mg
		Calories	40

tomato, canned

COMPOSITION AND NUTRIENT VALUE PER Cup (241 g)

Protein	2 g	Phosphorous	44 mg
Carbohydrate	10 g	Potassium	552 mg
Fat	1 g	Sodium	18 mg
Saturated Fatty Acids	— g	Vitamin A	2170 I.U.
Oleic Acid	— g	Vitamin B$_1$	0.12 mg
Linoleic Acid	— g	Vitamin B$_2$	0.07 mg
Iron	1.2 mg	Niacin	1.7 mg
Calcium	14 mg	Vitamin C	41 mg
		Calories	50

turnip greens

COMPOSITION AND NUTRIENT VALUE PER Cup (145 g), cooked

Protein	3 g	Phosphorous	75 mg
Carbohydrate	5 g	Potassium	N.D. mg
Fat	Trace g	Sodium	N.D. mg
Saturated Fatty Acids	— g	Vitamin A	8270 I.U.
Oleic Acid	— g	Vitamin B$_1$	0.15 mg
Linoleic Acid	— g	Vitamin B$_2$	0.33 mg
Iron	1.5 mg	Niacin	0.70 mg
Calcium	252 mg	Vitamin C	68 mg
		Calories	30

turnips

COMPOSITION AND NUTRIENT VALUE PER Cup (155 g), cooked

Protein	1 g	Phosphorous	51 mg
Carbohydrate	8 g	Potassium	345 mg
Fat	Trace g	Sodium	87 mg
Saturated Fatty Acids	— g	Vitamin A	Trace I.U.
Oleic Acid	— g	Vitamin B$_1$	0.06 mg

Linoleic Acid	— g	Vitamin B_2	0.08 mg
Iron	0.6 mg	Niacin	0.50 mg
Calcium	54 mg	Vitamin C	34 mg
		Calories	35

watercress

COMPOSITION AND NUTRIENT VALUE PER Cup (50 g), raw

Protein	1 g	Phosphorous	27 mg
Carbohydrate	1 g	Potassium	140 mg
Fat	Trace g	Sodium	25 mg
Saturated Fatty Acids	— g	Vitamin A	2500 I.U.
Oleic Acid	— g	Vitamin B_1	Trace mg
Linoleic Acid	— g	Vitamin B_2	1 mg
Iron	0.8 mg	Niacin	0.4 mg
Calcium	75 mg	Vitamin C	80 mg
		Calories	9

vegetable juices

All vegetable juices contain various vitamins, minerals, acids, and salts in varying amounts. They are especially rich in vitamins A and C, and potassium.

See Fruit Juices for remarks on unstrained juices or canned juice.

tomato juice

COMPOSITION AND NUTRIENT VALUE PER Cup. (243 g), canned

Protein	2 g	Phosphorous	80 mg
Carbohydrate	10 g	Potassium	540 mg
Fat	Trace g	Sodium	36 mg
Saturated Fatty Acids	— g	Vitamin A	1940 I.U.
Oleic Acid	— g	Vitamin B_1	0.12 mg
Linoleic Acid	— g	Vitamin B_2	0.07 mg
Iron	2.2 mg	Niacin	1.90 mg
Calcium	17 mg	Vitamin C	39 mg
		Calories	45

vegetable oils

In their natural, unhydrogenated, form, the principal sources of the essential fatty acids.*

corn oil

COMPOSITION AND NUTRIENT VALUE PER Tablespoon (14 g)

Protein	0 g	Phosphorous	0 mg
Carbohydrate	0 g	Potassium	0 mg
Fat	14 g	Sodium	0 mg
Saturated Fatty Acids	1 g	Vitamin A	0 I.U.
Oleic Acid	4 g	Vitamin B_1	0 mg
Linoleic Acid	7 g	Vitamin B_2	0 mg
Iron	0 mg	Niacin	0 mg
Calcium	0 mg	Vitamin C	0 mg
		Calories	125

cottonseed oil

COMPOSITION AND NUTRIENT VALUE PER Tablespoon (14 g)

Protein	0 g	Phosphorous	0 mg
Carbohydrate	0 g	Potassium	0 mg
Fat	14 g	Sodium	0 mg
Saturated Fatty Acids	4 g	Vitamin A	0 I.U.
Oleic Acid	3 g	Vitamin B_1	0 mg
Linoleic Acid	7 g	Vitamin B_2	0 mg
Iron	0 mg	Niacin	0 mg
Calcium	0 mg	Vitamin C	0 mg
		Calories	125

peanut oil

COMPOSITION AND NUTRIENT VALUE PER Tablespoon (14 g)

Protein	0 g	Phosphorous	0 mg
Carbohydrate	0 g	Potassium	0 mg
Fat	14 g	Sodium	0 mg
Saturated Fatty Acids	3 g	Vitamin A	0 I.U.
Oleic Acid	7 g	Vitamin B_1	0 mg
Linoleic Acid	4 g	Vitamin B_2	0 mg
Iron	0 mg	Niacin	0 mg
Calcium	0 mg	Vitamin C	0 mg
		Calories	125

safflower oil

COMPOSITION AND NUTRIENT VALUE PER Tablespoon (14 g)

Protein	0 g	Phosphorous	0 mg
Carbohydrate	0 g	Potassium	0 mg
Fat	14 g	Sodium	0 mg
Saturated Fatty Acids	1 g	Vitamin A	0 I.U.
Oleic Acid	2 g	Vitamin B_1	0 mg
Linoleic Acid	10 g	Vitamin B_2	0 mg
Iron	0 mg	Niacin	0 mg
Calcium	0 mg	Vitamin C	0 mg
		Calories	125

soybean oil

COMPOSITION AND NUTRIENT VALUE PER Tablespoon (14 g)

Protein	0 g	Phosphorous	0 mg
Carbohydrate	0 g	Potassium	0 mg
Fat	14 g	Sodium	0 mg
Saturated Fatty Acids	2 g	Vitamin A	0 I.U.
Oleic Acid	3 g	Vitamin B_1	0 mg
Linoleic Acid	7 g	Vitamin B_2	0 mg
Iron	0 mg	Niacin	0 mg
Calcium	0 mg	Vitamin C	0 mg
		Calories	125

vegetarianism
The theory and the practical attempt to live on foods of solely plant origin, a practice which logically excludes eating any foodstuff of animal origin. Strict vegetarians are few in number, most supplement their diets with dairy products (milk, eggs, cheese, yogurt etc.) Since the most effective proteins, the complete proteins, are primarily found in animal foods, most nutritionists feel that if one must be a vegetarian, it is best to be one who eats dairy products. Though it is possible to obtain a balanced diet while strictly abstaining from all foods of animal origin, it is very difficult.

viosterol
Artificial Vitamin D, produced by the irradiation of ergosterol, a sterol isolated from yeast. When ergosterol is heated with ultraviolet light, it is converted to calciferol (Vitamin D_2).

visual purple
The pigment composed of Vitamin A and protein located in the retina of the eye.
  See Night Blindness; Vitamin A

vitamins, general
A group of organic substances occurring naturally in animals and plants in small quantities and which are essential to the normal growth and functioning of the body. Each vitamin serves a distinct function in the body and thus cannot be substituted for by another vitamin, and all vitamins require the presence of minerals before they can be effectively utilized in the body. Fat-soluble vitamins* can be stored in the body for future use. Water-soluble vitamins cannot be stored and must be replaced on a daily basis. Deficiencies in any of the vitamins may cause or aggravate a wide variety of problems and diseases. Recommended daily allowances (RDA) have been established for several vitamins, but many nutritionists believe the

amounts recommended are too low to maintain the body in good health. Almost all nutritionists agree that those vitamins for which recommended daily allowances have not been established are equally essential to good health.

In August 1973 the Food and Drug Administration issued a great number of new regulations pertaining to the labeling, sales, and promotion of vitamins (and minerals), whether natural or synthetic. All are affected, but especially vitamins A and D. As of October 1, 1973 any Vitamin A preparation containing more than 10,000 I.U. must henceforth be labeled as a drug and be dispensed by prescription. The same applies to any Vitamin D preparation containing more than 400 I.U.

The new regulations pertaining to other vitamins (and minerals) are less strict and do not go into effect until the end of 1974. At that time the other vitamin and mineral preparations will be classified as drugs if they contain more than 150 per cent of the recommended daily allowance. And if they are so classified they will still be sold over the counter and not by prescription as in the cases of Vitamins A and D.

Just what these new regulations will accomplish is difficult to see. Anyone still wanting more than 10,000 I.U. of A and 400 I.U. of D can still take these amounts without prescription—the only restriction is that he won't be able to take these amounts in one pill or capsule.

See Synthetic Vitamins

Vitamin A

A fat-soluble vitamin which does not occur in nature by itself but which is formed from yellow substances (carotenes) occurring in plants, by the walls of the intestines and in the liver and kidneys. The liver is the main storage depot for Vitamin A; thus it is found in such high concentration in fish-liver oils.

Vitamin A has several known functions in the human body: it is essential for maintaining the mucous membranes of the mouth, nose, throat, lungs, ears and other body organs in healthy condition; it is necessary for healthy skin, bones and teeth and normal growth; it plays a part in reproduction and lactation; and it is indispensable for maintaining good vision, especially in dim light. Vitamin A combines with protein to form a pigment in the retina of the eye called visual purple. Light—whether artificial light or sunlight—reaching the eyes breaks down part of this pigment, setting up nerve impulses which inform the brain of what is seen. The formation and breakdown of visual purple is a continuous cycle whose efficiency is dependent on an adequate supply of Vitamin A.

Day and night vision both require Vitamin A, but night vision is entirely dependent on the visual pigment and thus on Vitamin A. Consequently, the earliest sign of even a mild deficiency is difficulty in seeing at night. Persons working in bright light or dim light require more Vitamin A than those workng in moderate light. Bright light destroys Vitamin A quickly and vision in dim light is entirely dependent on it.

SOURCES

Vitamin A itself is found only in animal foods; the best sources are liver and fish liver oils (cod or halibut). Butter, cheese, eggs, and milk are good sources.

Good sources of carotene—from which the body can make Vitamin A—are the green leafy vegetables, carrots, sweet potatoes, squash, tomatoes, and the yellow fruits. Corn is the only common cereal which contains carotene.

The amount of carotene, however, in any given plant food varies with the soil and climate conditions. For example, winter butter (produced when cows are eating dry feed) averages 2,000 I.U. per pound whereas summer butter (produced when they are eating fresh grasses) averages 12,000 I.U.'s per pound. Vegetables which have lost their color or have never been green may entirely lack carotene. Some carrots, for example, contain no carotene at all.

Cooking destroys Vitamin A; thus overcooking should be avoided.

REQUIREMENTS

The amount of Vitamin A needed by healthy persons varies. One important factor is body weight: the greater the weight the more Vitamin A required. Consequently, the recommended dietary allowance (RDA) for infants up to six months is 1400 I.U.; for children 6 months to three years, 2,000 I.U.; from four to six, 2,500 I.U.; from seven to ten, 3,300 I.U.; adolescents and adults, 4 to 5,000 I.U.; pregnant women, 5,000 I.U.; and lactating women, 6,000 I.U. (A 4-ounce serving of broiled calf's liver contains approximately 37,000 I.U.; 1 medium-sized egg, 562 I.U.; one cup of cooked carrots, 16,800 I.U.).

Many researchers and nutritionists recommend a daily intake of 20,000 I.U. They base this recommendation on at least three facts: (1) the need for Vitamin A varies widely among individuals; (2) excess Vitamin A is stored in the liver and can be used to advantage during times when intake is low; and (3) only massive doses taken over a period of time have proved toxic. (Massive doses are those somewhere in the range of 100,000 to 500,000 I.U.'s per day taken over a period of several months.)

DEFICIENCY

The earliest sign of vitamin A deficiency is usually night blindness. (A person who, when driving a car at night finds it difficult to see the road clearly after being "blinded" by oncoming lights, is suffering from a degree of night blindness.)

Mild deficiencies result in roughness and dryness of the skin, especially the elbows, knees, and buttocks. The hair becomes dry and the fingernails may become ridged. A degree of night blindness may appear.

More severe deficiencies lead to inflamed eyelids, eyestrain, frequently occurring sties, the drying up of the various mucous membranes of the throat, ears, and lungs and disturbances in digestion. Very severe deficiencies may lead to growth retardation in children and eye diseases (xerophthalmia and keratomalacia) severe enough to result in blindness. Deficiencies are caused by factors other than inadequate intake of Vitamin A or carotene. Vitamin

A is quickly destroyed unless protected by Vitamin E, and thus those with inadequate dietary Vitamin E usually suffer from Vitamin A deficiency as well. Also, those whose diets are low in fat frequently are deficient in Vitamin A because carotene is poorly utilized if there is an inadequacy of fat. And since bile salts are required for the absorption of both Vitamin A and carotene, persons suffering from obstructions of the bile ducts are very likely to be deficient in Vitamin A.

EXCESS AND TOXICITY

Toxic reactions with symptoms such as lethargy, abdominal pain, excessive sweating, brittle nails, painful joints, edema, and tenderness and swelling over the long bones and bone damage have occurred when massive doses have been taken over a long period of time.

Adults who have developed Vitamin A toxicity have usually taken 100,000 to 500,000 I.U.'s per day over a several month period. The treatment for toxic reactions is primarily the cutting off of any further intake of Vitamin A.

See Fats; RDA chart in front of book; Vitamin E

vitamin b complex

A group of fifteen or more water-soluble vitamins which, with the exception of B_{12}, occur together in the same sources in varying proportions. For example, in wheat germ, liver, and brewer's yeast. (Vitamin B_{12} occurs only in animal foods, of which liver is the richest source.) They are all coenzymes and were discovered by separation from what was once simply known as Vitamin B. Three of the B vitamins—choline, inositol, and para-aminobenzoic acid (PABA)—are not considered vitamins by some researchers.

Each of the B vitamins appears to have a separate function in the body but all are interdependent: a deficiency in any one leads to a deficiency in the others, and an excessive intake of any one increases the need for the others. None is stored in the body, and all must be replenished on a daily basis.

The role of the B vitamins in maintaining health is wide and varied. They are essential to the functioning of the digestive and nervous systems, to the proper functioning of the heart and all other muscles, and to the production of energy. And at least three of them—choline, inositol, and B_6—help maintain the blood cholesterol at normal levels.

Since the B vitamins seem equally needed by all the cells in the body, deficiencies can produce damage well before any notice is taken of it. Instead of a deficiency showing up markedly in one area of the body, the entire body mechanism operates below par and the entire body suffers a degenerative process. Very severe B vitamin deficiencies result in beriberi and pellagra, but the milder deficiencies, usually occurring in America, produce no such dramatic evidence. Though mild in comparison to deficiencies which result in beriberi and pellagra, the Vitamin B deficiencies common in America are very widespread. The ordinary diet offers a very small supply of the B vitamins, chiefly because the B-vitamin-rich unrefined grains which once were used for all our breads, cereals, and other foods made from grains have been supplanted by refined grains which almost entirely lack these vitamins. At the present time the only reliable sources of the B vitamins are wheat germ, brewer's yeast, liver, and rice polish. Moreover, as a nation, we consume great quantities of refined sugar and sugar, which while augmenting the need for certain B vitamins at the same time reduces appetite and consequently makes it even less likely that we will eat the necessary quantities of foods containing the B vitamins.

See The individual B vitamins: B_1, B_2, B_6, B_{12}, Biotin, Choline, Folic Acid, Inositol, Niacin, Para-aminobenzoic Acid, Pantothenic Acid

vitamin B_1 (thiamine)

A water-soluble vitamin which has the distinction of being the first vitamin discovered. (From the observations of a Dutch physician, Dr. Eijkman, who in 1897 discovered that hens who had been fed on leftover polished rice and who developed a disease similar to beriberi recovered when fed unpolished rice.)

Though the symptoms of thiamine deficiency are varied and numerous, thiamine seems to have but one function: as a coenzyme it helps to change glucose into energy or fat. From this function flows its importance in the distribution of oxygen in the body, in the proper functioning of the digestive system, in maintaining proper functioning of the nervous system, and in maintaining a balanced personality and a soundly functioning heart.

When thiamine is undersupplied the production of energy is slowed down. Pyruvic and lactic acids are formed during the breakdown of sugar. Thiamine, as a coenzyme, further breaks down the pyruvic acid into carbon dioxide and water, and converts the lactic acid into glycogen. If the body is deficient in thiamine these transformations are not completed; the acids remain in the tissues as irritants until excreted in the urine. More importantly, the production of energy is adversely affected, coming as it does from only partially burned sugar and fat. The result is fatigue.

This inefficient production of energy is a direct cause of poor digestion and poor elimination. The muscles of the stomach and intestinal walls, for example, lack the energy to contract properly and thus food cannot be properly mixed with the digestive juices and waste material remains in the large bowel too long. The result is gas pains, flatulence, and constipation.

The nerves derive their energy from sugar exclusively and without adequate thiamine their functions are impaired and the result is varying forms of neuritis.

Personality change, mental depression, forgetfulness, and the like occur with thiamine deficiencies for two reasons: the brain cells get their energy exclusively from sugar and the inability to efficiently convert sugar to energy affects them adversely; and the pyruvic and lactic acids which accumulate in the brain cells are toxic.

The heart, of course, is a muscle which must work continually. The inefficient production of energy resulting from thiamine deficiency does it no good, and the accumulation of pyruvic and lactic acids irritates it and is thought to cause both the increased pulse rate and enlarged heart which are symptoms of thiamine deficiency.

SOURCES

The best sources are brewer's yeast, wheat germ, and rice polish. Good sources are whole grains and whole grain products, pork, milk, nuts, liver, peas, lentils, soybeans, and dried beans. Useful quantities are contained in meat, fish, and green vegetables. Thiamine is highly soluble in water and is easily leached out of foods when they are washed or boiled. It also tends to be destroyed at temperatures above 100°C. Frying in a hot pan or cooking too long under pressure results in temperatures above this and thus should be avoided.

REQUIREMENTS

The recommended dietary allowance (RDA) is 0.4 milligrams per thousand calories for all ages with an additional 0.2 milligrams per day after the third month of pregnancy, and 0.4 milligrams daily during lactation.

For elderly persons, and those under stress or who are very active, most nutritionists recommend considerably higher doses. Ten milligrams per day has been suggested for these cases. (One-quarter cup of brewer's yeast contains 5.2 milligrams, 4 ounces of calf's liver, 0.27 milligrams).

DEFICIENCIES

The symptoms of deficiency range from mild to severe: indigestion, constipation, nervousness, irritability, fatigue, neuritis, mental depression, enlarged heart, and beriberi. Various degrees of thiamine deficiency, especially the milder forms, are common in the United States. The more severe forms of deficiency are common among alcoholics, of whom there are many millions.

TOXICITY

Excessive thiamine is excreted in the urine and no known toxicity exists.

See Beriberi; RDA chart in front of book.

vitamin B$_2$ (riboflavin)

A water-soluble vitamin which plays an important role in both protein and energy metabolism, and which is required for tissue oxidation and respiration. In combination with Vitamin A it is important in promoting good vision and healthy skin.

SOURCES

The richest sources are liver, brewer's yeast, and milk. Whole grains and green leafy vegetables (if cooked and the water is not discarded) are good sources. Fish and eggs also contain worthwhile quantities.

Some riboflavin is lost in cooking and in exposure to sunlight.

REQUIREMENTS

The recommended dietary allowance (RDA) ranges from 0.4 milligrams per day for infants, up to 1.8 milligrams per day for adolescents. 1.4 milligrams per day for women, and 1.8 milligrams per day for men. For pregnant women the RDA is 1.8 milligrams.

Many nutritionists find these recommendations far too low for optimum health and suggest 5 milligrams per day for adolescents and adults. (One quart of whole milk contains 1.64 milligrams and 4 ounces of calf's liver 4.73 milligrams.)

DEFICIENCIES

Riboflavin deficiency impairs cell oxidation and results in a set of symptoms called ariboflavinosis. Specifically, these are lesions affecting the mouth, lips, eyes, skin, and genitalia. These lesions appear as fissures or cracks radiating from the corners of the mouth onto the skin. At times they extend into the mucous membrane inside the mouth. They also appear as extended cracks on the upper and lower lips. In men, the scrotum becomes intensely itchy and scaly. And in women vulval dermatitis is a common riboflavin deficiency.

The first sign of deficiency may be a burning feeling in

the eyes. They may feel gritty, and they become bloodshot and water readily. Cataracts occur in severe deficiencies.

TOXICITY
Excess riboflavin is excreted in the urine. No known toxicity occurs.

See RDA chart in front of book.

vitamin B₃ through B₅

These designations are no longer used to identify members of the Vitamin B complex.

vitamin B₆ (pyridoxine)

A water-soluble vitamin which functions as a coenzyme on the metabolism of amino acids.* It aids in blood building and the utilization of fats, and it is of great importance to the normal functioning of the brain, nerves, and muscles.

Pyridoxine has been successfully used to ameliorate the symptoms of epilepsy and cerebral palsy, and to reduce and sometimes eliminate various unpleasant side-effects of pregnancy such as nausea, headache, and the like. It has also been used to relieve certain types of anemia.

SOURCES
The richest sources are brewer's yeast, wheat bran, wheat germ, liver, kidney, heart, and blackstrap molasses. Milk, eggs, cabbage, and beets contain useful amounts.

Vitamin B₆ resists heat well but canning, exposure to light, and long storage destroy significant amounts of it. Also, roasting or stewing meat destroys up to 50 per cent of the B₆ content.

REQUIREMENTS
The recommended dietary allowance (RDA) is 0.3 to 0.4 milligrams per day for infants; 0.6 to 1.2 for children; 1.6 to 2.0 for adolescents; 2.0 for adults; and 2.5 during pregnancy and lactation. Many nutritionists regard these recommendations as far too low and advise 5 to 10 milligrams per day for adults. According to some nutritionists, Vita-

min B_6 and magnesium are interdependent and thus both must be supplied in adequate amounts at the same time if either is to perform its functions.

DEFICIENCY

Experimentally induced B_6 deficiency has led to loss of weight and appetite, extreme nervousness, general weakness, lethargy, and other signs usually associated with deficiencies of other B vitamins. These include sore lips, mouth and tongue, peripheral neuritis, and skin disorders reminiscent of pellagra.

Vitamin B_6 deficiency in infants leads to hyperirritability, convulsions similar to those of epilepsy, and anemia.

Some people have a genetic need for a high intake of B_6. The signs (convulsions) are seen in the first week of life. Unless treated with B_6 immediately the child may suffer mental retardation.

TOXICITY

Men receiving 300 milligrams per day have shown toxic effects. This is a dose far in excess of any recommended B_6 therapy (usually no more than 100 milligrams per day) and far in excess of any amount one can obtain from dietary sources.

See Magnesium; RDA chart in front of book.

vitamins B_7 through B_9

Designations given in error to substances which never existed. The error apparently arose because a researcher thought that nine separately named factors had been identified in the B complex when in fact they had been numbered only through B_6.

vitamins B_{10} and B_{11}

Names once given to substances which were later shown to be a mixture of Vitamin B_{12} and folic acid.

vitamin B_{12} (cyanocobalamin)

The only vitamin containing a mineral (cobalt). It is soluble in water and resistant to heat, but is readily destroyed by sunlight, strong acids, and alkalis. It is essential for the functioning of all cells, but especially for the cells of the bone marrow, the central nervous system, and the intestinal tract. It is thought to be involved in the metabolism of protein, carbohydrates, and fats. It is of great importance in the metabolic processes involving nucleic and folic acid. B_{12} is stored in the liver, and to a lesser extent in the kidneys.

SOURCES
Liver is the richest source, closely followed by kidney. Milk, eggs, cheese and most meats are good sources.

REQUIREMENTS
The recommended daily allowance (RDA) is 3 micrograms (3/1,000,000 of a gram) for adults, and 4 during pregnancy.

Persons with pernicious anemia or megaloblastic anemia caused by B_{12} deficiency are usually cured by daily doses of five-tenths to two micrograms but 2 to 4 micrograms are needed to replenish the liver stores.

DEFICIENCY
The most serious manifestation of B_{12} deficiency is pernicious anemia, so called because it once was invariably fatal. Pernicious anemia leads to a general muscular weakness and signs of deterioration of the central nervous system. Skin pallor, heart palpitations, and eventually more severe heart disturbances are also symptoms, as are a sore, red, inflamed-looking tongue which eventually becomes smooth and glazed.

The disease is not considered to be caused by a simple dietary deficiency of B_{12}, but by either a genetic defect which impairs the secretion of the intrinsic factor* by the stomach, or by a simultaneous deficiency of folic acid, another member of the B complex. This latter view is given substantiation by the fact that strict vegetarians—those who consume only vegetable products and who exclude even all dairy products from their diets—often develop most of the signs of pernicious anemia but only infrequently develop the disease itself. Now strict vegetarians receive adequate supplies of folic acid from their diets but no B_{12}.

TOXICITY

B_{12} has not been shown to be toxic to man even when given in amounts far larger than those recommended for therapeutic purposes.

See RDA chart in front of book.

biotin

Also called Vitamin H. A colorless crystalline vitamin, usually considered a member of the B vitamin complex. It plays an essential role in the metabolism of proteins, carbohydrates, and fats.

SOURCES

Biotin is present in many foods and in relatively large quantities in yeast, egg yolk, milk, and liver. It is also synthesized in sufficient quantity in the human intestinal tract to meet normal requirements.

REQUIREMENTS

Relatively little work has been done on biotin, probably because it is synthesized in the intestinal tract in amounts considered sufficient for human needs. The 150 to 300 micrograms estimated daily need is provided by most diets.

DEFICIENCIES

They apparently occur only in two situations:

(1) In infants whose intestinal tracts have been deprived of biotin synthesizing bacteria by an excessive use of sulfa drugs or antibiotics.

(2) In persons whose diets are high in raw eggs. Raw egg whites contain avidin, a substance which combines with biotin, rendering it unavailable to the body.

The first signs of biotin deficiency are dry, peeling skin and mental depression. Experimental subjects in whom biotin deficiencies have been induced developed symptoms of mental depression, dry peeling skin, muscle pain, extreme fatigue, nausea, and distress around the heart. The mental depression was strong enough to be termed "panic." All symptoms disappeared a few days after biotin was administered.

TOXICITY
There is no known toxicity. Very large doses given to experimental animals have not produced any signs of toxicity. *See* Egg-white Injury

choline
It is part of the structure of lecithin* and as such very important in the metabolism of fat, and especially in dissolving cholesterol. Because it is an essential dietary factor it is classed as a vitamin, and usually as one of the B complex.

SOURCES
The richest sources of choline are brains, liver, kidney, wheat germ, brewer's yeast, and egg yolk.

REQUIREMENTS
The need for choline in the human diet has been recognized but no daily requirements have been established. The usual assumption is that choline deficiencies do not exist in humans because choline can be manufactured in the body from methionine, an amino acid which is part of all complete proteins. But this happens only if excess methionine is available, as well as Vitamin B_{12} and folic acid. And of course any or all of these vitamins may not be present in amounts adequate for the production of choline.

DEFICIENCIES
Deficiencies lead to fatty infiltration of the liver, impaired kidney functions, and high cholesterol counts. In laboratory animals induced choline deficiencies have resulted in severe kidney damage which frequently resulted in death, and abnormally high cholesterol counts and abnormally high blood pressure.

folic acid (Folacin)

A water-soluble vitamin of the B complex, folic acid is necessary for the division of body cells and for the production of RNA and DNA, the substances which carry hereditary patterns. As a coenzyme it is required for the utilization of sugar and amino acids. Folic acid is stored primarily in the liver.

SOURCES

Liver, kidney, green vegetables, torula yeast, and nuts are rich sources. Small amounts are present in meats, whole grain cereals, fruits and some roots.

Cooking causes considerable loss if the cooking water is thrown out and storage also causes a considerable loss. Drugs such as phenobarbital and Dilantin destroy folic acid quickly.

REQUIREMENTS

The recommended daily allowance (RDA) is 0.4 milligrams for adults, with an additional 0.4 milligrams during pregnancy. Many nutritionists, however, feel the amount should be as high as 5 milligrams per day.

DEFICIENCY

Severe folic acid deficiency results in macrocytic (large-cell) anemia which is characterized by stomatitis, glossitis, diarrhea, and changes in the intestines. (*See* Deficiency subhead under Vitamin B_{12} for folic acid's relation to pernicious anemia.) Less severe deficiencies result in fatigue, dizziness, shortness of breath, and a grayish-brown skin pigmentation. Pregnant women especially show this latter sign and folic acid deficiencies are especially common during pregnancy. They are also especially dangerous at this time and can lead to hemorrhaging, miscarriage, premature birth, hard labor, and a high infant mortality rate. The grayish-brown pigmentation of the skin, also known as the "pregnancy cap" is also frequently seen on women who use oral contraceptives, which increase the need for folic acid. Therapeutic doses of 5 milligrams per day are usually sufficient to remove all signs of the "pregnancy cap."

TOXICITY

Folic acid is not toxic to normal humans even in doses far larger than those used in therapy. Nevertheless, the FDA has made it illegal to sell any vitamin preparation containing more than 0.1 milligram of folic acid because greater doses may mask the neurologic signs of pernicious anemia.

See RDA chart in front of book.

inositol

It is part of the structure of lecithin,* along with choline, and as such is of importance in the metabolism of fat and especially in the dissolving of cholesterol. As an essential dietary factor it is classed as a vitamin, and usually as one of the B complex.

Though much more inositol is found in the human body than any other vitamin except niacin, the need for it in human nutrition is not precisely known, nor of course have any requirements been established.

Induced inositol deficiencies in laboratory animals result in loss of hair, eczema, constipation and abnormalities of the eyes.

The richest sources of inositol are liver, brewer's yeast, wheat germ, whole grains, oatmeal, corn, and unrefined molasses.

niacin (nicotinic acid)

A water-soluble vitamin of the B complex which functions as a coenzyme in the oxidation of carbohydrates, niacin is important in tissue respiration; and is needed for proper brain functions, the nervous system, and for a healthy skin.

It has been established that very large oral doses of niacin will lower blood cholesterol.

SOURCES

The richest sources are brewer's yeast, liver, kidney, and wheat germ. Good sources are whole grains, fish, eggs, lean meat, and nuts. Beans, peas, and other legumes contain useful amounts.

(The human body is able to convert the amino acid tryptophane into niacin, and it is thought that 60 milligrams of dietary tryptophane is the equivalent of 1 milligram of niacin. Since tryptophane is a protein, persons with diets rich in proteins receive a substantial contribution to their niacin needs. Poor people in the United States, however, usually have diets low in protein.)

Niacin resists heat well, but is leached out into cooking water.

REQUIREMENTS

The recommended dietary allowance (RDA) is 5 to 8 milligrams per day for infants; 9 to 16 milligrams for children; 18 to 20 milligrams for adolescents; 18 milligrams for adult males; 13 milligrams for females, with an extra 2 milligrams for the last six months of pregnancy, and an extra 4 milligrams during lactation. (These recommendations are based on the need for 6.6 milligrams per 1000 calories, and not less than 13 milligrams if the calorie intake is between 1000-2000.)

Most nutritionists consider the RDA allowances too low and recommend that adolescents and adults have 40 to 100 milligrams per day. (1/2 lb. of lean steak contains 8.4 milligrams; 4 ounces of calf's liver 19 milligrams; and 1/4 cup of brewer's yeast 12.9 milligrams.)

DEFICIENCY

Niacin deficiency leads to pellagra,* which results from severe deficiency of the vitamin. The early symptoms of mild and moderate deficiencies are the same as the early symptoms of pellagra: suspicion, hostility, irritability, insomnia, loss of memory, and anxiety; abdominal pain, a burning sensation in the tongue; and dry and scaly patches where the skin is exposed to sunlight. As the deficiency becomes more severe, the nervous system symptoms progress to insanity; the digestive symptoms to diarrhea; the tongue becomes red and raw-looking, and the skin patches may become cracked and fissured.

TOXICITY

The margin is so wide between therapeutic doses (e.g., 100 milligrams, three times a day) and toxic doses that niacin is considered nontoxic.

See Pellagra; RDA chart in front of book.

pantothenic acid

A member of the B complex of vitamins, it is a part of coenzyme A and is necessary for the release of energy from sugar and fat. PABA* and choline* cannot be utilized without it, and it is vital to the proper functioning of the adrenal glands.

SOURCES

Liver, kidney, heart, wheat germ and bran, whole grains and whole grain products, green vegetables, and brewer's yeast are good sources. However, pantothenic acid is unstable when exposed to heat, and is easily destroyed in canning or overcooking.

REQUIREMENTS

No recommended daily allowance (RDA) has been established. The more conservative nutritionists recommend 10 milligrams per day, while others feel that at least 50 milligrams per day is needed. The more stress one is under, the greater appears to be the need for pantothenic acid.

DEFICIENCY

Volunteers in whom pantothenic acid deficiencies were induced developed fatigue, abdominal pains, cramps, and nausea, irritability, depression, constant colds, and paresthesia of the hands and feet. As the pantothenic acid-deficient diet continued, the symptoms got worse and after six weeks all the volunteers became very ill. Deficiencies have also been associated with hypoglycemia.*

TOXICITY

There is no known toxicity in man.

para-aminobenzoic acid (PABA)

PABA is part of the molecule of folic acid and an essential factor in the growth of microorganisms. It is therefore classed as a vitamin. And since it is thought that one of its functions is to promote the formation of folic acid, it is considered part of the B complex.

Because black-haired animals lacking it became gray, and when given sufficient doses regained their hair color in 70 per cent of the cases, PABA was widely publicized as the anti-gray-hair factor. Further research has indicated that premature gray hair results from multiple vitamin deficiencies. At least four B vitamins are implicated: PABA, biotin, folic acid, and pantothenic acid.

PABA renders sulfa drugs ineffective and for this reason the FDA does not permit any vitamin supplements which contain more than 30 milligrams of PABA to be sold without prescription. This is somewhat odd since sulfa drugs have largely been replaced by other antibacterial drugs, because they produce severe PABA deficiency symptoms—extreme fatigue, anemia, and eczema. (PABA and sulfanilamide are chemically very similar, and sulfanilamide is effective because it takes the place of PABA in the bodies of bacteria.)

PABA deficiencies are thought to cause gray hair, eczema, and anemia but the need for it in human nutrition has not been established. Consequently, there are no set requirements.

Foods such as liver, kidney, whole grains, and brewer's yeast, which are rich in the other vitamins of the B complex, also provide good amounts of PABA.

TOXICITY

There has been no indication that it is toxic, even when given in huge (up to 48,000 milligrams) therapeutic doses.

bioflavonoids

Once called Vitamin P, they are a group of plant flavonoid substances that affect the strength of the walls of the blood capillaries. They are widely distributed in nature as pigments in fruits and vegetables, and flowers and barks.

Bioflavonoids reduce the need for Vitamin C and make it more effective. Thus they strengthen the capillary walls and thereby protect the body against infections. Bioflavonoids given to athletes have helped to speed the healing of muscle strains, joint injuries, and skin abrasions.

Some researchers believe their effect is pharmacological, and that they are not dietary essentials. Perhaps a greater number disagree with this view.

SOURCES
The richest sources are the pulp, especially the white of the rind of citrus fruits; black and red currants, rose hips, asparagus, and apricots are good sources. The bioflavonoids are destroyed when boiled or when exposed to air.

REQUIREMENTS
The need for bioflavonoids in the human diet has not been established and therefore there are no official requirements. Most nutritionists think they are needed on a daily basis and recommend the daily consumption of some raw fruits or vegetables to obtain them.

vitamin C (ascorbic acid)
A water-soluble vitamin which has many functions in the human body. It plays an important role in the formation of collagen, a stiff jellylike substance which as a connective tissue holds together the cells of the body; it is important to the development of healthy bones and teeth; it functions in the formation and maturation of red blood cells; it promotes resistance to infection; and aids the rapid healing of wounds and broken bones.

Vitamin C is not stored in the body. When the cells become saturated with it, the excess is excreted through the urine. Almost all drugs seem to destroy Vitamin C and people who smoke, drink, or resort to frequent ingestions of aspirin need much more Vitamin C than those who do not. Some researchers regard Vitamin C as their antibiotic of choice and claim that it is helpful in combating any kind of infectious disease, from the common cold to meningitis. Many papers have been published on these claims and to some degree they seem justified. At the very least Vitamin C certainly alleviates many of the symptoms common to a wide variety of infections: high fevers, loss of appetite, fatigue, and the like. On the other hand, a good many researchers flatly state that the therapeutic value of Vitamin C is greatly overrated—especially in respect to the claim that sufficiently high doses act as a preventative to the common cold. They say that controlled tests show that Vitamin C has no benefit in this regard. (Our own, thoroughly unscientific experience with Vitamin C and the common cold is that it doesn't seem to help much once one has a cold, but that our incidence of colds dropped dramatically after we began taking 500 milligrams of Vitamin C per day.)

SOURCES

All fresh, growing foods contain Vitamin C. The richest souces are the citrus fruits, guavas, ripe bell peppers, and rose hips. Tomato juice, fresh strawberries, and cabbage are fair sources. Vitamin C is sensitive to heat and air. Thus, for example, cut fruits quickly lose large amounts of their Vitamin C, as do cooked vegetables. And since it is water-soluble, the overwashing of salad stuffs and fruits leaches away a goodly portion of the vitamin. Therefore uncooked vegetables and raw fruits should be part of the diet.

REQUIREMENTS

The recommended daily allowance (RDA) is 45 milligrams per day for adolescents and adults, with an additional 15 milligrams per day during pregnancy and 35 milligrams during lactation; and from 35 to 40 milligrams per day for infants and children. Many nutritionists recommend far larger daily intakes, ranging from 200 milligrams per day to 500 milligrams per day for adults. (A glass of fresh orange juice contains approximately 130 milligrams per 8 ounces; a typical serving of tomatoes or salad greens, 30 to 60 milligrams.)

DEFICIENCY

Severe Vitamin C deficiency results in scurvy,* a disease now rare since fresh fruits and vegetables are widely available. Mild deficiency results in bleeding of the gums, easy bruising, slow healing of wounds, loss of appetite, small red spots on the skin caused by the bleeding of the small blood vessels, muscular weakness; and susceptibility to infections.

TOXICITY

Extremely high doses have produced no toxic effects. After the body is saturated with the vitamin the excess is secreted via the urine. (In some persons, high doses of Vitamin C act as a diuretic.) Excessive use of Vitamin C has been associated in some persons with kidney stones.

vitamin D

A fat-soluble vitamin essential to the absorption, retention, and proper utilization of calcium. It is universally agreed that Vitamin D is vital to the health of growing children, who develop rickets if deficient in it, but there is disagreement on the adult need for it. Some researchers believe that the adult need is so low that casual exposure to sunlight will give sufficient amounts. Most, however, take heed of the fact that adults deficient in Vitamin D develop osteomalacia,* the adult equivalent of rickets, and infer from this that adults do indeed have a need for substantial amounts of Vitamin D.

SOURCES

Vitamin D occurs naturally only in the fat of some animal foods. Fish-liver oils and milk fortified with Vitamin D are the richest sources. Eggs, milk, cheese, and butter provide small quantities, but usually too small to be of much use. Sunlight is another source. Vitamin D is formed by the ultraviolet rays of the sun in the oils on the skin, which are then absorbed back into the skin. In winter, however, these rays do not penetrate the atmosphere. Moreover, if one bathes before going into the sunshine, the oils are removed and no Vitamin D is formed; and if one bathes immediately after, the oils are removed before the vitamin can be absorbed into the body. In short, sunshine is no reliable source of Vitamin D in our bathing civilization.

REQUIREMENTS

The recommended dietary allowance (RDA) is 400 I.U., for everyone from infants to twenty-two-year old adults, and 400 I.U. for pregnant or lactating women. Almost all nutritionists recommend 400 I.U. for all adults as well as for all children. Some recommend as much as 4000 to 5000 I.U. daily for all adults.

DEFICIENCY

In children, it leads to rickets; in adults to osteomalacia. In general, deficiency adversely affects the entire bone structure, including the teeth. It may also lead to a weak and flabby muscle structure.

TOXICITY

Excessive quantities can be toxic, causing symptoms such as weakness, fatigue, nausea, weight loss, irritability, diarrhea, dizziness, and abdominal cramps. The calcium blood is raised and because of this calcium may be laid down in the soft tissues. The condition may lead to death.

Quantities of 2000 I.U. per day per kilogram (2.2 lbs) of body weight can be toxic to adults and children. And quantities of 25,000 I.U. per day taken over a long period of time have proven toxic to adults.

vitamin E

The term is applied to any of eight fat-soluble physiologically active tocopherols of which the alpha is both the most common and most effective. The metabolic role of Vitamin E is not yet fully understood but its sole and vital function seems to be to prevent destruction by oxygen of unsaturated fatty acids and other fatlike substances. These include Vitamin A, the essential fatty acids, and the hormones of the pituitary, adrenal, and sex glands.

Many claims have been made for the beneficial powers

of Vitamin E. Most of them have been disputed by the National Academy of Sciences.

(*See* Deficiency for a discussion.)

SOURCES

The major sources are unrefined vegetable oils (soybean, cottonseed, corn), wheat germ, whole grains, and nuts. Fresh greens, the legumes, and eggs possess small quantities. The refining processes used in the food industry destroy Vitamin E. And, with the exception of the alpha tocopherols, they are destroyed by heating, freezing, storage, and exposure to air.

REQUIREMENTS

The recommended dietary allowance (RDA) is 4 to 5 I.U. in infants; 7 to 10 I.U. for children; and 12 to 15 I.U. for adults. Many nutritionists recommended 50 to 100 I.U. daily; some from 140 to 210 I.U. daily; and at least one seems to recommend from 600 to 1600 I.U. daily.

Vitamin E requirements are increased by the intake of polyunsaturated fats, but these fats are also the best sources of Vitamin E.

DEFICIENCY

In studies done on rats with induced vitamin E deficiency, the males became sterile and the females, though they conceived normally, often suffered miscarriages. The young they did bear were premature and often suffered severe vital-organ damage. Older animals with Vitamin E deficiency developed anemia, liver and kidney damage, enlarged prostates, and muscle degeneration. The administration of Vitamin E reverses these symptoms.

It has been claimed that these same symptoms occur in humans deficient in Vitamin E, but the committee on Nutritional Misinformation of the Food and Nutrition Board, National Academy of Sciences, has said that these claims are misleading and "not backed by sound experimentation or clinical observation." The grounds for this conclusion were numerous. Among them were the following: that relevant tests on humans had been few and inconclusive; that the use of large doses of Vitamin E in treating human sterility and impotence had been unproductive; and that though severe deficiency caused muscle wasting in most animals studied, persons with muscular dystrophy have normal supplements of Vitamin E and do not benefit from increased supplements. The Committee on Nutritional Misinformation also stated that the claim that Vitamin E is useful in preventing or treating heart disease is not based on scientific fact.

On the other hand, nutritionists such as Adelle Davis cite numerous histories to the contrary of the above. Being laymen we are in no position to decide the issue. No one disagrees, however, that Vitamin E's role as an antioxidant is vital to health.

TOXICITY
Very little is known about the effects of excessive intake of Vitamin E in humans and it is not thought to be toxic. Very large doses (4000 I.U. daily for three months) have been reported to cause diarrhea and soreness in the mouth, tongue and lips.

vitamin G
Former name for Vitamin B_2.

vitamin H
See Biotin

vitamin K
A fat-soluble vitamin necessary for the production of prothrombin, a key substance in blood clotting. Like the other fat-soluble vitamins (A, D, and E), it requires fat intake and bile salts to be absorbed and utilized by the body.

SOURCES
Vitamin K is widely distributed in green vegetables and is also synthesized by bacteria in the intestine. Dietary deficiency rarely occurs.

REQUIREMENTS

No recommended daily allowance has been established since it is believed that the minute amounts synthesized by the intestines and from food are sufficient to maintain a normal prothrombin level. The exception is newborn infants who have a Vitamin K deficiency because their intestinal bacteria are not yet well established and because their mothers were deficient in Vitamin K. Such infants are given a therapeutic dose.

DEFICIENCY

In infancy the most serious complication resulting from Vitamin K deficiency is cerebral hemorrhage. It has been suggested that the routine administration of Vitamin K during the last two months of pregnancy would greatly reduce the incidence of such complications.

Any defect in the absorption of fats or any obstruction of the bile ducts may lead to deficiency. In the latter case, surgery to relieve the obstruction usually results in severe bleeding unless Vitamin K is given prior to surgery.

TOXICITY

Excessive doses of synthetic Vitamin K have led to hemolytic anemia and kernicterus in infants.

vitamin P
See Bioflavonoids

vitellin
A protein of egg yolk comprising approximately four-fifths of the total protein.

vodka
An alcoholic beverage made from neutral spirits (distilled alcohol). In Russia, this is derived from fermented potato mash, but vodka is also made from wheat, rye, and corn mashes.

COMPOSITION AND NUTRIENT VALUE PER 1 1/2 fl. ounces (42 g)

Protein	0 g	Phosphorous	0 mg
Carbohydrate	Trace g	Potassium	Trace mg
Fat	0 g	Sodium	Trace mg
Saturated Fatty Acids	0 g	Vitamin A	0 I.U.
Oleic Acid	0 g	Vitamin B_1	0 mg
Linoleic Acid	0 g	Vitamin B_2	0 mg
Iron	0 mg	Niacin	0 mg
Calcium	0 mg	Vitamin C	0 mg
		Calories	80 proof 100
			86 proof 105
			90 proof 110
			100 proof 125

water

A clear, colorless, nearly odorless and tasteless liquid without which most plant and animal life cannot live. Chemically a compound of hydrogen and oxygen (H_2O), it forms more than 60 per cent of the body weight of humans, and obviously plays an important role in metabolism. It has been demonstrated that the younger the animal, the richer it is in water; and that the fatter the animal, the smaller is the percentage of water.

As a solvent water aids in the absorption of water-soluble nutrients and in the elimination of water-soluble waste through the urine (and to some extent through the feces.) And by means of the evaporation of water through the skin in perspiration and via the lungs in exhalation, water plays an indispensable role in the control of body temperature.

Water provides neither vitamins nor calories, but it does provide various minerals: magnesium, and calcium in hard water, and fluoride in water that either naturally contains it or to which it has been added by man. In addition, some specific mineral and spring waters contain mineral salts (carbonates, silicates, and chlorides) and iron.

A moderately active person in good health takes in an average of 5.5 pints of water per day. Approximately 3 pints of this comes from water and beverages containing water (coffee, tea, soft drinks, etc.), and 2.5 pints from solid foods (vegetables, fruits, meat, etc.) and liquid foods (soup, milk, etc.) containing water.

About 60 per cent of this intake is eliminated through the urine, 25 per cent through the skin (perspiration), 12 per cent through the lungs (vapor in the air exhaled) and 3 per cent in the feces.

When there is an unusual loss of water from the body (excessive perspiration in hot weather or from undue physical activity), the water should be replaced. And since water contains salt, it, too, should be replaced.

See Perspiration; Salt

water-soluble vitamins

The members of the B vitamin complex and Vitamin C. There is no specific storage site in the body for the water-soluble vitamins. They are dispersed in solution through the blood and tissues.

See Fat-soluble Vitamins

weight-control drugs

See Amphetamines

weight watchers

An organization with a program designed to help people lose weight. The diet recommended by Weight Watchers is considered by most nutritional authorities to be excellent. In any event Weight Watchers has enjoyed a phenomenal success with even the most recalcitrant of overeaters.

wheat

The generic name for various annual cereal grasses of the genus *Triticum,* but especially *Triticum aestivum* which is widely cultivated in a number of varieties.

Wheat is the most important of the cereal crops in the Western world, as rice is in the Eastern. In its unrefined state, wheat flour is a very nutritious product, but the modern milling and refining process discards the bran and the germ, leaving a product that is almost pure starch and of little nutritional value.

See Bran Flakes; Flour, Refining and Bleaching; Wheat Germ

wheat germ
The embryo of the wheat kernel, that part which gives rise to the new plant (as chicks rise from eggs). It constitutes approximately 2 per cent of the kernel, but is nutritionally by far the most important part of it, being rich in the B complex of vitamins and the richest known source of Vitamin E as well as a good source of complete protein.

Wheat germ that has been ground into flour or any other powder form should be kept in a tightly covered container and stored in the refrigerator. Otherwise oxygen will combine with the oils containing the Vitamin E and it will become rancid and lose much Vitamin E.

wheat germ

COMPOSITION AND NUTRIENT VALUE PER Cup (68 g)

Protein	17 g	Phosphorous	744 mg
Carbohydrate	34 g	Potassium	550 mg
Fat	7 g	Sodium	5 mg
Saturated Fatty Acids	2 g	Vitamin A	0 I.U.
Oleic Acid	1 g	Vitamin B$_1$	1.4 mg
Linoleic Acid	3 g	Vitamin B$_2$	0.5 mg
Iron	5.5 mg	Niacin	3.1 mg
Calcium	57 mg	Vitamin C	0 mg
		Calories	245

whisky (or whiskey)
An alcoholic beverage distilled from grain—usually rye, corn or barley. The name whisky comes from a Gaelic word meaning "the water of life."

COMPOSITION AND NUTRIENT VALUE PER 1 1/2 fl. ounce (42 g)

Protein	0 g	Phosphorous	0 mg
Carbohydrate	Trace g	Potassium	Trace mg
Fat	0 g	Sodium	Trace mg
Saturated Fatty Acids	0 g	Vitamin A	0 I.U.
Oleic Acid	0 g	Vitamin B$_1$	0 mg
Linoleic Acid	0 g	Vitamin B$_2$	0 mg
Iron	0 mg	Niacin	0 mg
Calcium	0 mg	Vitamin C	0 mg
		Calories	80 Proof 100
			86 Proof 105
			90 Proof 110
			100 Proof 125

whole foods
See Organic Foods

wine
The fermented juice of any of several varieties of grapes.
Table wines (e.g. bordeaux, burgundy) usually range from
11 per cent to 14 per cent alcohol by volume (22 to 28
proof), dessert wines (e.g. port, sherry fortified by the addition of brandy made from grapes) from 17 per cent to
21 per cent (34 to 42 proof).

wine, (dessert, fortified)

COMPOSITION AND NUTRIENT VALUE PER 3 1/2 fl. ounces
(103 g)

Protein	Trace g	Phosphorous	N.D. mg
Carbohydrate	8 g	Potassium	N.D. mg
Fat	0 g	Sodium	N.D. mg
Saturated Fatty Acids	0 g	Vitamin A	— I.U.
Oleic Acid	0 g	Vitamin B$_1$	0.01 mg
Linoleic Acid	0 g	Vitamin B$_2$	0.02 mg
Iron	— mg	Niacin	0.20 mg
Calcium	8 mg	Vitamin C	0 mg
		Calories	140

wine (table)

COMPOSITION AND NUTRIENT VALUE PER 3 1/2 fl. ounces (102 g)

Protein	Trace g	Phosphorous	N.D. mg
Carbohydrate	4 g	Potassium	N.D. mg
Fat	0 g	Sodium	N.D. mg
Saturated Fatty Acids	0 g	Vitamin A	— I.U.
Oleic Acid	0 g	Vitamin B$_1$	Trace mg
Linoleic Acid	0 g	Vitamin B$_2$	0.01 mg
Iron	0.4 mg	Niacin	0.10 mg
Calcium	9 mg	Vitamin C	0 mg
		Calories	85

xerophthalmia
An eye disease characterized by an extreme dryness of the conjunctiva (the mucous membrane lining the inner surface of the eyelid and the exposed surface of the eyeball) and caused by Vitamin A deficiency. It is the precursor of kertomalacia, a disease which can cause blindness.
   See Vitamin A

yeast
   See Brewer's yeast

yogurt
A food with a custardlike texture made from milk curdled with lactic-acid-producing bacteria, especially *Lactobacillus bulgaricus.* Yogurt is rich in vitamins of the B complex and a good source of protein. It also establishes a medium in the intestinal tract which inhibits the growth of harmful bacteria and which aids the absorption of minerals.

   yogurt, of partially skimmed milk:

COMPOSITION AND NUTRIENT VALUE PER Cup (245 g)

Protein	8 g	Phosphorous	270 mg
Carbohydrate	13 g	Potassium	50 mg
Fat	4 g	Sodium	19 mg
Saturated Fatty Acids	2 g	Vitamin A	170 I.U.
Oleic Acid	1 g	Vitamin B_1	0.10 mg
Linoleic Acid	Trace g	Vitamin B_2	0.44 mg
Iron	0.1 mg	Niacin	0.2 mg
Calcium	294 mg	Vitamin C	2 mg
		Calories	125